Daily Bread

A Daybook of
Recipes and Reflections for Healthy Eating

M.J. Smith

CHRONIMED PUBLISHING

Daily Bread: A Daybook of Recipes and Reflections for Healthy Eating © 1997 by M.J. Smith, RD

All rights reserved. Except for brief passages for review purposes, no part of this publication may be reproduced, stored in a retrieval system, or transmitted, in any form or by any means, electronic, photocopying, recording, or otherwise, without the prior written permission of Chronimed Publishing.

Library of Congress Cataloging-in-Publication Data
Smith, M.J.
Daily bread / by M.J. Smith

p.   cm.

Includes index.

ISBN 1-56561-113-6; $19.95

Edited by: Jolene Steffer
Cover Design: Emerson Wajdowicz Design
Text Design & Production: David Enyeart
Art/Production Manager: Claire Lewis
Printed in the United States

Published by
Chronimed Publishing
P.O. Box 59032
Minneapolis, MN 55459-9686

10   9   8   7   6   5   4   3   2   1

Every effort has been made to contact the copyright holders for permission to reprint borrowed material. We regret any oversights that may have occurred and would be happy to rectify them in future printings of this work.

Daily Bread is dedicated to those who
first showed me a life of spirited faith and joyful food—
my dad and mother, Frederic and Mary Agnes Budweg Rewoldt.

ACKNOWLEDGMENTS

This book was first conceived in a summer night's dream, a vision sparked and fueled by my friend Claire Lewis at Chronimed Publishing. Special thanks to Claire and the women's prayer group that keeps her soul fed.

The process of melding these reflections and recipes at first reminded me of trying to mix up the perfect salad dressing, fearing the oil and vinegar would never mix. But the concept was kept alive and encouraged by my friends and advisors, whom I thank now:

Sharon Cumberland from The Mustard Seed, Strawberry Point, Iowa; Carolyn Frye from The Master's Touch, Decorah, Iowa; Jill Sasse and Marie Mick, Guttenberg, Iowa; Liz Goodfellow, Author, Guttenberg, Iowa; Julie Cull, RD/Author, Glen Haven, Wisconsin; Anne Blocker, RD/Author, Waukon, Iowa; Michele Gaffney, Home Economist/Editor, Manchester, Iowa; Lois Vahrenkamp, Children's Author, Austin, Texas; Jane Siebrecht, Elementary Teacher, Garnavillo, Iowa; My pastor Harold and his wife, Linda McMillin, St. John's Lutheran; All my friends in Stephen Ministry; Members of the Upper Iowa District Dietetic Association; Deb Moser and Liz Webster, my home and office neighbors, for daily laughter

ABOUT THE AUTHOR

M.J. Smith is a Registered Dietitian, cookbook author, working mother, and volunteer Stephen Minister.

Her career as a dietitian has included teaching at the university level, self-publishing a monthly menu and recipe service, and consultation to hospitals and food businesses. She has written seven cookbooks, including *All-American Low-Fat & No-Fat Meals in Minutes*. This best-selling cookbook ushered in '90s style low-fat cooking. Her subsequent titles include: *60 Days of Low-Fat, Low-Cost Meals in Minutes; 366 Low-Fat Brand-Name Recipes in Minutes; The Miracle Foods Cookbook; Year-Round Low-Fat & No-Fat Holiday Meals in Minutes; Around the World Low-Fat & No-Fat Meals in Minutes;* and *Diabetic Low-Fat & No-Fat Meals in Minutes*.

She has a home page on the World Wide Web entitled The All American Low-Fat Kitchen that provides daily menus and information for her readers. The home page address is www.agmall.com/lowfatkitchen. Her e-mail address is mjsmithrd@worldnet.att.net.

In 1996, after Stephen Ministry and Stephen Leader training, she became interested in writing for the spiritual diet. Stephen Ministry is a transdenominational lay ministry that equips Christians to live out the commandment: "Love one another." Ms. Smith currently devotes one or two days a week to the ecumenical Stephen Ministry in her community of Guttenberg, Iowa, a small historic German town along the bluffed banks of the Mississippi River.

Ms. Smith is married to Dr. Andy Smith, a family physician. They have two school-aged children. Her favorite Bible verse from the Old Testament hangs next to her outbound door: For the eyes of the Lord range throughout the entire earth, to strengthen those whose heart is true to him (II Chronicles 16:9). Her favorite verse from the New Testament is the Great Commission from her Lutheran confirmation: Go ye, therefore, and teach all nations, baptizing them in the name of the Father, Son, and Holy Spirit (Matthew 28:19).

To the reader: The ideas expressed in *Daily Bread* are not, in all cases, exact quotations, as some have been edited for brevity. In all cases, the author has attempted to maintain the speaker's original intent. Material for this book was obtained from secondary sources in some instances. For clarifications or to learn more about the source of the daily reflections, please write to the author.

WHAT IS *DAILY BREAD*?

Daily Bread is meant to be a calorie-free, but oh-so-delicious treat you can enjoy every day. Make it your kitchen counter's best friend. Allow the orange juice and toast crumbs to discolor its pages.

Open it up and find today's date as you make the coffee. Pause to greet the morning with a new reflection. Whether it be Mahalia Jackson lyrics or the King James Version gospel, you will delight in the variety of inspirations collected here. Embrace the familiar Psalms, verses, and quotes. Contemplate the new stories and verses you'll find spaced between.

The daily menus are for all of us who struggle with that nagging question, "What will we have for dinner?" The menus are healthy, balanced, and all that 'good stuff,' because I am a dietitian and have faced that same daily assignment for 15 years. Most of us wake up and know that sometime, somewhere in the middle of everything else that fills our day, we'll have to think about planning dinner. Just beyond the balance and nutrition in these menus is a quick and tasty method. I don't know a soul who has three hours to prepare dinner.

After the reflections and menus, there are recipes, or simple ways to help you celebrate food and spirit every day. It may be a food idea, an exercise or health tip, or a shortcut for kitchen work and cleaning. You will learn something new to put into immediate use.

This daybook is divided into six bimonthly themes:

January-February/Comfort and Renewal
March-April/Nurturing Our Commitment to Healthy Changes
May-June/Celebrating Our Connections
July-August/Taking a Full Breath of God's World
September-October/Gathering a Harvest
November-December/ Thankful Celebration

As the days and months go by, you will change focus with each season and holiday. Today will be special but there will be something new tomorrow. Make notes along the margins. Cross out "baked potatoes" and write in "instant mashed" whenever you like. Please return to this book again next year. Or pass it on to someone whose kitchen counter is bare.

Food and faith, like music and language, unite our culture. *Daily Bread* represents the best of food and faith, as I have come to experience it. Like an oil and vinegar salad dressing, when you shake it all up, I hope you find the taste delicious.

Comfort and Renewal

**Create in me a clean heart O God;
and renew a right spirit within me.
—Psalm 51:10**

In January and February, we comfort and renew ourselves. We nourish our post-holiday blues with Jesus' New Testament teachings. We forgive an old hurt with Archbishop Desmond Tutu.

The menus have something hot and smooth for cold winter days and something easy to chew and digest for our weary bodies. We will rest after the season of celebration.

We take time to look at our eating style, examine our relationship with the bathroom scale, and create some new ways to appreciate food.

By mid-February, we throw off our fears and choose only to believe. We make soup and bread, macaroni and cheese, and chicken pot pies. Our spirits will be renewed.

Hamburger Soup
4 2-cup servings

Start this new year with a promise to make it as healthy as it can be. Let this comforting soup simmer as you put away holiday decorations or enjoy a New Year's Day bowl game.

1/2 pound lean ground beef
1 medium onion, chopped
2 ribs celery, diced
8 ounces fresh mushrooms, sliced thin
1 teaspoon basil

1 teaspoon dill weed
1/4 teaspoon celery salt
10 ounces frozen mixed vegetables
2 14-ounce cans no-added-salt chunky tomatoes
1/2 cup pearl barley

1. In a large stockpot, brown ground beef with onion, celery, and mushrooms. Drain off any fat from meat. Add all remaining ingredients to the stockpot and bring to a boil.

2. Reduce heat to a simmer for at least 20 minutes or until barley is tender. Simmer covered soup for up to 2 hours.

Calories per serving: 250 Fat: 7 g. Sodium: 67 mg.
For exchange diets, count: 2 lean meat, 1 vegetable, 1 1/2 starch
Preparation time: 15 minutes Cooking time: 20 minutes

Menu of the Day

Hamburger Soup

Hot Breadsticks with
Soft Margarine

Applesauce with Cinnamon
on top

Skim Milk

Comfort and Renewal

The real voyage of discovery consists not in seeking new landscapes, but in having new eyes. —Marcel Proust

A New Way to Repeat an Old Custom: The January Diet

Look through the list and appreciate all that's going right with your eating.

_____ I eat a good breakfast.

_____ I keep healthy low-fat snacks around.

_____ Lunch and dinner are thought out, planned ahead.

_____ My eating is under control between 4 p.m. and the evening meal.

_____ My bedtime snack is a sensible one.

_____ I'm getting five fruits and/or vegetables a day.

_____ I don't catch every little sniffle that comes along, partly because my diet is rich in nutrients.

_____ I'm getting three good sources of calcium (dairy products) every day.

_____ I'm enjoying a high protein food (other than milk) at lunch and dinner.

_____ I like high fiber foods and my gastrointestinal health is A-OK.

_____ I've found low-fat substitutes for the high-saturated-fat favorites in my diet (cheese, salad dressing and mayonnaise, butter and stick margarine, fatty meats, ice cream, deep fried foods, regular chips).

_____ Foods that give me great pleasure are included in my diet in a healthy way.

Menu *of the* Day

Frozen Pizza with Your Own Chopped Veggie Topping and Extra Basil
There's nothing wrong with a frozen pizza once in a while. But pizza needs some help in the nutrient department: shredded carrots, onion, and green or red peppers.

Fresh Greens
with Reduced-Fat Dressing

Peach Slices with
Creme Caramel Yogurt on top

Skim Milk

Do You Love Your Body?

How do we find peace in loving our bodies just the way they are, and yet continue to work at treating them like temples?

In "One Woman's Story," Renate Shafter shares how she grew to love her body by turning away from the media's narrow standard for female beauty and embracing God's concept of beauty.

Proverbs 31:30 points out, "Favour is deceitful and beauty is vain: but a woman that feareth the Lord, she shall be praised."

By renewing her mind daily and striving to love her body, Renate was led to healthy eating and exercise habits.

Health and vitality are yours to claim, but we must first forgive and forget society's hang-ups with thinness.

Today's Christian Woman, May/June 1996, page 29.

Menu *of the* Day

Cheddar Cheese Soup with
California Blend Vegetables
*Prepare soup by mixing 1 can
of reduced-fat cheddar cheese soup
prepared according to package directions, with 2 cups of frozen
California blend veggies. Add veggies 5 minutes before serving time.*

Wheat Rolls
Sliced Lean Ham
Sweet Pickle Spears
Kiwifruit Marinated in
Sugar-Free Gingerale
Skim Milk

January 4

Low-Fat French Toast
4 2-slice servings

Use this on Sunday after church or as a quick comforting supper. The Gallup Organization reports that 42 percent of Americans attend worship services, up from 40 percent in 1992. Celebrate every Sunday with Christ and the ones you love.

2 eggs or 1/2 cup liquid egg substitute
1/2 cup skim milk
1/2 teaspoon vanilla

1 teaspoon oil
8 slices bread (The best French toast is from bread that has been left out to dry.)

1. In a shallow bowl, mix egg, milk, and vanilla with a fork until smooth.

2. Pour oil into a no-stick skillet and heat over medium-high heat. Use a pastry brush if necessary to coat surface of pan with oil. Reduce heat to medium.

3. Dip the bread into the egg mixture and place in skillet. Brown both sides of bread, and top with your favorite topping.

Calories per serving: 193 Fat: 5 g. Sodium: 358 mg.
For exchange diets, count: 2 starch, 1 fat
Preparation time: 15 minutes

Menu of the Day

Low-Fat French Toast
Grilled 95% Lean Ham
Fresh Fruit Toppings for
French Toast: Sliced Bananas,
Strawberries, or Pears
Maple Syrup Topping
Vanilla Yogurt Topping
Skim Milk

Healthy Prayers

When we pray regularly and thoughtfully, we glorify our bodies.

Research over the last 25 years at Harvard Medical School has established that when a person engages in prayer, a specific set of physiologic changes ensue. These include: decreased metabolism, decreased heart rate, decreased rate of breathing, and a slowing of brain waves. These changes are evidence of the healing effects of prayer. And in fact, these body changes are the opposite of those induced by stress. Use prayer to help yourself respond positively to the stress in your life.

> Dear Lord,
>
> Help us experience your power, force, and energy more fully in our bodies and in our lives.
>
> Amen.

Menu of the Day

Baked Skinless Boneless Chicken Breasts
prepared with a shake-on crumb mixture, wheat germ or crushed cornflakes coating

Quick Rice with flakes of Thyme and Reduced-Fat Margarine

Baby Carrots with Reduced-Fat Ranch Dressing as a dip

Green Grapes

Hot Skim Milk Cocoa

Perfect Tea

We cannot fully function if we are holding on to anger and pain. We simply must learn to forgive and to forgive boldly to be able to move on. If there is someone you need to forgive, do so this minute. And meditate on your decision with a cup of perfect tea.

Loose green or black tea or tea bags   Teapot
Cold tap water

Use a china, heatproof glass, or porcelain pot rather than a metal one. Scald the pot first with boiling water. For each serving, use 3/4 cup water and 1 teaspoon loose green tea or 1 tea bag. Place required quantity of cold water in a teakettle and bring to a full boil. Meanwhile, place tea in the scalded teapot, pour boiling water directly over the tea, and allow to steep for 5 minutes. Serve from the teapot (use a small strainer if you're using loose tea) into china teacups. Add milk, sugar, or lemon juice as desired.

Calories, Fat, Sodium: 0
For exchange diets, count: Free
Preparation time: 5 minutes

Menu *of the* Day

Baked Potatoes topped with Browned Lean Ground Beef and Spaghetti Sauce
Warm up the house with baked potatoes. Try adding fresh sliced mushrooms or green peppers to the beef and spaghetti sauce.
French Bread
Sliced Cucumbers with Reduced-Fat Red Wine Vinegar Dressing
Fresh Banana
Perfect Tea

*Come unto me, all ye that labor and are
heavy laden, and I will give you rest.
—Matthew 11:28*

January 7

Cheesy Chicken and Rice Casserole with Broccoli
4 1 1/2-cup servings

Comfort your family with this quick chicken casserole.

1 medium onion, chopped
2 ribs celery, diced fine
8 ounces fresh mushrooms, sliced thin
1 teaspoon soft margarine
16-ounce package chopped broccoli

1 cup quick rice, uncooked
5-ounce can white meat chicken, undrained
2 ounces light American cheese, shredded
11-ounce can reduced-fat cream of chicken soup
2 cans water

1. Preheat oven to 375°. (Recipe can also be microwaved.)

2. In a no-stick skillet, sauté onion, celery, and sliced mushrooms in margarine until tender.

3. Using a large casserole dish, combine sautéed vegetables with all remaining ingredients, stirring well.

4. Bake for 30 minutes or microwave on high power for 15 to 18 minutes, until mixture is bubbly and broccoli has just turned bright green.

Calories per 1 1/2-cup serving: 180 Fat: 7 g. Sodium: 427 mg.
For exchange diets, count: 1 starch, 1 vegetable, 1 very lean meat,
1 fat; Preparation time: 45 minutes

Menu of the Day

Cheesy Chicken and Rice
Casserole with Broccoli
Wheat Toast
Shredded Cabbage with
Reduced-Calorie Dressing
Pineapple Chunks
Skim Milk

January 8

Be of Good Cheer Glazed Lemon Muffins
18 muffins

2/3 cup sugar
1/3 cup vegetable oil
1 egg or 1/4 cup liquid egg substitute
1 cup low-fat lemon (or orange) yogurt
1 tablespoon grated fresh lemon (or orange) peel
1 teaspoon baking soda
2 cups flour

Glaze:
1/4 cup lemon (or orange) juice
2 tablespoons sugar

1. Preheat oven to 375°.

2. In mixing bowl, cream sugar and oil. Beat in egg, yogurt, and lemon peel.

3. Combine soda and flour, then stir into batter just until all is moistened.

4. Spoon batter into greased or lined muffin tins. Bake for 20 minutes.

5. To glaze: Use a toothpick to poke 5 holes in each muffin. Combine lemon juice and sugar in a glass measuring cup and microwave for 25 seconds to dissolve sugar. Stir. Pour a small amount of glaze over each muffin.

Calories per muffin: 125 Fat: 4 g. Sodium: 45 mg.
For exchange diets, count: 1 starch, 1 fat
Preparation time: 40 minutes

Menu of the Day

Your Favorite Recipe
for Tuna and Noodles
*Try using reduced-fat cream soups
as a binding agent*
Be of Good Cheer
Glazed Lemon Muffins
Radishes
Mandarin Orange Slices
Skim Milk

Go Ahead and Ask the Lord to Help

Ask yourself: "Am I inviting the Holy Spirit into all of my eating encounters?"
Use this prayer to bring peace and understanding to your food rituals.

Dear Lord,

Allow your Holy Spirit to guide us:

As we plan favorite meals

and as we struggle with what to fix

As we shop for groceries

and as we put them away

As we stumble through breakfast

and as we gobble down lunch

As we prepare an evening meal

and as we clean up the table

As we scrounge the kitchen for a night snack

and as we wake up hungry in the night

As we entertain family and friends with food

and as we attend social functions

Thank you for the peace, comfort, guidance, and encouragement that can only come through daily communion with you. Amen.

Menu of the *Day*

Flour Tortillas stuffed with
Fat-Free Refried Beans and
Reduced-Fat Cheddar Cheese
Chunky Salsa Topping
Chopped Fresh Greens and
Tomatoes
*A better bet than lettuce
for iron and vitamin A is
fresh chopped spinach.*

Frozen Vanilla Yogurt with
Chocolate Sauce
Flavored Decaf Coffee

---

*I will walk among you, and will be your God,
and ye shall be my people.
—Leviticus 26:12*

Vegetable Couscous

8 1¼-cup servings

Couscous is a very fine grain made from semolina flour.

Let us imagine God walking with us, as he promised in Leviticus.
Celebrate the old world flavor of couscous.

1 tablespoon olive oil
1 1/2 cups finely chopped vegetables (suggest carrots, onion, and celery)
2 minced cloves garlic or 1/2 teaspoon minced garlic
1 teaspoon cumin
1/2 teaspoon paprika
1/4 teaspoon dry mustard
1/4 teaspoon ginger

1/8 teaspoon cayenne pepper
1 cup fat-free chicken broth
1 cup shredded potato
1 cup chopped tomato
2 1/4 cups water
1/2 teaspoon salt
10-ounce package couscous
1/4 teaspoon cinnamon

1. In large skillet heat oil. Add vegetables; cook over medium heat about 5 minutes. Add garlic, cumin, paprika, mustard, ginger, and pepper; cook 30 seconds.

2. Add chicken broth and potato; bring to a boil. Reduce heat to low and simmer 15 minutes. Stir in tomato; cover and simmer on low while cooking couscous.

3. In medium saucepan bring water and salt to a boil; stir in couscous. Cover; remove from heat and let stand 5 minutes. Add cinnamon; fluff with fork.

4. Stir into vegetables. Serve immediately.

Calories per serving: 166 Fat: 2 g. Sodium: 93 mg.
For exchange diets, count: 1 1/2 starch, 2 vegetable
Preparation time: 15 minutes Cooking time: 20 minutes

Menu of the Day

Broiled Sirloin
Vegetable Couscous
Fresh Strawberries
Skim Milk

Let me be weighed in an even balance,
that God may know mine integrity.
—Job 31:6

January 11

Does Weight Matter?

Notice what God tells us about weight in Job 31:6 above.

The bathroom scale can be a back-stabbing morning companion. Somehow those numbers encourage us to think of ourselves as good or bad, depending on where the arrow points.

Author Monica Dixon, MS, RD, in her book, *Love the Body You Were Born With,* asks us:

> What in the world would you do if you didn't weigh yourself every day?
> Just try on your favorite pair of pants. Pay attention to how those favorite
> pants feel every time you wear them and you will have a winning feed-
> back tool.

While some people may need to lose weight to improve their health and quality of life, for the majority of women dieting is an inappropriate means to an impossible dream.

The key is to eat a wide variety of wholesome foods to protect your health. You do not need another diet plan to do that and you should not exist on rabbit food!

Weigh yourself as rarely as possible. Instead, look in the mirror, think of Job, and reflect on your integrity.

Menu of the *Day*

Lean Ground Pork Tacos
Use just half of a taco seasoning
packet for 1 pound of ground pork.
Add fresh onions, peppers, and cel-
ery to the pork for a fresh flavor
without the sodium.

Reduced-Fat Cheddar Cheese,
Lettuce, Tomato, Chunky Salsa,
and Reduced-Fat Sour Cream

Sugar-Free Instant Pudding over
Mango Slices

Sugar-Free Lemon Lime Soda

Be of good courage, and he shall strengthen your heart, all ye that hope in the Lord.
–Psalm 31:24

Monterey Skillet Vegetables
8 1-cup servings

We can strengthen our hearts with this antioxidant-rich entree! Vitamins A, C, and E are powerful repair agents for cholesterol-damaged arteries and veins. This is a recipe passed to me by a fellow dietitian, author, mentor, and Christian, Mabel Caviani.

8 small zucchini
1 tablespoon vegetable oil (prefer safflower)
1 large yellow onion, coarsely chopped
1 large green pepper, chopped
4-ounce can diced green chilies
14-ounce can diced tomatoes in juice
8-ounce can whole kernel corn, drained well

1/2 teaspoon garlic powder
1/2 teaspoon salt
1/4 teaspoon black pepper
8 ounces reduced-fat Monterey Jack cheese, shredded
Garnish: paprika

1. Wash and trim ends from zucchini. Cut crosswise into 1/4-inch slices and set aside.

2. In a large skillet, heat oil over medium-high heat and sauté onions with chopped pepper and green chilies for 2 minutes. Add tomatoes and continue cooking 2 minutes. Add zucchini and corn and cook over medium heat uncovered for 10 minutes. Stir in garlic powder, salt, and pepper and continue cooking until heated through and most of the liquid has been reduced. Sprinkle the vegetables with cheese and then sprinkle the cheese with paprika.

3. Once the cheese is melted, remove the skillet from heat to the table and serve. This makes a wonderful light supper with a crusty whole wheat roll and fresh fruit. If this is garden season, substitute fresh tomatoes and corn for the canned varieties.

Menu *of the* Day

Monterey Skillet Vegetables
Fresh Onion Roll
with Soft Margarine
Red Grapes
Skim Milk

Calories per serving: 162 Fat: 7 g. Sodium: 482 mg.
For exchange diets, count: 1 vegetable, 1 lean meat, 1 starch
Preparation time: 15 minutes Cooking time: 20 minutes

Create a New Eating Style

If you could just start the whole process over and create a new world of eating in seven days, how would your healthy eating pattern evolve?

Here is some help in getting started:

Day 1. Take time to savor every bite of food as a precious gift.

Day 2. Stop eating with the first sign of fullness.

Day 3. Prepare just enough food so that none goes to waste.

Day 4. Taste new foods with a sense of discovery and excitement.

Day 5. Select a diet with the richest sources of essential nutrition.

Day 6. Accept food as the friend that fuels you 3 to 5 times every day.

Day 7. Delight in the responsibility of feeding your loved ones.

Menu of the Day

Baked White Fish Fillet
A baked fish trick: spread reduced-fat tartar sauce or salad dressing over thawed fillet, then sprinkle with bread crumbs. Bake uncovered at 425° F. until flaky, about 25 minutes.

Steamed Red Skinned Potatoes
Fresh Broccoli steamed tender crisp seasoned with Butter-Flavored Spray
Cherry Flavored Low-Fat Yogurt
Mint Tea

Give me neither poverty nor riches;
feed me with food convenient for me.
—Proverbs 30:8

Low-Fat Macaroni and Cheese

4 ¾-cup servings

This recipe for macaroni and cheese works with any 16-ounce box
and reduces the fat in a kid-favorite by 75 percent!

1 package Kraft macaroni and cheese dinner
4 cups water

1 tablespoon soft margarine
1/3 cup skim milk

1. Bring water to a boil in a medium saucepan. Stir in macaroni. Reduce heat to medium-low and cook for 8 minutes.

2. Drain noodles and return to the saucepan or a serving bowl. Stir in cheese packet, margarine, and milk. Serve.

Calories per serving: 210 Fat: 3 g. Sodium: 460 mg.
For exchange diets, count: 2 starch, 1 fat
Preparation time: 15 minutes

Menu of the Day

Low-Fat Macaroni and Cheese
Mixed Vegetables
Rye Bread with Soft Margarine
Granny Smith Apple Slices and
Low-Fat Caramel Dip from the
produce section
Skim Milk

I have a dream that my four little children will one day live in a nation where they will not be judged by the color of their skin, but by the content of their character. —Martin Luther King, Jr.

January 15

Pork Chops with Smothered Cabbage
4 servings

4 3-ounce lean pork chops
1/8 teaspoon salt
1/2 teaspoon pepper

16-ounce can sauerkraut or 4 cups grated fresh cabbage
1 fresh potato, grated

1. Preheat oven to 350°.

2. In a medium skillet, brown pork chops over medium heat. Season with salt and pepper.

3. Meanwhile in an 11- by 7-inch baking dish, combine kraut or fresh cabbage with grated potato. Use a spoon to spread mixture evenly over the bottom of the dish. Arrange browned chops on top of the kraut mixture. Cover and bake for 1 hour.

Calories per serving: 287 Fat: 1 g. Sodium: 856 mg.
(To reduce sodium, choose cabbage instead of sauerkraut.)
For exchange diets, count: 3 vegetable, 3 lean meat
Preparation time: 15 minutes. Baking time: 60 minutes

Menu *of the* Day

Celebrate this day with a favorite menu of Dr. King's.

Pork Chops
with Smothered Cabbage
Cornbread Muffins from a box
Steamed Fresh or Frozen Turnip
Greens dotted with Vinegar
Custard Pudding from a box

Give us this day our daily bread.
—Matthew 6:11

Potato Bread in the Machine
24 half slices

Who doesn't enjoy fresh bread? It can be so delicious, so nourishing, and so satisfying without a lot of added fat. The machines have become very affordable and can be adapted to large or small loaves. Maybe it's time to buy yourself a present.

1 cup water
1 egg
3 cups white bread flour
1/4 cup instant mashed potato flakes
1 1/2 teaspoons nonfat dried milk

3 tablespoons sugar
1 1/2 teaspoons salt
1 1/2 teaspoons dry yeast
1 tablespoon margarine

1. Recipe is meant for large (3 cups flour) loaf. Add ingredients to pan in order listed (recipe tested with Hitachi Automatic Home Bakery). If your machine calls for dry ingredients first, then invert the order of ingredients.

2. Program for "Bread" or regular setting. Push "Start," and remove bread from machine approximately 4 hours later.

Calories per 1/2-slice serving: 120 Fat: 1 g. Sodium: 150 mg.
For exchange diets, count: 1 1/2 starch
Preparation time: 10 minutes Baking time: 4 hours

Menu *of the* Day

Grilled Ham Slices with Crushed
Pineapple and Mustard on top
Baked Potato Sprinkled with
Fresh or Dried Chives
Potato Bread
Peach and Banana Slices
Cranapple Juice

Take Time to Ignore Busywork!

January days beg us to sit back, rest, and reflect. Give yourself an afternoon to slow down and ponder these four ways you can creatively neglect busywork that really doesn't matter.

*1. **Know what to overlook.*** Friends coming by for dinner? The crumbs under the dining room table won't be noticed.

*2. **Choose your battles.*** Hold pesky phone calls and that pile of mail until you plan a week's menu, write the grocery list, get to the market, and put the food away.

*3. **Spend less time immersed in the superficial.*** We can run around all day just picking up clutter. Start today by announcing a specific time for everyone in the house to pick up after themselves. Put on the tunes and everyone dig in to help.

*4. **Be committed to avoiding overcommitment.*** You really don't have to fly by the seat of your pants all the time. Focus your energy on what is most important, and forget feeling guilty about what's not getting done. Practice saying "I choose not to" instead of "I can't" or "I don't have enough time."

Enjoy your new freedom to make clear decisions about the gifts, people, and commitments God gives you.

Menu *of the* Day

Pick this entire meal up from the deli. We all need to take a day off and dust off our "busy" bodies. The deli meal won't kill you. But leave the greasy chicken skin on your plate.

Crispy White Meat Chicken
Mashed Potatoes
Any Veggie Salad with
a Clear Dressing
Dinner Rolls
Orange Sherbet
or Angel Food Cake
Skim Milk

I have found that among other benefits, giving liberates the soul of the giver.
—Maya Angelou, Wouldn't Take Nothing for My Journey Now

Wee Angel Orange Rolls
10 rolls

When you yearn to bake something, but fear eating the whole thing, try this recipe. Enjoy them at a family meal, then give the rest away.

1 pound loaf frozen sweet roll dough
2 tablespoons melted margarine
1/4 cup sugar
1 teaspoon cinnamon
Non-stick cooking spray

Frosting:
1 cup powdered sugar
Zest of 1 orange
1 tablespoon melted margarine
Juice from 1 orange to thin frosting to spreading consistency

1. Thaw bread dough according to package directions.

2. Roll out on floured surface to 14- by 8-inch rectangle. Spread dough with melted margarine; sprinkle with sugar and cinnamon. Roll up dough and pinch shut. Cut rolls into 1 1/2-inch pieces and arrange in a 9-inch round baking pan that has been sprayed with cooking spray.

3. Cover rolls, transfer to a warm location, and allow to rise about 2 1/2 inches high, about 30 minutes.

4. Bake in preheated 350° oven for 20 to 25 minutes.

5. Combine ingredients for the frosting in a small mixing bowl. (Orange zest is tiny narrow strips of the colored part of the orange rind.) Spread frosting over the rolls while they are still warm.

Calories per 1-roll serving: 212 Fat: 4 g. Sodium: 253 mg.
For exchange diets, count: 2 starch, 1/2 fruit, 1/2 fat
Preparation time: 15 minutes Rising time: 30 minutes
    Baking time: 20 minutes

Menu of the Day

Chicken Noodle Soup
Soda Crackers
String Cheese
Wee Angel Orange Rolls
Sliced Kiwifruit
Skim Milk

What I say is, if a man really likes potatoes,
he must be a pretty decent sort of fellow.
—A.A. Milne, Not That It Matters

January 19

Irish Potato Soup
4 1-cup servings

4 medium potatoes, peeled and cubed fine
1 small onion, chopped
1 rib celery, chopped
1 small carrot, finely grated
1/2 cup no-added-salt chicken broth

1/4 teaspoon salt (optional)
1/4 cup flour
1 tablespoon margarine, melted
2 cups skim milk
Garnish: fresh parsley

1. In a 2-quart kettle or microwave dish, steam vegetables with broth and optional salt until tender.

2. Combine flour, margarine, and milk in shaker container. Stir into vegetables, bring to a boil, and then reduce to simmer for 5 minutes.

3. Ladle into bowls and garnish with fresh parsley.

Calories per 1-cup serving: 186 Fat: 4 g. Sodium: 236 mg. with salt; 113 mg. without salt
For exchange diets, count: 2 starch, 1 fat
Preparation time: 25 minutes

Menu of the Day

Irish Potato Soup
Toasted Onion Bagel
with Soft Margarine
Baby Carrots cut into thin strips,
dotted with Reduced-Fat
Western Dressing
Frozen Blueberries
Decaf Cappuccino from a box

Let not your hands be weak;
for your work shall be rewarded.
—2 Chronicles 15:7

Two O'Clock Blues

Skipping breakfast or skimping on lunch can lead to low blood sugar, also known as hypoglycemia. This can be a problem even if you don't have diabetes. The condition may also be induced with heavy exercise or 60 to 90 minutes following the intake of sugar-rich foods.

Signs of Hypoglycemia:
light-headedness
sweating
shaky hands
irritable
intense hunger
dizziness
feeling faint

Food Remedies:
Quick source of natural sugar such as:
1 full cup of orange or apple juice, taken with a protein-rich food, such as:
low-fat cheese
milk
low-fat yogurt
cold lean ham
hard boiled egg
cottage cheese

Menu of the Day

Your favorite Meatloaf topped
with your favorite Barbecue Sauce
*Any meatloaf recipe will work in
the new perforated meatloaf pans.
Drain away that dangerous
saturated fat.*

Butternut Squash
seasoned with Allspice
Kaiser Rolls with Soft Margarine
Chilled Fruit Cocktail
Skim Milk

January 21

Create Comfort in your Kitchen

Do you save those metal baking powder tins? Have you stashed away enough glass jars to fill a room in the basement? Whether you have too much stuff or what you have is in a state of chaos, the result is the same. Your living space lacks order!

1. Don't make excuses. If you are not using something on a regular basis (at least once a year) get rid of it. Got enough plastic containers to outfit the neighborhood? Donate some to the church or shelter.

2. Find the best place once and for all for everything. Store items close to where you are going to be using them. Are your top drawers full of items rarely used? Reorganize so the top drawers contain the items used most often.

3. Handle things once. When unpacking groceries, divide bulky items such as ground beef, freezing it in portion sizes immediately. Don't leave anything in a temporary holding area.

4. Get a recipe file. Every kitchen needs a box for those favorite recipes. Don't worry if they aren't all printed uniformly on index cards. You'll quickly recognize a news or magazine clipping in the recipe box.

5. Inspect your kitchen counters and walls. Items on the countertop or displayed on the walls should have a valid reason for being there, whether it is for function or looks.

Menu of the Day

Clean Out the Cupboard or Freezer.
Use up that boxed pasta dish you bought on sale a year ago. Clean up the roast beef that's been in the freezer since the birthday party. Toast the leftover rye bread. Open a can of fruit from the back of the shelf. Use your saved time to create an orderly kitchen.

January 22

Rejoice not that the spirits are subject unto you;
but rather rejoice, because your names are written in heaven.
—Luke 10:20

Happiness is an Attitude, Not a Condition.

It's cleaning the oven while listening to an aria, or spending a pleasant hour organizing your spice cupboard.

Happiness is your whole family assembled at the dinner table, with everyone finally free of their winter colds.

Happiness is no leftovers, or just enough turkey for your sandwich tomorrow.

It is in this very moment, not in the distant promise of "someday when." How much luckier we are and how much more happiness we experience, if we can fall in love with the life God allows us today.

Menu of the *Day*

Everybody's happy with this one!

Smoked Turkey and Reduced-Fat Cheese Sub Sandwiches with your favorite Trimmings

Reduced-Fat Potato Chips

Sugar-Free Chocolate Pudding

Vegetable Juice Cocktail

Ten Commandments for Healthy Eating

1. Portion a few potato chips, rather than eating from the bag.

2. A glass of milk for breakfast and bedtime goes a long way toward meeting our calcium need.

3. Kids do better on bananas than cookies after school.

4. Brushing your teeth after meals makes the next feeding seem far off.

5. Eating at our desk or in front of the TV erases any potential for mealtime magic.

6. Keeping your favorite fresh fruits in the fridge instead of ice cream in the freezer is 97 percent danger free.

7. Chewing gum during meal preparation leaves more food for the table.

8. Waking up hungry is a delightful way to start the morning.

9. Overfeed loved ones with hugs and kisses instead of brownies.

10. A brisk walk does more than clear the lungs.

Menu of the Day

Baked Fish Square on a Bun
with Reduced-Fat Tartar Sauce
Baked French Fries
Sliced Tomatoes with Reduced-Fat
Italian Dressing
Fruit Cocktail in its own juice
Skim Milk

We count them happy which endure.
–James 5:11

Chocolate Almond Angel Cake

12 servings

A healthy eating style need not be an endurance test. Can't remember the last time you had real chocolate? Celebrate your fortitude with this dessert.

18-ounce 2-step angel food cake mix
Water according to package directions
2 teaspoons almond extract
1/3 cup cocoa

1 cup reduced-fat whipped topping
  (or try fat-free topping)
1/4 cup cocoa
1 teaspoon almond extract
Garnish: 1/2 cup fresh raspberries

1. Preheat oven to 375°.

2. In a large mixing bowl, combine water and almond extract with egg white mixture. Beat until stiff peaks form.

3. Empty the packet of flour mixture into a small bowl and use a wire whisk to mix well with 1/3 cup cocoa. Sprinkle the flour and cocoa slowly and evenly over the egg whites, beating slowly after each addition.

4. Pour batter into prepared angel food cake pan and bake according to package directions. Cool cake upside down for at least 1 hour, then remove from pan.

5. Fold 1/4 cup cocoa and almond extract into whipped topping with a wire whisk; use a spoonful as a topping for the cake. Garnish with raspberries.

Calories per serving: 206 Fat: 4 g. Sodium: 261 mg.
For exchange diets, count: 2 starch, 1 fat
Preparation time: 15 minutes Baking time: 40 minutes

Menu *of the* Day

Pan Grilled Chicken Breast Fillet
seasoned with rosemary served
over a Quick Rice and Vegetable
Side Dish from a box
French Bread with Soft Margarine
Chocolate Almond Angel Cake
Skim Milk

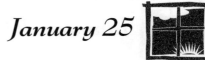

Creamy Chicken and Vegetables
4 servings

This is a creamy, comforting winter supper.

4 skinless, boneless chicken breast halves
1/8 teaspoon garlic powder
1 teaspoon dried rosemary
Non-stick cooking spray
10-ounce can reduced-fat cream of mushroom
  soup

1/2 cup skim milk
1 tablespoon lemon juice
1/4 teaspoon dried basil
16-ounce bag frozen San Francisco blend
  vegetables

1. Sprinkle chicken with garlic and rosemary.

2. Spray skillet with cooking spray and heat over medium-high heat for 1 minute.

3. Cook chicken for 10 minutes or until browned. Set aside on a platter.

4. Add soup, milk, lemon juice, basil, and vegetables to the skillet. Heat to a boil. Return
chicken to pan and cover. Cook over low heat for 10 minutes or until the chicken is done.

Calories per serving: 237 Fat: 5 g. Sodium: 467 mg.
For exchange diets, count: 4 very lean meat, 2 vegetable, 1/2 starch
Preparation time: 10 minutes Cooking time: 20 minutes

Menu of the *Day*

Creamy Chicken and Vegetables
Wheat Toast
Fresh Apple Slices
with Pineapple Chunks
Skim Milk

Be of good cheer: it is I; be not afraid.
—Mark 6:50

Food Choices: A Matter of Attitude

Be real. Very small changes in your food patterns over time will add up to better health.

Be adventurous. Expand your tastes and menus to explore the variety of foods available to you.

Be flexible. Balance what you eat with your physical movement over several days. No need to fret about just one meal or one day.

Be sensible. Enjoy all of your favorite foods in healthy portions.

Choose movement whenever you can! Your dog would love a walk. Or call an old friend and make a date to go swimming.

Menu of the Day

Grilled Sirloin Steak
Baked Potato with Soft Margarine
Fresh Stir-Fried Veggies
from the market
*Find some cheer today in a
fresh stir-fried vegetable
combination: pea pods, bean
sprouts, bamboo shoots, and a red
pepper quick cooked in a no-stick
skillet seasoned with teriyaki
sauce or fresh ginger.*

Frozen Strawberries
with Sliced Bananas
Skim Milk

Pork and Vegetables in the Skillet
4 servings

Why not share the peace of this meal with someone
in your circle of life who is lonely or shut-in during the winter?

1 pound boneless pork cubes
16-ounce can oriental broth, divided
6 cups fresh vegetables, cut into 1-inch pieces
   (such as green onion, celery, carrots, bok choy,
   mushrooms, pea pods, and broccoli)

2 tablespoons cornstarch

1. In a nonstick skillet over medium heat, stir-fry pork until browned, then set aside.

2. Add 3/4 cup of broth and all the vegetables to the skillet and bring to a boil. Cover and cook 3 minutes, just until vegetables have turned color.

3. In a glass measure, mix cornstarch and remaining broth. Add slowly to the pan, stirring constantly until mixture thickens.

Calories per serving: 290 Fat: 9 g. Sodium: 467 mg.
For exchange diets, count: 4 lean meat, 3 vegetable
Preparation time: 10 minutes Cooking time: 15 minutes

Menu of the Day

Pork and Vegetables in the Skillet
Quick Rice
Fresh Orange Slices
Fortune Cookies
Skim Milk

January 28

*Again—nothing you do or think or wish
or make is necessary to establish your worth.*
—A Course in Miracles

A Grateful Self

Oprah Winfrey shared a wonderful secret to her peaceful life. She keeps a Journal of Gratitude. Every day, she takes some time to record all the things she's grateful for.

We don't live in a perfect world. But adjusting our focus to what's going right—the big and little things for which we are thankful—does set a tone for peace and joy.

Next time you're in a stationery store, pick up a journal with blank pages... or start recording along the margins of this book every day.

Thank God with your heart, head, and hands for loving children, a faithful spouse, the health of aging parents, the bird at the feeder, a caring pastor, a neighbor that waves "Good Morning," a boss that likes to laugh, a warm turtleneck, and your moment of peace to connect with gratitude.

Menu of the *Day*

Broiled Hamburger on a Bun with
your favorite Toppings
*Anyone can make a simple ham-
burger and enjoy its perfection.*

Whole Kernel Corn with Diced
Green Pepper and Green Onions
Granny Smith Apple Slices
Skim Milk

Unleash Your Creativity

While that pot roast is cooking, reflect on ways to put your imagination to work:

1. *Remind yourself of your dreams every day.*

2. *Write in a journal every day.* Many great philosophers kept journals. Writing keeps your ideas flowing. Think of journalizing as "brain dumping."

3. *Set aside time to be completely alone.* For two hours every week, do something by yourself. Our creativity flourishes when we are alone.

4. *Hang out with creative people.* Work on friendships with people who may inspire and uplift you.

5. *For a week, turn off the radio and TV, stop reading the mail, and put a halt to the negative distractions of our culture.*

Menu *of the* Day

Beef Pot Roast with Chunks of
Potato, Carrot, Onion, and Celery
*Any pot roast can be made tender
with this method: Arrange roast
and vegetables in a baking pan.
Pour in 1 can of beer. Cover and
roast at 325° for 5 hours.*

Fresh Bread from Frozen Dough
with Soft Margarine

Warm Applesauce flavored with
Rum Extract over Ice Milk

Hot Tea

Do all that is in thine heart; for the Lord is with thee.
—2 Samuel 7:3

Peanut Butter Brownies
24 brownies

Taste all the comfort and joy of those chocolate peanut butter cups.

Non-stick cooking spray
18-ounce package reduced-fat brownie mix
3 tablespoons chunky peanut butter

2 eggs
1/2 cup skim milk

1. Preheat oven to 350°. Spray 9- by 13-inch baking pan with cooking spray.

2. In a medium mixing bowl, combine all ingredients, stirring until moist. Spread batter in prepared pan and bake for 27 to 30 minutes. Do not overbake.

Calories per serving: 117 Fat: 3 g. Sodium: 18 mg.
For exchange diets, count: 1 starch, 1 fat
Preparation time: 10 minutes Baking time: 30 minutes

Menu of the *Day*

Pan Grilled Turkey Breasts
with Barbecue Sauce
Bowtie Pasta
Green Salad
with Reduced-Fat Dressing
Pear Sauce
Peanut Butter Brownies
Skim Milk

5 Minute Banana Bars
36 squares

Is it your turn to take bars to the church or school? These can't be beat.

Non-stick cooking spray
18-ounce package reduced-fat yellow cake mix
2 ripe bananas, mashed
3 eggs or 3/4 cup liquid egg substitute

1 cup water
1 tablespoon vanilla extract
Optional topping: 1/4 cup chopped pecans or walnuts

1. Preheat oven to 375°.

2. Spray a 15- by 8-inch baking pan with cooking spray.

3. Combine all ingredients in a large mixing bowl. Beat on high power for 2 minutes. Pour into prepared pan. Sprinkle with nuts if desired.

4. Bake for 40 minutes or until bars test done with wooden pick.

Calories per 1-bar serving: 72 Fat: 2 g. Sodium: 107 mg.
For exchange diets, count: 1 starch
Preparation time: 5 minutes Baking time: 40 minutes

Menu *of the* Day
Baked Potato with Diced Ham and Cheese topping
Fat-Free Sour Cream
Radishes and Celery Sticks
5 Minute Banana Bars
Skim Milk

We are exiles until we can come into God,
the heart's true home.
—Richard Foster, Coming Home, A Prayer Journal

Make Ahead Apple-Flavored Maple Syrup
4 cups of syrup or 32 2-tablespoon servings

2 cups apple juice
4 cups brown sugar

2 teaspoons maple extract
1 teaspoon butter-flavored extract (optional)

1. In a medium saucepan, bring apple juice to a rapid boil.

2. Add brown sugar all at once and stir until it is dissolved. Remove from heat and stir in maple extract and optional butter-flavored extract.

3. Pour into a clean quart jar and let stand for 24 hours at room temperature before using. Store in the refrigerator for up to 6 months.

Calories per serving: 110 Fat: 0 Sodium: 11 mg.
For exchange diets, count: 1 1/2 fruit
Preparation time: 10 minutes Standing time: 24 hours

Menu *of the* Day

Pancakes made from reduced-fat
baking mix grilled in a
no-stick skillet
recipe is on the box

Make Ahead Apple-Flavored
Maple Syrup
Grilled Canadian Bacon
Pineapple Slices
Skim Milk

Jump Start Spring Fever,
Regardless of What the Groundhog Says

1. If you need to inject daily exercise into your life, why not get up 30 minutes earlier in the morning to take a walk? Find a neighbor or a friend who needs a walking buddy.

2. Forget the drive-through carwash and do it yourself on the next sunny day.

3. Park at the farthest end of the grocery store or church parking lot and enjoy the extra steps.

4. Are you spending time in front of a computer? Reward yourself with 5 minutes of moving around for every hour you spend computing.

5. Take a walk on your lunch break.

6. Take time to play. Everyone loves to throw a Frisbee.

7. Consider a walk after the evening meal with a member of your family.

Menu *of the* Day

Spaghetti and Meatballs with your favorite Pasta Sauce
French Bread with Soft Margarine
Green Salad with Red Wine Vinegar Dressing
Mango Slices
Skim Milk

If ye have faith as a grain of mustard seed, ye shall say to this mountain, remove hence to yonder place; and it shall remove. —Matthew 17:20

Keep Moving Toward Spring

1. Do something outdoors. Pick up stray sticks and branches, or clean out a pesky gutter.

2. Ride your bike on the first nice day.

3. Keep yourself busy while watching the tube. Consider a project like mending or sorting photos.

4. Wash a window, vacuum a dusty carpet, or sweep up the sidewalk.

5. Use the exercise equipment you already own.

6. Rent a new exercise video to break up your routine.

7. When planning your next weekend, work in physical activity for everyone.

8. Make strong friendships with those who affirm your desire and need to keep moving!

Menu of the *Day*

Baked Breaded Fish Square
from a Box
*Van de Kamp and Healthy
Choice offer low-fat varieties.*

Tricolor Corkscrew Pasta
seasoned with Tarragon
Salad Greens
with Reduced-Fat Dressing
Peach Slices in Juice
Skim Milk

*Rest. Rest. Rest in God's love. The only work you are required now
to do is to give your most intense attention to His still, small voice within.*
—Madame Guyon

February 4

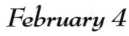

Pear Cake
24 slices

Non-stick cooking spray
18-ounce package reduced-fat yellow cake mix
1 teaspoon ground cinnamon
1 teaspoon ground nutmeg
1 cup apple juice
3 ripe pears, mashed smooth (may substitute
   peaches or nectarines)

Glaze:
1/4 cup apple cider or juice
1/4 cup brown sugar

1. Preheat oven to 350°. Spray 9- by 13-inch baking pan with cooking spray.

2. Combine all ingredients in a large mixing bowl and beat for 2 minutes until smooth.
Pour into prepared pan and bake for 35 minutes.

3. While cake is warm, poke holes in the top with a fork.

4. Mix cider and brown sugar together until smooth; pour slowly over the cake. Allow cake
to cool completely and then slice into 24 servings.

Calories per 1-slice serving: 96 Fat: 2 g. Sodium: 140 mg.
For exchange diets, count: 1/2 starch, 1 fruit
Preparation time: 10 minutes Baking time: 35 minutes

Menu *of the* Day

Tomato Soup
Grilled Reduced-Fat
Cheese Sandwiches
*Lightly spread both sides
of the cheese sandwiches with
soft margarine and grill slowly
and gently over medium heat
in a no-stick skillet.*

Celery Sticks
Pear Cake
Skim Milk

All things are possible to him that believeth.
—Mark 9:23

Easy Chicken Pot Pie

6 slices

1 2/3 cups frozen mixed vegetables, thawed
1 cup diced cooked chicken
10-ounce can reduced-fat cream of chicken soup

1 cup reduced-fat baking mix
1/2 cup skim milk
1 egg or 1/4 cup liquid egg substitute

1. Preheat oven to 400°.

2. Mix vegetables, chicken, and soup in 9-inch round pie pan or baking dish.

3. In a small bowl, stir together remaining ingredients with a fork until well blended. Pour into pie plate.

4. Bake for 30 minutes or until golden brown.

> Calories per 1-slice serving: 285 Fat: 8 g. Sodium: 681 mg.
> For exchange diets, count: 2 lean meat, 2 starch
> Preparation time: 15 minutes Baking time: 30 minutes

Menu *of the* Day

Easy Chicken Pot Pie
Sliced Cucumbers
with Italian Dressing
Fresh Pears with Lemon Yogurt
Skim Milk

Roasted Potatoes Poupon

6 1/2-cup servings

1/4 cup Grey Poupon or dark mustard
2 tablespoons apple juice or white wine
6 medium red skinned potatoes, cut into cubes

1 medium onion, sliced
Chopped parsley

1. Preheat oven to 400°.

2. In a small bowl, combine mustard and apple juice or wine.

3. In large bowl, combine potatoes, onions, and mustard mixture, tossing to coat well. Spread evenly on a baking sheet.

4. Bake for 45 minutes. Serve topped with parsley.

Calories per serving: 87 Fat: 1 g. Sodium: 70 mg.
For exchange diets, count: 1 starch
Preparation time: 5 minutes Baking time: 45 minutes

Menu *of the* Day

Broiled Pork Chops
Roasted Potatoes Poupon
Shredded Cabbage with
Reduced-Fat Coleslaw Dressing
Sherbet
Skim Milk

*For God so loved the world, that he gave his only begotten son,
that whosoever believeth in him should not perish,
but have everlasting life. —John 3:16*

A Promise to Eat Spontaneously

1. Never deprive yourself of something you really want to eat: eat and enjoy it fully. Be pleased with yourself for knowing what you wanted and fulfilling your desire.

2. Never force yourself to eat something you do not want.

3. Make physical comfort a goal. Try to eat exactly the amount of food that will please you most, avoiding feelings of being stuffed or starved.

4. Be aware that you choose what you eat. If you are thinking to yourself: "I shouldn't be eating this," then choose to put it down.

5. Recall how you felt before you became concerned about diet and weight and body image. Try to recreate that feeling of trusting your appetite again.

These promises are continued tomorrow.

Menu of the Day

Salmon, Halibut, or Cod Fillets
skillet-simmered with a small can
of Chunky Tomatoes, Fresh Diced
Pepper, Onion, and a dash of
Lemon Juice until flaky
Brown Rice
White Dinner Roll with Soft
Margarine
Mandarin Oranges marinated
in Sugar-Free Lemon-Lime
Soft Drink
Skim Milk

To clasp the hands in prayer is the beginning
of an uprising against the disorder of the world.
—Karl Barth

February 8

Day 2 of Keeping Your Promise to Eat Spontaneously

6. Avoid the temptation to strictly control fat grams and calories. There will be some food encounters that nicely match a calorie or fat gram prescription, and many others that won't.

7. Think of all foods as having positive and negative attributes, and avoid labeling certain foods as all good or all bad.

8. Remember that how and what you choose to eat has nothing to do with your value. You are a good person.

9. Weigh yourself as rarely as possible.

10. As you learn to eat spontaneously in response to true hunger, don't sweat the setbacks. Remember that you are always doing the best you can, which is 100 percent good enough.

—"A Promise to Eat Spontaneously" from *Making Peace with Food* by Susan Kano.
©1989 by Susan Kano. Reprinted by permission of HarperCollins Publishers, Inc.

Menu *of the* Day

Baked Potatoes with toppings:
Reduced-Fat Shredded Cheese,
Lean Roast Beef, Green Onions,
Salsa
Garlic Toast
Red Apple Slices
Skim Milk

All things work together for good to them that love God.
–Romans 8:28

How to Brew Great Coffee

Espresso is a blend of coffee beans typically roasted medium to dark.
It is also a beverage made by forcing hot water through a bed of finely ground
and densely packed espresso coffee.

1. Always start with the finest, freshest beans.

2. Use a clean coffee brewer; built-up resins and oily deposits can make your coffee taste bitter.

3. It is best to grind coffee just before brewing. A coarser grind will yield lighter coffee; a finer grind will produce a stronger brew. If coffee is ground too fine, the coffee may suffer from overextraction and will tend to be bitter. It may also clog filters.

4. Use fresh tap or bottled water to make coffee.

5. Use one rounded tablespoon of ground coffee for each eight ounces of water. Adjust the amount of coffee to suit your taste.

6. Drink coffee while it is fresh. Coffee is best held in a thermal carafe away from air and heat.

Menu *of the* Day

Lean Browned Ground Pork
with your favorite Marinara Sauce
and Cooked Rice stuffed into a
Green Pepper
Mix equal parts browned ground
pork, cooked rice, and marinara
sauce together, and stuff into
green peppers. Bake at 400°
for 40 minutes.

Steamed Baby Carrots
Strawberry Ice Milk
Espresso

All I really need to know about how to live and
what to do and how to be I learned in kindergarten.
—Robert Fulghum

February 10

Kindergarten Rules of Family Eating

Always cut the last piece of dessert in two and share it.

Encourage all members of the family toward healthy eating by support and involvement rather than food control games.

Don't reach across the table for the hot rolls. Wait until they are passed, then enjoy every bite.

Everyone cleans up their own mess, whether it's wiping up toast crumbs or rinsing their dishes and placing them in the dishwasher.

If the taco chips were purchased for Joe, leave them for Joe.

If you can't say something nice about the sweet potato casserole, don't say anything at all.

Wash your hands every time before you eat or cook.

Pray before every meal.

Try a new food as often as you can.

Menu of the Day

Pan-Grilled Minute Steaks with
Sliced Mushrooms and Onions on
a Toasted French Roll with your
favorite Condiments
Steamed Cauliflower
with Soft Margarine
Granny Smith Apple Slices
Skim Milk

February 11

More About Brussels Sprouts

Brussels sprouts are a member of the cruciferous vegetable family. Members of this cabbage family (that derives its name from the four-petaled flowers that look like a crucifer or cross) are thought to protect against cancer. Other vegetables with this property include arugula, bok choy, broccoli, cabbage, cauliflower, collards, kale, kohlrabi, mustard greens, radishes, rutabaga, turnip, turnip greens, and watercress.

Nutrition studies suggest the cabbage family vegetables provide a protective effect specifically against colon and rectal cancer. They are also fat free and have varying amounts of calcium, iron, and folic acid.

Brussels sprouts and all members of the cruciferous family have a strong cooking aroma. It is best to eat them soon after you buy them. Steam them quickly, just until tender-crisp or until they have started to change color. Leftovers are less than desirable after one day.

Favorite seasonings for steamed Brussels sprouts include fresh squeezed lemon juice, chicken broth, bits of lean bacon, sprinkles of balsamic vinegar, caraway seed, and dill.

Menu *of the* Day

Cold Salmon, Diced Celery, and
Reduced-Fat Cucumber Dressing
on a Toasted Bagel
*Water pack tuna is also
tasty with diced celery and
a cucumber dressing.*

Steamed Brussels Sprouts
Sugar-Free Skim Milk Pudding
from a box
Grape Juice

Mary Lincoln's Chicken Fricassee
Serves 4, 1 chicken breast each

2 whole chicken breasts, skinned, boned, and
halved
1/4 teaspoon salt
1/4 teaspoon pepper
1/4 teaspoon nutmeg

1/4 teaspoon mace
1/4 teaspoon sweet marjoram
1 cup evaporated skim milk
Optional garnish: fresh parsley

1. Season chicken with salt, pepper, nutmeg, mace, and marjoram.

2. Place in a large skillet. Pour milk over chicken. Cook over medium-low heat for 20 minutes, until chicken is tender. Garnish with fresh parsley.

Calories per serving: 186 Fat: 3 g. Sodium: 261 mg.
For exchange diets, count: 3 1/2 lean meat
Preparation time: 10 minutes Cooking time: 20 minutes

Menu of the *Day*
Mary Lincoln's Chicken Fricassee
Mashed Potatoes
Green Beans
White Rolls
Diced Peaches over Low-Fat
Caramel Nut Frozen Yogurt
Skim Milk

The History of "Dieting"

Since the dawn of history people have been obsessed about their weight
and searched in folly for the perfect diet pill. Consider these calamities.

Third Century B.C. Philon the Byzantine makes a "hunger and thirst checking pill" with sesame, honey, oil, almonds, and sea onions.

1890s: Thyroid extract, from the glands of farm animals, becomes popular among fashionable weight-conscious women because it is thought to speed up metabolism. Physicians prescribe it until they learn that prolonged use causes heart palpitations and anxiety.

1914: Jean Down's Get Slim Pink Lemonade becomes the rage in New York City.

1920: Arsenic is found to help ladies squeeze into their corsets. It is available in tablet form.

1920: To fit into their skinny flapper dresses, women begin reaching for cigarettes instead of sweets.

1930: Physicians prescribe the insecticide dinitrophenol for weight loss. Severe side effects include liver and kidney damage as well as blindness.

1940 to 1960: Women use amphetamines to curb appetite. Anxiety, paranoia, and hypertension follow.

Menu *of the* Day

Reduced-Fat Cream of Mushroom
Soup and Soda Crackers
Sliced Lean Ham on Rye with
Mustard or Horseradish
Baby Carrots
Sliced Kiwifruit
Skim Milk

Cherry Cheese Pie
12 slices

8-ounce carton nonfat lemon yogurt
8 ounces nonfat cream cheese, softened to room
   temperature
1 envelope unflavored gelatin

1/4 cup very cold water
1/2 cup white grape juice concentrate
1 prepared graham cracker crust
21-ounce can cherry pie filling

1. Combine yogurt and cream cheese in a large mixing bowl. Beat until blended and smooth. Set aside.

2. In a small saucepan, sprinkle gelatin over cold water. Allow to soften for 1 minute, then cook over low heat, stirring constantly until gelatin is dissolved. Remove from heat; stir in grape juice concentrate and yogurt mixture, beating well.

3. Pour into prepared crust. Cover and refrigerate for at least 1 hour or up to overnight. Top with chilled cherry pie filling just before serving.

Calories per 1-slice serving: 243 Fat: 6 g. Sodium: 184
For exchange diets, count: 2 starch, 1 fruit, 1/2 fat
Preparation time: 20 minutes Chilling time: 60 minutes

Menu *of the* Day

*Go out to dinner, then come
home and enjoy Cherry Cheese Pie.
Valentine's Day restaurant
dining can be healthy. Start out with
a favorite appetizer, green salad, or
vegetable soup and then consider
sharing an entrée between you and
your sweetheart.*

Tuna Quesadillas
8 servings

Non-stick cooking spray
2 6-ounce cans chunk light tuna, drained well
4-ounce can chopped green chilies, drained
4 ounces reduced-fat cheddar cheese, shredded

4 ounces reduced-fat mozzarella cheese, shredded
1/2 cup sliced green onions
1 package fat-free tortillas (8 tortillas)
Salsa on the side to pass

1. Preheat oven to 375°.

2. Lightly spray a baking sheet with cooking spray.

3. In a large bowl, combine tuna, chilies, cheese, and green onion.

4. Divide the filling onto the top half of each tortilla within 1/4 inch of the edge. Fold tortillas in half over the filling and place on the baking sheet. Bake for 8 minutes or until the tortillas are golden brown and the cheese is melted.

5. Serve the tortillas by cutting into two wedges. Pass the salsa if desired.

Calories per serving: 187 Fat: 3 g. Sodium: 327 mg.
For exchange diets, count: 2 lean meat, 1 starch
Preparation time: 15 minutes Baking time: 8 minutes

Menu *of the* Day

Tuna Quesadillas
Chopped Lettuce and Tomatoes
Raspberries and Vanilla Ice Milk
Cranapple Juice

God give us the grace to accept with serenity the things that cannot be changed; courage to change the things that should be changed; and wisdom to distinguish the one from the other. —Reinhold Niebuhr

February 16

The Healthy Snack Attack

There are loads of guilt-free snacks to fuel you between meals. The trick is to select foods with just enough quick carbohydrate to perk you up in a hurry along with some protein or complex carbohydrate to make the full feeling last. Try these at home or at the office.

Sliced strawberries and nonfat vanilla yogurt
Pineapple chunks stirred into nonfat ricotta cheese
Peaches and low-fat cottage cheese
Veggies dipped into soft cheese
Tuna and wheat crackers
Skim milk with sugar-free quick chocolate powder
Bananas dipped in reduced-fat peanut butter
Cereal with dried fruit and 1% or skim milk

Frozen yogurt cone
String cheese and rye crackers
Baked tortilla chips warmed with shredded reduced-fat cheddar cheese and dots of salsa
Pretzels dipped in vegetable-flavored nonfat cream cheese
Baked potato chips with nonfat onion dip

Menu of the *Day*

Braised Pork Steak with Apples and Onions in Red Wine
Tenderize and flavor ordinary pork steak by slow cooking it in a skillet with a sliced apple, onion, and red wine.

Butternut Squash
Green Beans
Dinner Roll
Apricots in Juice
Skim Milk

Comfort and Renewal

I have fought a good fight, I have finished my course.
I have kept the faith. —2 Timothy 4:7

Rinsing Ground Beef to Reduce Fat and Saturated Fat

Nutritionists at Iowa State University perfected this method to rinse ground beef. Rinsing 80% lean ground beef reduced the fat content to 5 grams per 3-ounce portion (compared to 15 grams with no blotting or rinsing).

1. Brown ground beef in a skillet over medium heat for 10 minutes or until no longer pink, stirring occasionally.

2. Meanwhile, place 4 cups of water in a 1-quart glass measuring cup or bowl. Microwave on high power for 6 minutes or until very hot, but not boiling.

3. Using a slotted spoon, remove beef crumbles to a large plate or other container lined with 3 layers of white paper towels. Let sit 1 minute, blotting top of beef with an additional paper towel.

4. Transfer beef to a mesh strainer or colander. Pour heated water over beef to rinse fat. Drain for 5 minutes, then proceed as recipe directs.

Menu of the *Day*

Ground Beef Hard Shell Tacos
Reduced-Fat Cheddar Cheese
Chopped Tomato, Peppers, and
Lettuce
Frozen Bananas
Low-Fat Chocolate Milk

All About Grapefruit

What could be simpler than the grapefruit? Slice it open and dig in. New varieties of super sweet grapefruit like the Rio Star are most popular today. Grapefruit are either white, pink, or red; seeded or seedless. The color of the rind doesn't indicate ripeness. In many grapefruit, the outside color isn't a clue to the inside. But the Rio Star can be recognized by its exterior blush. Fruit should feel firm but springy. Minor blemishes on the rind are acceptable, but avoid those with soft spots or bruises. Choose thin-skinned fruits that seem heavy for their size.

Grapefruit does not ripen once it is picked, and quality diminishes with storage. By the time it reaches your refrigerator, a typical grapefruit will remain in its prime for about two weeks.

One-half grapefruit has 45 calories and is loaded with vitamin C and potassium. Pink grapefruit is a good source of vitamin A.

To broil grapefruit:

Cut into halves, spread with honey, and broil about two inches away from the heat for 5 minutes or until the top is bubbly.

Calories per 1/2-grapefruit serving: 55 Fat: 0 Sodium: 1 mg.
For exchange diets, count: 1 fruit
Preparation time: 5 minutes

Menu *of the* Day

Round Steak slow cooked
with Dry Onion Soup Mix
Whole Kernel Corn
Dinner Roll
Broiled Grapefruit
Skim Milk

Eat Right/Sleep Tight

1. With good sleep your goal, try to eat a basic breakfast, a substantial lunch and light evening meal containing protein such as fish, poultry or lean red meat. Avoid heavy, spicy rich meals at days end.

2. For a bedtime snack, try a glass of sparkling water, a cup of herbal tea, a glass of warm skim milk, Ovaltine, crackers and cheese, or a piece of toast. Try combining carbohydrates and protein such as cheese and crackers or cereal and milk. Your stomach should be neither full nor empty.

3. Tryptophan is the amino acid converted to serotonin that promotes sleep and is found in protein foods.

4. Avoid sugar-rich foods in the evening as you may experience rebound low blood sugar and wake up really hungry.

5. Avoid alcohol and caffeine. They are known to disrupt sleep.

Used with permission from *How to Get a Good Night's Sleep* by Richard Graber and Paul Gouin, M.D. Chronimed Publishing, 1995.

Menu of the *Day*

Broiled Breast of Turkey
Steamed Baby Carrots
sprinkled with Garlic and Basil
Bowtie Pasta
Mandarin Oranges
over Lemon Sherbet
Skim Milk

All Week Salad
8 1-cup servings

2 pounds baby carrots
2 tablespoons water
1 green pepper, seeded and diced
1 red pepper, seeded and diced
1 medium onion, chopped fine
11-ounce can reduced-fat, reduced-sodium tomato
  soup

1/4 cup brown sugar
1/4 cup red wine vinegar
1 teaspoon celery seed
1 teaspoon Worcestershire sauce
1 teaspoon dry mustard
1/2 teaspoon pepper

1. Place baby carrots in a microwave-safe container. Sprinkle with 2 tablespoons of water and microwave on high power for 4 minutes. Remove cover and drain water. Carrots will be tender-crisp. Transfer carrots to a large salad bowl with a tight fitting cover.

2. Add peppers and onion to cooled carrots.

3. In a small mixing bowl, combine all remaining ingredients. Pour over vegetables, toss, and refrigerate for up to 1 week.

    Calories per serving: 120 Fat: 1 g. Sodium: 277 mg.
    For exchange diets, count: 2 vegetable, 1 fruit
    Preparation time: 15 minutes

Menu of the Day

Deli Plate of Low-Fat Cold Cuts
Reduced-Fat Cheeses
Dill Pickles
Your favorite Bagels
All Week Salad
Purple Grapes
Skim Milk

Fight the good fight of faith.
—I Timothy 6:12

Roasted Winter Vegetables
8 ¾-cup servings

2 tablespoons olive oil
1/4 cup balsamic vinegar
1/4 teaspoon salt
1/2 teaspoon pepper
1 teaspoon fennel seeds
1 yellow pepper, quartered and seeded

1 red pepper, quartered and seeded
1 Samuel acorn squash, peeled and sliced into chunks
1 large onion, quartered
6 whole baby turnips
1/2 cup fresh thyme, chopped, or 2 tablespoons dried thyme flakes

1. Preheat oven to 350°.

2. In a medium mixing bowl, mix together oil, vinegar, salt, pepper, and fennel. Add the vegetables and toss to coat.

3. Place coated vegetables in a roaster container, cover, and roast 30 minutes or until tender. Remove from oven, sprinkle with thyme, and serve.

Calories per serving: 99 Fat: 3 g. Sodium: 98 mg.
For exchange diets, count: 1 starch, 1/2 fat
Preparation time: 10 minutes Roasting time: 30 minutes

Menu of the *Day*

Ground Pork Burger
on a Wheat Bun
Winter Vegetables
Green Salad
with Reduced-Calorie Dressing
Breadsticks
Grape Juice

Associate yourself with men of good quality if you esteem your own reputation; for 'tis better to be alone than in bad company.
—George Washington, Rules of Civility

February 22
George Washington's Birthday

George Washington's Beefsteak Pie
6 slices

2 strips bacon, diced
1/2 pound sirloin steak, cut into 1-inch pieces
1/4 cup flour
1 cup red wine
2 small onions, diced
2 bay leaves
1/2 cup chopped parsley
1/2 cup chopped celery, including leafy tops

1 cup sliced mushrooms
1/4 teaspoon salt
1 teaspoon black pepper
1 teaspoon marjoram
Non-stick cooking spray
1 1/2 cups reduced-fat baking mix
1/2 cup beef broth

1. Preheat oven to 375°.

2. In a large skillet, cook bacon until crisp.

3. Roll chunks of sirloin steak in flour, then add to bacon and sauté for 3 minutes, until well browned. Next, add wine, onions, bay leaves, parsley, celery, mushrooms, salt, pepper, and marjoram. Cover and simmer mixture for 10 minutes.

4. Meanwhile, spray an 11- by 7-inch baking dish with cooking spray.

5. Use a fork to combine baking mix and beef broth in a small bowl. Mix just until liquid is absorbed; dough will be sticky. Pour beef and vegetable mixture into prepared baking dish. Use a spoon to dollop biscuit dough on top of beef and vegetable mixture. Bake for 20 minutes or until biscuits are golden brown.

Calories per 1-slice serving: 306 Fat: 8 g. Sodium: 825 mg.
(To reduce sodium, use no-added-salt beef broth and omit salt.)
For exchange diets, count: 2 starch, 2 lean meat, 2 vegetable
Preparation time: 20 minutes Baking time: 20 minutes

> ### *Menu of the Day*
> George Washington's
> Beefsteak Pie
> Pickled Beets
> Yellow Cake with
> Chocolate Pudding on top
> Strong Coffee

A poor diet plus vitamin supplements is still a poor diet.
–Dr. Art Ulene, The Today Show, April 10, 1997

Baked Bananas
8 ¾-cup servings

Even your desserts can be rich in nutrients, like this one.

3/4 cup orange juice
1 teaspoon vanilla
Non-stick cooking spray
4 firm ripe bananas, peeled
1/2 cup flour

1/2 cup oatmeal
1/3 cup brown sugar
1/2 teaspoon nutmeg
1/4 teaspoon salt
3 tablespoons soft margarine

1. Preheat oven to 375°.

2. In a 1-cup glass measure, combine orange juice and vanilla. Set aside.

3. Slice bananas lengthwise and place cut side up in a baking dish that has been sprayed with cooking spray.

4. Combine flour, oatmeal, brown sugar, nutmeg, and salt. Work in margarine with a pastry blender or fork.

5. Drizzle bananas with orange juice, then spoon oatmeal mixture over the bananas.

6. Bake for 20 minutes and serve warm.

Calories per serving: 151 Fat: 3 g. Sodium: 101 mg.
For exchange diets, count: 2 fruit, 1/2 fat
Preparation time: 10 minutes Baking time: 20 minutes

Menu *of the* Day

Low-Fat Cottage Cheese
with Chives
Wheat Crackers
Tomato Juice
Baked Bananas
Herb Tea

Prayer is relationship. It is being with God.
—Maxine Dunnam from Living Prayer

February 24

Applesauce Bars
24 bars

Non-stick cooking spray
2 cups oatmeal
3/4 cup wheat flour
1/2 cup packed light brown sugar
1/2 cup chopped pecans
1/2 cup raisins
2 1/2 teaspoons baking powder

1/2 teaspoon cinnamon
1/4 teaspoon nutmeg
1/2 teaspoon grated orange zest
1 cup skim milk
2 eggs
6 tablespoons soft margarine, melted
1 1/2 cups no-added-sugar applesauce

1. Preheat oven to 350°.

2. Spray a 9- by 13-inch baking pan with cooking spray.

3. Combine oatmeal, flour, brown sugar, nuts, raisins, baking powder, spices, and orange zest in a large bowl and set aside.

4. Combine milk, eggs, margarine, and applesauce in a blender. Process until smooth. Stir into the dry ingredients.

5. Spread batter into the prepared pan and bake for 30 minutes. Dust bars with powdered sugar if desired.

> Calories per serving: 132 Fat: 6 g. Sodium: 46 mg.
> For exchange diets, count: 1 starch, 1 fat
> Preparation time: 15 minutes Baking time: 30 minutes

Menu *of the* Day

Lasagna Frozen Dinner
*Lean Cuisine and Weight
Watchers offer several varieties.*

Garlic Bread
Green Salad
with Reduced-Fat Dressing
Applesauce Bars
Sparkling Grape Juice

Begin at once to live, and count each day
as a separate life. —Lucius Annaeus Seneca

Chicken Enchiladas
4 servings

2 chicken breasts, halved, boned, skinned,
    and diced
1/4 teaspoon minced garlic
1 teaspoon vegetable oil
4 large fresh tomatoes

1 large onion, chopped
1 canned chipotle chili pepper
8 corn tortillas
Non-stick cooking spray
4 ounces reduced-fat cheddar cheese

1. Preheat oven to 425°.

2. In a large skillet, combine diced chicken, garlic, and vegetable oil. Cook over medium heat for 4 minutes or until the chicken is no longer pink.

3. Meanwhile, in a blender, blend tomatoes, onion, and chipotle pepper. Process until smooth.

4. Stuff corn tortillas with chicken and roll shut. Place seam side down in an 11- by 7-inch baking dish that has been sprayed with cooking spray.

5. Pour tomato puree over the tortillas. Sprinkle with cheese and bake for 15 minutes or until sauce is bubbly and cheese is melted.

Menu *of the* Day

Chicken Enchiladas
Chopped Lettuce, Tomato, and
Green Onions
Leftover Fresh Fruits, sliced and
marinated in a Sugar-Free Soft
Drink
Skim Milk

Calories per serving: 318 Fat: 9 g. Sodium: 200 mg.
For exchange diets, count: 3 lean meat, 2 starch
Preparation time: 15 minutes Baking time: 15 minutes

We will run and not grow weary / We will walk and will not faint
For the Lord will go before us / And his joy will be our strength
—Tricia Allen and Martin Nystrom, "We Will Wait"*

February 26

Let the Spirit Go With You on Your Walks

Put on the headphones and let these artists inspire you!

"Hymns in Colour," Smitty Price and Harlan Rogers

"Faith Hope and Love," Lyn Westafer

"Seeds of Love," New Tradition

"20 Years of Hope," Maranatha Music

"Joseph and the Amazing Technicolor Dreamcoat," Original Broadway Cast

"Lift Him Up," Ron Kenoly

"Too Long in Exile," Van Morrison

"The Preacher's Wife," Whitney Houston

"Greatest Gospel Hits," Malaco Records

"The Secret is Out," Vanessa Bell Armstrong

Menu of the *Day*

Cheeseburgers! Lean Ground
Beef and Reduced-Fat American
Cheese on a Bun
Sugar Snap Peas
with Dried Mint
Cranberry Juice Cocktail

---

* © 1992 Integrity's Hosanna! Music/ASCAP All rights reserved.
International copyright secured. Used by permission.

*"God kind of said, 'Kelsey, you know what? I am going to take over.'
And I listened this time, and it's been a wonderful journey since then."*
—Kelsey Grammer, star of "Frasier"

Honey Mustard Pork Medallions

4 servings

1 pound boneless pork loin, cut into 4 rounds
2 minced garlic cloves or 1/2 teaspoon
   minced garlic

1/3 cup reduced-sodium soy sauce
1/4 cup Dijon-style mustard
1/4 cup honey

1. Preheat broiler.

2. Place boneless pork rounds on a broiler pan. Broil 3 inches from broiler element for 5 minutes.

3. Meanwhile, combine remaining ingredients in a small mixing bowl. Brush pork rounds with honey mustard sauce and turn. Broil for 5 more minutes, brush with glaze, and test for doneness.

4. Serve with reserved sauce.

Calories per serving: 292 Fat: 9 g. Sodium: 1113 mg.
For exchange diets, count: 4 lean meat, 1 fruit
Preparation time: 15 minutes

Menu of the Day

Honey Mustard Pork Medallions
Brown Rice
Steamed Broccoli and Cauliflower
Apricot Halves
stuffed with Raisins
Skim Milk

The Truth About Spirituality

Can you tell what's Christian from what's not? Ruth E. Van Reken asks
this question in *Today's Christian Woman* (November/December 1996).

The Lies of "spirituality": All paths lead to God. You control your own destiny. The
Truth of the Bible says there is only one way to God; we are saved through Christ Jesus
alone. We are to submit to God who is the immortal Creator and Ruler of all.

The Lies of "spirituality": Everyone has his or her own truth. The Truth of the Bible
tells us that truth comes through Jesus Christ and God's work. Jesus said he is the truth.
He is the same yesterday, today, and forever.

*The Lies of "spirituality": Quiet your mind and let your inner feelings and instincts be
your guide.* The Truth of the Bible reminds us the Holy Spirit will guide us into all truth.

The Lies of "spirituality": Love yourself first. Pursue self-fulfillment above all else. The
Truth of the Bible reminds us to love the Lord your God with all your heart, soul, mind,
and strength; and love your neighbor as yourself.

As we move into a new month, a new season will greet us. Comfort and renewal have been
accomplished.

Menu *of the* Day

Turkey Franks on a Hot Dog Roll
Steamed Red Cabbage
with Caraway Seed
Crushed Pineapple over Frozen
Lemon Yogurt
Skim Milk

Nurturing Our Commitment to Healthy Changes

The sound of spring is within earshot. March brings a fever for newness of life. Let the fresh air herald your commitment to living healthy. During the next two months, feel yourself branching out to food and movement choices that are best for you. With the Lord at your side, your personal power to be healthy will be double-strength.

Ever wonder just exactly how to compute Target Heart Rate or Body Mass Index? Need a review on what foods are high in fiber or how much water you need? Those nutritional topics are part of this two-month section on maximizing physical well-being.

During Lent, fish recipes are featured. Seafood is more satisfying calorie for calorie than any other protein food. Of course, you can have corned beef and cabbage for St. Patrick's Day. Delicious end-of-winter soups and early spring salads find their way onto these pages as well. Asparagus becomes widely available and makes an out-of-the-ordinary soup or salad. And who doesn't go wild with the first sign of delicious spring berries, melons, and rhubarb?

Keeping our commitment to good health is made sure with the power of prayer. This two-month section ends with a whole series of techniques and topics for exploring personal and group prayer, as well as a list of known health benefits of daily prayer.

Be sure to write in the margins of the pages as you turn them. The recipes and information will be enriched as you experience and react to a new taste or idea for the first time.

God calls us to a faith in health in Acts 14:9: "He had faith to be healed." Our joy in stewardship is sometimes in direct proportion to the joy in our bones.

This is the day the Lord hath made. Choose today to be healthy and strong.

You are only sure of today;
do not let yourself be cheated out of it.
—Henry Ward Beecher

March 1

Glance back at your January checklist:

_____ I eat a good breakfast.

_____ I keep healthy low-fat snacks around.

_____ Lunch and dinner are thought out, planned ahead.

_____ My eating is under control between 4 p.m. and the evening meal.

_____ My bedtime snack is a sensible one.

_____ I'm getting five fruits and/or vegetables a day.

_____ I don't catch every little sniffle that comes along, partly because my diet is rich in nutrients.

_____ I'm getting three good sources of calcium (dairy products) every day.

_____ I'm enjoying a high protein food (other than milk) at lunch and dinner.

_____ I like high fiber foods and my gastrointestinal health is A-OK.

_____ I've found low-fat substitutes for the high-saturated-fat favorites in my diet (cheese, salad dressing and mayonnaise, butter and stick margarine, fatty meats, ice cream, deep fried foods, regular chips).

_____ Foods that give me great pleasure are included in my diet in a healthy way.

Menu *of the* Day

Sautéed Chicken Breasts with
Mushrooms and Celery seasoned
with Lemon Juice and
Curry Powder over Quick Rice
Shredded Cabbage
with Reduced-Fat Dressing
Chilled Fruit Cocktail in Juice
Skim Milk

March 2

March is a Springboard

You're going beyond the renewal and comfort of winter toward a genuine commitment to good health. Today begin with a look at physical activity and body movement.

God blessed all of us with beautiful bodies and by moving them (notice I don't like the "e" word) on a regular basis, we accomplish several goals:

we have fun... taking a walk with a dear friend, or throwing the football with our sons and daughters.

we feel better physically and mentally... relieving anxiety and daily tensions.

we promote the joy of movement... and become unhampered by physical limitations, feeling at home in our own bodies.

we develop unconditional body acceptance and appreciation.

we improve nearly all measures of good health... such as blood pressure, bone density, blood cholesterol and sugar levels, respiratory capacity, and immune function!

Menu of the Day

Drained Salmon or Tuna
with Minced Onion and
Reduced-Fat Mayonnaise
on an Onion Bagel
Baby Carrots
Honeydew Melon
Skim Milk

Every Little Move You Make

Today, you will embrace healthy everyday patterns of movement
and cast away the lazy ones.

We take the stairs whenever we can and give our heart muscles a little excitement.

We take our mid-morning beverage break, we stroll around the office building or walk out to get the mail to wake up our tired muscles and neurons.

We hang up the clothes to dry whenever we have time and weather.

We give an umph and move the family room furniture to vacuum up the dust bunnies as soon as they collect.

We wash just one or two windows when they get smeary and enjoy a clean view.

We bend and stoop to clean the inside corners of the car when we're preparing for a special trip.

We plan movement activities into the family's weekly schedule, with something as simple as Saturday morning house cleaning or a Sunday evening game of ping-pong.

We participate in group activities like walking or skating or swimming or dancing or aerobics with our friends and family.

Menu of the Day

Lean Beef Roast
with Red Potatoes
slowcooked in the Crockpot
seasoned with Teriyaki Sauce
Steamed Stir-Fry Vegetables
Wheat Roll with Soft Margarine
Sugar-Free Instant Vanilla
Pudding with Raisins
and Cinnamon
Herb Tea

March 4

A time to keep silence, and a time to speak.
–Ecclesiastes 3:7

No Time Like the Present

There is no time like this moment to find a friend to take walks with. And if you already have a walking partner, today is the day to thank God for the blessing of friendship.

If you don't have a current walking partner, and need to find one, here is some sure-fire persuasion.

Walking is the most natural form of exercise.

There is no special equipment or expense involved (beyond a good pair of walking shoes).

You can start very slowly, no matter what shape you're in.

You can stop with the first sign of discomfort because your primary goal is the joy of movement.

By seeking a walking partner of similar stature, you are likely to walk at the same pace.

There will be days when your partner is not available, but don't forget, the Lord can accompany you with a favorite gospel or spiritual tune through the headphones.

Menu *of the* Day

Your favorite Meatloaf
Mashed Potatoes
Steamed Peas and Pearl Onions
Sliced Delicious Apples,
Celery, and Dates with
Low-Fat Yogurt on top
Mineral Water

Let not your hands be weak,
for your work shall be rewarded.
–2 Chronicles 15:7

March 5

The Next Step

Today, you are going to add hand weights to your daily walk to entertain your upper body muscles. There are half or one pound soft bracelet weights available for about ten dollars in the sporting goods section of discount department stores.

And if you don't want to go shopping, just grab a couple cans of soup or vegetables from the pantry. Hold on to them and gently swing your arms with each step. Feel those upper arms pull and tighten.

If you've found a partner and started walking, reward yourself with a new sweatshirt or walking suit that perks you up. Or surprise your friend and pick up a couple of matching sweatbands.

Vary your route now and then. Take a new road, and notice the grandeur of the world around you.

Do you have cotton mouth when you get back from your walk? Don't forget to push the water. Besides the fluid losses from sweat, your body's increased respiration demands fluid. Half of America is running around slightly dehydrated with signs of sluggishness.

Menu *of the* Day

Soft Shell Tacos with
Diced Cooked Chicken,
and Green Chilies
Reduced-Fat Cheddar Cheese,
Chopped Lettuce and Tomato,
and Chunky Salsa
Vanilla Ice Milk
with Chocolate Syrup
Decaf Coffee

March 6

Making the Most of Your Movement

As you become comfortable with walking, and maybe add the hand weights, you can monitor the intensity of your workout by taking your pulse.

There has been lots of attention an the "aerobic benefit" of walking. This simply means that new heart muscle is forming in response to the intensity of the exercise. The advantage of elevating your heart rate during brisk walking is that the heart rate stays elevated for one to three hours after you're home. Fat and calories are burned at an increased rate as well. We measure "aerobic benefit" by what is known as your individual target heart rate. This is simple to do if you can multiply and take your pulse.

What is your target heart rate for exercise?

Subtract your age from 225 (for example, 225 − an age of 50 = 175). If you are perfectly healthy, multiply the result by .75. If you have high blood pressure or any history of heart disease, multiply the result by .70 (for example, 175 x .75 = 131). The target heart rate in this example would be 131.

To take your pulse, find the space between the bony spots on the thumb side of your wrist and upper hand. Simply place your index and middle finger together over the spot until you feel the pulse. It's best to count the pulse for at least 30 seconds and then multiply it by two. Do this at least 10 minutes into your walk. If your pulse reaches the target heart rate, then you are working hard enough to achieve the aerobic benefits.

Menu *of the* Day

Broiled Pork Chops sprinkled
with Thyme and Marjoram
Whole Kernel Corn with Diced
Green Pepper
Fresh Tangelo
Skim Milk

Cheddar and Dill Vegetable Soup
4 1½-cup servings

16-ounce package frozen mixed
  or California blend vegetables
11-ounce can reduced-fat cream of chicken soup

1 cup skim milk
4 ounces reduced-fat cheddar cheese, shredded
1 teaspoon dill weed

1. Combine all ingredients in a stockpot.

2. Heat uncovered on medium-low, stirring occasionally just until bubbly. May serve at once. ***Do not boil.***

Calories per serving: 182 Fat: 6 g. Sodium: 563 mg.
For exchange diets, count: 1 skim milk, 2 vegetable, 1 fat
Preparation time: 10 minutes

Menu of the *Day*

Cheddar and Dill
Vegetable Soup
Rye Toast with Soft Margarine
Red Grapefruit Sections
Skim Milk

Fresh or Frozen Fish?

During Lent, fresh and frozen fish are promoted in grocery specials. Is fresh fish really better than frozen? The answer depends on how it has been handled, processed, shipped, marketed, and stored.

Fish that are caught several days from shore and immediately processed—flash frozen on board ship and stored at very low temperatures—are superior to never-frozen fish that have taken a long route to the table.

When buying frozen fish, avoid packages that are not solidly frozen or are displayed above the chill line of the freezer case. Do not thaw frozen seafood until you are ready to use it. Thaw frozen fish in the refrigerator. A 1-pound package will take 10 hours.

Fish with freezer burn will be tough and tasteless. Never refreeze fish once it has been thawed. Fresh fish should be packed well on ice, but not in contact with water from melted ice.

Fresh fish sold whole on the bone will stay fresher than fish cut into fillets. Put it in the coldest part of the refrigerator immediately and eat it within one or two days.

Menu *of the* Day

White Fish Fillet Broiled with Soft Margarine, and Old Bay or Lemon Pepper Seasoning
Firm white fish fillets you can trust for taste and texture include cod, halibut, sole, mahi-mahi, orange roughy, sea bass, and walleye. Darker meatier varieties suitable for broiling include salmon, shark, swordfish, snapper, and tuna.

Baked Potato with Reduced-Fat Sour Cream
Steamed Asparagus
Fresh Blueberries
Skim Milk

Surely goodness and mercy shall follow me all the days of my life
and I will dwell in the house of the Lord forever.
—Psalm 23:6

March 9

Ambrosia Toss
8 1/2-cup servings

11-ounce can mandarin oranges, drained well
1 large banana, sliced in 1/2-inch-thick slices
1 cup green grapes, cut in half

1 cup fat-free whipped topping
1/4 cup reduced-fat mayonnaise
Optional garnish: 2 tablespoons toasted coconut

1. Combine all ingredients in a pretty salad bowl; gently mix and serve or chill. This salad should be enjoyed within 8 hours of preparation to ensure fresh appearance and taste.

2. To toast coconut: sprinkle coconut over the bottom of a metal pie plate. Broil under low heat for 3 minutes. Remove and cool. Use as a garnish on the salad.

Calories per serving: 48 Fat: 2 g. Sodium: 62 mg.
For exchange diets, count: 1/2 starch
Preparation time: 5 minutes

Menu *of the* Day

Leftover Meatloaf or
Pork Sandwich
Ambrosia Toss
Sliced Cucumbers with
Reduced-Fat Italian Dressing
Skim Milk

*O Lord! Enable me to be more and more singly,
simply, and purely obedient to thy service.*
—Elizabeth Fry

What is BMI (Body Mass Index)?

Physicians and dietitians have traditionally used body weight as one means to check nutritional health. But the scale does not reveal the whole picture. The location and amount of body fat are actually better predictors of health risk than body weight. A new index of nutritional health is the BMI or body mass index. This measure is being used more and more in nutrition research to study weight-related health problems.

The BMI factors in the amount of body fat you have and is to be used only as a guideline for assessing nutritional health.

This is how to calculate BMI:

1. Convert your body weight to kilograms (1 kilogram = 2.2 pounds)

Example 155 pounds ÷ 2.2 = 70 kilograms

2. Convert your height to meters (1 meter = 39.37 inches)

Example: 70 inches ÷ 39.37 = 1.77 meters

3. Divide your weight in kilograms by your height in meters to find BMI

Example: 70 kilograms ÷ 1.77 meters = 39 BMI

The National Center for Health Statistics defines Risk for Health Problems Related to Body Weight as follows:

BMI	Risk
20-25	Very low risk
26-30	Low risk
31-35	Moderate risk
36-40	High risk
40+	Very high risk

Menu of the Day

Chunky Marinara Sauce
with Vegetables over
Thin Spaghetti

French Bread Broiled with
Reduced-Fat Mozzarella Cheese

Kiwifruit Topped with
Piña Colada Yogurt

Sugar-Free Lemon-Lime
Soft Drink

Always be a first-rate version of yourself,
instead of a second-rate version of somebody else.
—Judy Garland

March 11

Antioxidants—They Protect What's Inside You!

Today's menu is rich in Vitamins A, C, and E—those powerful antioxidants that protect us from cancer at the cellular level. An easy way to visualize antioxidant activity is to imagine these vitamins stamping out harmful effects of the contaminants and pollutants known to be the first domino in the formation of the cancer.

The Harvard Report on Cancer Prevention (November 1996) finds that healthier lifestyles could prevent half of all cancers and cancer deaths. Thirty percent of all cancer deaths are due to adult diet and obesity, and five percent are due to sedentary lifestyle.

God bless us with the common sense to protect ourselves and reduce our risk of cancer by choosing not to smoke, keeping our weight healthy, and eating plenty of antioxidant-rich fruits and vegetables.

Menu *of the* Day

Grilled Turkey Breast basted
with Orange Juice and
Reduced-Sodium Soy Sauce
Sweet Potatoes sprinkled
with Allspice
Fresh Spinach Salad with bits of
Bacon and Reduced-Fat Dressing
Strawberries
Apricot Nectar

March 12

Make Fiber Your Friend

Today's menu is rich in fiber. You know, roughage, those gas-producing foods that your grandma used to eat only on the days she stayed at home.

Today, we emphasize fiber at every meal, as it contributes to satiety (feeling fuller longer), smooths out blood glucose levels (an extra benefit if you have diabetes), and promotes blood flow to the digestive system, keeping it healthy.

Top Ten Ways to Add Fiber Every Day

1. Include a raw vegetable at both lunch and dinner.
2. Include a raw fruit at snack time such as apples, pears, peaches with the skins, or berries of any kind.
3. Eat a high fiber cereal for breakfast or at bedtime.
4. Include dried beans, peas, or lentils at least twice a week.
5. Use 100% whole wheat bread.
6. Use brown rice and pasta instead of white.
7. Use whole wheat buns, bagels, and muffins instead of white.
8. Load up on items that "crunch" at the salad bar.
9. Substitute wheat pilaf, couscous, or bulgar for plain white potatoes.
10. Keep dried fruits like apricots or raisins in the car and cupboard to stave off hunger.

Menu *of the* Day

Make your own
Boston Bean Casserole
Boston Bean Casserole is as simple as your favorite combination of canned beans in sauce slow cooked with a spoonful of molasses, dried onion, and chunks of lean ham.

Cornbread from a mix
with Soft Margarine
Radishes and Celery Sticks
Sliced Nectarine with the peel
Skim Milk

A merry heart doeth good like a medicine
but a broken spirit drieth the bones.
–Proverbs 17:22

March 13

Purple Cow
4 1-cup servings

After your walk, look forward to the refreshment of a fruit drink.
This recipe is just as tasty with orange, cranberry, or pineapple juice.

2 cups purple grape juice

1 cup nonfat frozen vanilla yogurt (may use sugar-free frozen yogurt)

1. Combine ingredients in a blender container. Blend until smooth and pour into 4 tumblers.

Calories per serving: 156 Fat: 0 Sodium: 38 mg.
For exchange diets, count: 2 fruit, 1/2 skim milk
Preparation time: 10 minutes

Menu of the *Day*

Cold Sliced Turkey on a
Submarine Roll with Bean
Sprouts, Cucumbers, and Tomato
and your favorite Condiments
Reduced-Fat Potato Chips
Stewed Tomatoes
Purple Cow

Nurturing Our Commitment to Healthy Changes

New wine must be put into new bottles.
—Luke 5:38

Are You Hydrated?

The average adult loses about 2 1/2 quarts (or 10 cups) of water daily through perspiration (this is without any exercise), urination, bowel movements, and breathing. Fluid losses are greater during hot weather, when you're exercising, during cold weather, in recirculated air environments (like airplanes), during pregnancy and breast-feeding, during any illness, and when eating a high-fiber diet. The body doesn't have room to store extra water, so fluid must be replaced often. If you consume more water than you need, your kidneys simply dump the overload.

Twelve cups of water daily will cover most adult needs. This water comes from drinking water and other beverages and from water present in foods.

How can you tell if you're becoming dehydrated? Watch for these progressive symptoms:

Thirst

Dry mouth, flushed skin, fatigue, headache

Increased body temperature, rapid breathing and pulse rate

Dizziness, increased weakness, labored breathing

Muscle spasms, swollen tongue, delirium, wakefulness

Poor blood circulation, failing kidneys

If you're tired of drinking water, just slice a piece of melon. It's 92 percent fluid!

Menu of the Day

Tuna and Noodle Casserole prepared with Reduced-Fat Cream of Mushroom Soup and Green Peas
Wheat Roll with Soft Margarine
Pear Slices drizzled with
All Fruit Raspberry Preserves
Skim Milk

*There is no mode of life in the world
more pleasing and more full of delight than
continual conversation with God. —Brother Lawrence*

March 15

Walking With God

As you're walking and talking with God, be mindful of
the many known physical benefits of movement:

Accelerates metabolic rate, even several hours
after exercise

Increases the rate at which you burn up stored
fatty acids

Decreases appetite

Builds up lean body mass, which speeds up
metabolism

Reduces stress and boredom

Motivates adherence to a healthy eating style

Changes your appetite to desire healthy foods

Improves your heart health by actually increasing
the size of your heart muscle

Increases the HDL (good cholesterol) in your
blood

Improves circulation of oxygen to all body cells

Improves circulation of essential nutrients to all
body cells

Improves muscle tone, agility, and balance

Increases stamina and endurance for daily
activities

Increases your resistance to minor illnesses by
boosting your immune system

Reduces emotional stress

Increases alertness

Menu *of the* Day

Grilled Lean Ham basted with
All Fruit Orange Marmalade
Boiled Small Potatoes with Parsley
Steamed Carrot Coins
Grapefruit Slices sweetened
with Cinnamon
Skim Milk

May God hold you in the palm of his hand.
—Irish Proverb

Leek and Potato Soup
8 1½-cup servings

Leeks are those giant green onions in the produce section. Shop for leeks with clean white bottoms and crisp fresh-looking green tops. Refrigerate, unwashed, in a plastic bag for up to a week. To prepare, cut off and discard the root ends. Trim the tops back, leaving about 3 inches of green leaves. Strip away and discard the coarse outer leaves, leaving the tender inner ones. Wash and trim the leeks under cold running water, separating layers and carefully rinsing out dirt. Enjoy steamed leeks with tarragon as a seasoning. My friend Mary Sadewasser discovered this wonderful recipe for leeks.

4 cups no-added-salt chicken broth
4 large potatoes, peeled and diced
1 large leek, chopped
1 grated carrot
1 tablespoon dried parsley
1 1/2 cups evaporated skim milk

1 1/2 cups skim milk
1 cup cooked diced chicken
1/2 teaspoon white pepper
1/4 teaspoon salt
Optional garnish: carrot curls

1. In a large pan, bring broth to simmering. Add potatoes, leeks, and carrots. Cover and simmer for 20 minutes.

2. Partially mash potatoes in broth. Add parsley and milks. Add chicken, pepper, and salt and continue to cook for 5 minutes. Garnish bowls of soup with carrot curls.

Calories per serving: 177 Fat: 2 g. Sodium: 827 mg.
For exchange diets, count: 1 starch, 1 skim milk
Preparation time: 15 minutes Cooking time: 30 minutes

Menu of the Day

Leek and Potato Soup
Raisin Scones from the bakery
Fresh Vegetable Relishes
Lime Sherbet
Green Tea

Today, reflect on the blessing and example of St. Patrick,
who used the three leafed shamrock to represent the Holy Trinity
in converting the Druids to Christianity.

March 17

Corned Beef and Cabbage
8 servings

If you are unfamiliar with corned beef, it is a brisket or round cut of beef cured in a seasoned salt solution or brine. The term "corned" comes from the English use of the word meaning any small particle (the salt). It is bright rosy red in color and is often sealed in clear vacuum packs and is usually found in the grocery store near the hams.

2 pounds corned brisket of beef, wiped with damp
    paper toweling
2 quarts cold water
6 peppercorns
6 whole allspice

1 bay leaf
1 large yellow onion, peeled and quartered
1 large cabbage, trimmed of coarse leaves, cored,
    and cut into 8 wedges
Optional garnish: prepared horseradish sauce

1. Place brisket in a very large kettle. Fill with water. Add peppercorns, allspice, bay leaf, and onion. Cover and bring to a boil over high heat. Reduce heat to low and simmer for 10 minutes. Skim off top layer of fat. Recover and simmer for 3 hours or until tender. Again, skim off any fat from the cooking water.

2. Add cabbage during last 15 minutes of cooking.

3. Arrange cabbage wedges around the outside of a large platter. Carve corned beef against the grain in thin slices. Garnish slices with horseradish sauce.

Calories per serving: 209 Fat: 9 g. Sodium: 122 mg.
For exchange diets, count: 3 lean meat, 2 vegetable
Preparation time: 10 minutes Cooking time: 3 1/2 hours

> ### *Menu* of the *Day*
> Corned Beef and Cabbage
> Potato Bread and Soft Margarine
> Pickled Beets from the jar
> Sliced Kiwifruit
> Skim Milk

Nurturing Our Commitment to Healthy Changes

By their fruits, ye shall know them.
—Matthew 7:20

Healthy Decision-Making

Spring renews our commitment to healthy patterns of movement and food choices. The season's change may also signal other life transitions, whether it be sprucing up the house, trading the car, or planning for a memorable summer.

Susan L. Lichtman shares thoughtful points for healthy decision making in the November 1996 issue of *Lutheran Woman Today* (page 14). Our alliance with Christ gives us a place of peace where we can prepare for the challenges ahead, and begin discovering what the next, right, healthy thing to do might be. Be willing to find the resources that God offers, in whatever form they appear.

1. Every person's journey is unique. Just because something has worked for someone else, does not mean that it's a good idea for you. Take advice from others as a suggestion, not a mandate.

2. Know what you can control, and what you cannot. As difficult as it can be to accept, we only control a limited amount of our experience. Take the time to discern what you can change, and make peace with your own limits.

3. Remember to care for yourself. Research studies clearly demonstrate that persons who are caring for others often ignore themselves. Include space and time to identify and address your own needs. The ones you love and care for need you to be as healthy in body, mind, and spirit as you can be.

Healthy Decision-Making continues tomorrow.

Menu of the Day

Swiss Burgers
(Lean Broiled Pork Burgers topped with Part-Skim Swiss Cheese)
Steamed Stir-Fry Vegetables
Raspberry Sorbet with Peach Slices
Skim Milk

Whosoever heareth these sayings of mine and doeth them,
I will liken him unto a wise man, which built his house upon a rock.
—Matthew 7:24

March 19

Day 2 of Healthy Decision-Making

4. Avoid "solutions" that can be harmful. This may appear self-evident, but think how easy it is to reach for a box of chocolates or a bottle of wine when life becomes stressful. Many things that are harmless when you are in a safe emotional place can create a disaster when you are in crisis. It is also easy to beat yourself up mentally after making trouble-some choices. Taking good care of your body and mind helps you hear God's voice in a situation.

5. One small manageable positive decision often leads to another. Breaking demands down into smaller pieces helps even the largest problem become "solution friendly." Making one healthy choice will help you better understand what your next step will be, and often gives you the positive energy you need to move forward.

6. Seek out support. Whether it is a neighbor, pastor, family member, or counselor, talk to people that you trust and who are willing to listen to your concerns. Gaining insight from another perspective is helpful. And seeking out support allows others an opportunity to minister to you.

7. God is present through every step in the process, even without invitation. The power, mercy, and love of God are always available, whether we want it or not. Thankfully, our behavior does not change God's willingness to be present for us during life's challenges.

Menu of the **Day**

Chef Salad: Tossed Lettuce,
Celery, Carrots, Cherry Tomato,
Radishes, and Peppers with thin
strips of Lean Ham and
Reduced-Fat Cheese
Wheat Crackers
Sliced Cantaloupe
Skim Milk

I believe in love, even when there's no one there.
And I believe in God; I believe in God, even when He is silent.
—from "I Believe," lyrics by unknown author

Asparagus Vinaigrette

4 1-cup servings

2 pounds fresh asparagus
1 tablespoon water
1 onion, chopped fine
1/4 teaspoon garlic powder
1/2 teaspoon salt, optional
1 1/2 teaspoons Dijon mustard

2 tablespoons lemon juice
1 tablespoon vegetable oil
1 teaspoon red wine
1/2 teaspoon vinegar
1/4 cup chopped fresh parsley

1. Trim and wash asparagus, then steam in microwave with water in a covered microwave dish on high power for 5 minutes.

2. Place spears in a flat shallow serving dish and sprinkle with finely chopped onion.

3. Combine all other ingredients except parsley in a blender container and pour over the asparagus. Chill in refrigerator for 20 minutes. Garnish with parsley and serve.

Calories per serving: 95 Fat: 4 g. Sodium: 179 mg. with salt; 57 mg. without salt
For exchange diets, count: 2 vegetable, 1 fat
Preparation time: 10 minutes Chilling time: 20 minutes

Menu of the Day

Broiled Salmon Steaks with
Dill Weed and fresh-squeezed
Lemon Juice
Asparagus Vinaigrette
Breadsticks with Soft Margarine
Frozen Yogurt
Orange-Pineapple Juice

It's only when we truly know and understand that we have a limited time on earth—and that we have no way of knowing when our time is up—that we will begin to live each day to the fullest, as if it was the only one we had.
—Elisabeth Kubler-Ross

March 21
First Day of Spring

Stand Up for Strawberry Pie
8 servings

Celebrate spring fever with strawberry pie.

Crust:
1 1/2 cups crushed cornflakes
2 tablespoons margarine, melted
1 tablespoon sugar

Topping:
8-ounce container low-fat vanilla yogurt

Filling:
4 cups sliced strawberries
2/3 cup sugar
1 cup water
3 tablespoons cornstarch
3 tablespoons corn syrup
3 tablespoons strawberry gelatin (may use sugar-free)

1. Preheat oven to 375°.

2. Combine ingredients for crust in a 9-inch pie plate. Press into pan and bake for 10 minutes until browned. Cool.

3. Put sliced berries into the crust.

4. Combine sugar, water, cornstarch, and corn syrup in a saucepan and boil for 2 minutes, stirring constantly. Remove from heat and stir in gelatin. Pour over berries.

5. Chill for 1 1/2 hours. Top with vanilla yogurt before serving.

Calories per serving: 194 Fat: 4 g. Sodium: 94 mg.
For exchange diets, count: 2 fruit, 1/2 starch, 1 fat
Preparation time: 20 minutes Chilling time: 1 1/2 hours

Menu *of the* Day

Your favorite Reduced-Fat Soup
out of a can with
Chopped Vegetables added
Grilled (Reduced-Fat) Cheese
Sandwich on Rye Bread
Stand Up for Strawberry Pie
Skim Milk

Nurturing Our Commitment to Healthy Changes

*Spring is when you feel like whistling
even with a shoe full of slush.*
—Doug Larson

Crunchy Banana Pudding
12 ½-cup servings

14-ounce can fat-free sweetened condensed milk
1 1/2 cups cold water
4-serving size package instant vanilla pudding mix

1 cup fat-free whipped topping
3 medium bananas
1/2 cup reduced-fat granola

1. In a large bowl, combine sweetened condensed milk and water. Add pudding mix; beat well and chill for 5 minutes. Fold in whipped topping.

2. Spoon 1 cup of mixture into a glass serving bowl. Top with one-third of bananas. Repeat the layering twice, ending with pudding.

3. Cover and chill for at least 1 hour.

4. Garnish with granola just before serving.

Calories per serving: 191 Fat: 3 g. Sodium: 71 mg.
For exchange diets, count: 2 fruit, 1 starch
Preparation time: 15 minutes Chilling time: 1 hour

Menu of the Day

Carryout Chicken
(discard the skin)
Hot Spiral Pasta
seasoned with Oregano
Fresh Raw Broccoli Chunks with
Reduced-Fat Ranch Dressing
Crunchy Banana Pudding
Decaf Coffee

*My Savior has not only provided for me pardoning love,
but renewing grace; nine-tenths of the believer's prayer is for purity of heart.
–R. Hill from* Coming Home *by Richard J. Foster*

March 23

Stromboli
4 3-ounce servings

1/2 pound lean ground beef
1 medium onion, sliced thin
4 ounces fresh mushrooms, sliced thin
2 cloves fresh garlic, minced, or 1/2 teaspoon
  minced garlic
1/4 teaspoon black pepper

1 cup prepared spaghetti sauce (I prefer Thick and
  Hearty Ragu)
1 pound loaf of French bread, cut in half lengthwise
2 ounces part-skim mozzarella cheese, shredded

1. In a Dutch oven, brown beef. Drain well and set aside.

2. In same Dutch oven, sauté onion and mushroom with garlic and pepper. Stir in drained meat and spaghetti sauce. Heat until bubbly.

3. Spread meat mixture over both halves of French bread and top with cheese. Broil six inches under low heat for 10 minutes. Slice and serve.

Calories per serving: 332 Fat: 10 g. Sodium: 402 mg.
For exchange diets, count: 2 starch, 2 vegetable, 2 lean meat
Preparation time: 15 minutes Cooking time: 10 minutes

Menu *of the* Day

Stromboli
Shredded Cabbage with Reduced-
Calorie Coleslaw Dressing
Fresh Banana
Low-Fat Chocolate Milk

Nurturing Our Commitment to Healthy Changes

O God, our help in ages past, Our hope for years to come
Our shelter from the stormy blast, And our eternal home.
–"O God, Our Help in Ages Past" by Isaac Watts (1674-1748)

Beef Burgundy Stew
8 1½-cup servings

There's nothing that envelops us into our home like a wild spring storm. Make one last beef stew before summer comes and it's too hot to start the oven.

1 pound boneless beef chuck or round, cut into
   1 1/2-inch pieces
1/2 teaspoon minced garlic or 2 garlic cloves,
   minced
2 tablespoons flour
1 cup beef broth
1/2 cup Burgundy wine

2 tablespoons tomato paste
2 bay leaves
1/2 teaspoon dried thyme
2 large potatoes, peeled and cut into wedges
8 ounces baby carrots
1 small onion, sliced into thin wedges
2 tablespoons parsley

1. Preheat oven to 350°.

2. In a large oven-proof stockpot, brown beef with garlic over medium heat.

3. In a small mixing bowl, combine flour, broth, wine, and tomato paste. Use a whisk to stir the mixture smooth.

4. Pour flour mixture over the browned meat. Add all remaining ingredients and stir to blend.

5. Cover and bake for 2 to 3 hours.

Calories per serving: 144 Fat: 4 g. Sodium: 190 mg.
For exchange diets, count: 2 very lean meat, 1 starch
Preparation time: 20 minutes Baking time: 2 hours

Menu *of the* Day

Beef Burgundy Stew
Baking Powder Biscuits
Sliced Apples
Chocolate Ice Milk
Skim Milk

God loves you, is present in you, lives in you, dwells in you, calls you, saves you, and offers you an understanding and light which are like nothing you ever found in books or heard in sermons. –Thomas Merton

March 25

Crunchy Wild Rice Salad

8 1-cup servings

Today's recipe is a great prescription for any leftover meat.

1 cup uncooked brown and wild rice blend
1/4 teaspoon seasoned salt
2 cups diced cooked meat of choice (suggest chicken, ham, or roast pork)
1 1/2 cups green grapes, halved

8-ounce can sliced water chestnuts, drained well
2 ribs celery, sliced thin
3/4 cup reduced-fat mayonnaise
1 tablespoon lemon juice
1 teaspoon sugar

1. Cook rice according to package directions (usually 30 to 40 minutes). Drain well, fluff with a fork, and cool to room temperature.

2. In a large salad bowl, combine cooled rice with salt, meat, grapes, water chestnuts, and celery.

3. In a small mixing bowl, blend mayonnaise, lemon juice, and sugar. Fold dressing into rice mixture and serve or chill until serving time.

Calories per serving: 229 Fat: 9 g. Sodium: 261 mg.
For exchange diets, count: 1 vegetable, 2 lean meat, 1 starch
Preparation time: 15 minutes Cooking time: 30 to 40 minutes

Menu *of the* Day

Crunchy Wild Rice Salad
Toasted Bagel with
Reduced-Fat Cream Cheese
Apple Slices
Skim Milk

Nurturing Our Commitment to Healthy Changes

For the beauty of the earth / For the beauty of the skies,
For the love which from our birth / Over and around us lies
Christ, our Lord, to you we raise / This our sacrifice of praise.
—"For the Beauty of the Earth" by Folliott S. Pierpoint (1835-1917)

Couscous with Peppers and Mint
8 ½-cup servings

2 1/4 cups water
10-ounce box couscous
7-ounce jar roasted peppers, drained and diced

1 tablespoon dried mint
1/2 teaspoon minced garlic
1 tablespoon soft margarine

1. Add water to a round 2-quart microwave-safe casserole dish. Microwave on high until water comes to a boil.

2. Add all ingredients to the boiling water. Stir to mix. Cover and let stand for 5 minutes. Fluff couscous lightly with a fork before serving.

Calories per serving: 145 Fat: 2 g. Sodium: 12 mg.
For exchange diets, count: 1 starch, 1 vegetable, 1/2 fat
Preparation time: 5 minutes Cooking time: 10 minutes

Menu *of the* Day

Grilled Lean Ham and Reduced-
Fat Cheddar Cheese Sandwich
Couscous with Peppers and Mint
Dried Apricots
Grape Juice

Outside the open window
The morning air is all awash with angels.
–*Richard Wilbur from* Cooking With Angels *by Julie Abbinante*

March 27

Cream of Asparagus Soup
8 1-cup servings

Enjoy fresh asparagus now. Look for firm, brittle spears that are bright green almost their entire length, with tightly closed tips. Wrap the ends in a slightly damp paper towel, seal the bunch in a plastic bag, and refrigerate (unwashed) for up to 3 days.

2 pounds clean tender asparagus, chopped in 1/4-inch slices
3 green onions, chopped fine
1 tablespoon vegetable oil
1 cup nonfat cottage cheese

1 cup evaporated skim milk
46-ounce can no-added-salt chicken broth
1/4 teaspoon curry powder
1/4 teaspoon white pepper
1 teaspoon dill weed

1. In a large stockpot, sauté chopped asparagus and green onion in oil for 6 to 8 minutes.

2. Put half of the cooked onion and asparagus into a blender container with the cottage cheese and milk. Process until smooth.

3. Add broth to the stockpot and stir to mix. Using a whisk, gradually add vegetable and milk mixture to the broth and vegetables. Heat just to scalding, stirring continually to prevent scorching. Reduce heat immediately. Stir in seasonings, and serve.

Calories per serving: 86 Fat: 2 g. Sodium: 134 mg.
For exchange diets, count: 1/2 skim milk, 1 vegetable, 1/2 fat
Preparation time: 15 minutes Cooking time: 15 minutes

Menu of the **Day**

Cream of Asparagus Soup
Homemade Wheat Bread from frozen dough with Soft Margarine
Red Raspberries
over Orange Sorbet
Skim Milk

Nurturing Our Commitment to Healthy Changes

I will give you rain in due season, and the land shall yield her increase, and the trees of the field shall yield their fruit. —Leviticus 26:3-4

Michele's Mushroom Salad

8 ½-cup servings

1 pound mushrooms, wiped clean and sliced
1/4 pound part-skim Swiss cheese, grated
2 bunches green onion, chopped fine
1/2 bunch parsley, minced

Dressing:
2 tablespoons olive oil
1/4 cup vegetable broth or dark beer
1/3 cup red wine vinegar
3 teaspoons Cavenders™ Greek seasoning

1. Layer mushrooms, grated cheese, green onions, and parsley in a salad bowl.

2. Combine ingredients for dressing in a shaker container and add to salad 15 minutes before serving. Toss, cover, and chill until serving.

Calories per serving: 71 Fat: 5 g. Sodium: 468 mg.
For exchange diets, count: 1 vegetable, 1 fat
Preparation time: 10 minutes Chilling time: 15 minutes

Menu *of the* Day

Grilled Sirloin Steak
Michele's Mushroom Salad
Broiled French Bread
with Soft Margarine
Blueberries with
Lemon Yogurt Topping
Herb Tea

Give me neither poverty nor riches;
feed me with food convenient for me.
—Proverbs 30:8

March 29

Eternal Pancakes
6 batches of pancakes, 10 4-inch cakes per batch

Find a large covered plastic container and whip up this pancake and waffle mix.
Store it in the cupboard and use it for a quick meal.

7 cups flour
2 cups nonfat dry milk powder
1 tablespoon salt

1/2 cup baking powder
1/2 cup sugar

1. Combine ingredients in a plastic container and mix well. Cover until use.

2. To prepare pancake batter, mix 1 1/2 cups of mix with 1 egg (or 1/4 cup liquid egg substitute), 1 cup of water or fruit juice, and 1 tablespoon of vegetable oil in a mixing bowl.

3. Stir until smooth, then cook in a non-stick skillet with non-stick cooking spray.

Calories per 2 4-inch pancake serving: 94 Fat: 2 g. Sodium: 271 mg.
For exchange diets, count: 1 starch
Preparation time: 15 minutes per batch

Menu *of the* Day

Eternal Pancakes
with All Fruit Preserves
Broiled Lean Bacon
Low-Fat Cottage Cheese Sundae
with assorted Fresh Fruit toppings
such as Strawberries, Pineapple,
Peaches, Bananas, and Grapes
Flavored Coffee

Nurturing Our Commitment to Healthy Changes

*I will praise Thee; for I am
fearfully and wonderfully made.
—Psalm 139:14*

Rhubarb Dream Dessert

8 servings

As soon as those tender rhubarb shoots turn pink,
weed around the plant, and pull some shoots for a spring dessert.

Non-stick cooking spray
4 cups fresh rhubarb, washed and chopped fine
  (may substitute fresh apples, berries, or peaches)
1/3 cup sugar
1/4 cup flour
1/8 teaspoon salt
1/2 teaspoon cinnamon

1/4 teaspoon nutmeg
2 eggs, beaten, or 1/2 cup liquid egg substitute
1 small package sugar-free strawberry gelatin
Topping:
2 tablespoons margarine
2 tablespoons brown sugar
1/3 cup oatmeal

1. Preheat oven to 350°.

2. Spray an 8- by 8-inch baking dish with cooking spray. Place chopped rhubarb in bottom of dish.

3. Combine all remaining ingredients except topping in a mixing bowl, blending well. Pour over rhubarb. Mix together topping ingredients just until crumbly. Sprinkle over rhubarb.

4. Bake for 35 minutes. Serve with low-fat frozen yogurt or fat-free whipped topping.

Menu *of the* Day

Grilled Breast of Turkey with
Honey Mustard on the side
Butternut Squash
Dinner Rolls with Soft Margarine
Rhubarb Dream Dessert
Iced Tea

Calories per serving: 137 Fat: 5 g. Sodium: 86 mg.
For exchange diets, count: 1 fruit, 1/2 starch, 1 fat
Preparation time: 15 minutes Baking time: 35 minutes

*There are some things we can't do, change, or
understand and those are God's parts to take care of.
—Patsy Clairmont from* Under His Wings

March 31

Garden Shrimp Salad
4 2-cup servings

Lighten up dinner with this shrimp salad. It will also work with mock crab.

8 ounces uncooked angel hair pasta
1 cup zucchini, cubed
1/2 medium yellow bell pepper, chopped
4 green onions, sliced
12 ounces frozen cooked shrimp, thawed

1/4 cup black olives, chopped
1/2 cup prepared reduced-calorie Dijon vinaigrette
   salad dressing
1 cup quartered cherry tomatoes
Romaine lettuce leaves

1. Break raw angel hair pasta into thirds. Cook as directed on package; drain. Rinse with cold water.

2. In a large bowl, combine pasta, zucchini, bell pepper, onions, shrimp, and black olives. Pour dressing over salad; toss gently to coat.

3. Cover and refrigerate 2 hours to allow flavors to blend.

4. When ready to serve, add tomatoes to salad. Gently toss again and serve on lettuce leaves.

Calories per serving: 145 Fat: 2 g. Sodium: 113 mg.
For exchange diets, count: 1 starch, 1 vegetable, 1 lean meat
Preparation time: 15 minutes Chilling time: 2 hours

Menu *of the* Day

Garden Shrimp Salad
Reduced-Fat Crescent Rolls
Fresh Nectarine
Skim Milk

Laughter is the brush that sweeps away the
cobwebs of the heart. —Mort Walker, King Features

Have a Good Laugh

An April Fool's laugh activates your muscles, increases your heart rate, and deepens your respiration, increasing oxygen exchange. All of these responses are similar to the desirable effect of athletic exercise. When you laugh, the muscles in your face, legs, and stomach get a mini-workout. So do your diaphragm, thorax, and circulatory and endocrine systems. Laughing could be called "internal jogging."

How can joy and laughter become characteristic of our lives?

Joy comes from being in God's presence. David's heart was glad; he had found the secret to joy. True joy is far deeper than happiness and laughter. We can feel joy in spite of our deepest troubles. Happiness is temporary because it is based on external happenings. But joy is lasting because it is based on God being present within us. As we contemplate his daily presence, we will find contentment. As we understand the future he has for us, we will experience joy. A life full of laughter and true joy is one spent following God.

Menu *of the* Day

Hamburger on a Bun with
crazy toppings such as
Sliced Radishes, Hot Pickled
Peppers, and Steak Sauce
Reduced-Fat Potato Chips
Carrot Sticks
Banana Splits made with
Reduced-Fat Frozen Yogurt,
Fresh Strawberries, and Fat-Free
Chocolate Syrup
Flavored Mineral Water

*We act as though comfort and luxury were the chief requirements of life,
when all that we need to make us happy is something to be enthusiastic about.*
–Charles Kingsley

April 2

Seven Strategies to Shed Seven Pounds by May Day

Surprisingly, the best way to take off weight is by making small adjustments in the way you eat and live. Here are seven strategies to help you feel in shape for spring.

Strategy 1: Try eating breakfast. If you skip breakfast, what you miss at the start of the day, you more than make up at the next meal. Nutritionists at the University of Colorado found that breakfast eaters consumed a diet lower in fat and higher in carbohydrates than breakfast skippers. Researchers believe that having breakfast may reduce the impulse to snack on high-calorie, high-fat, nutrient-poor foods.

Obesity specialist Dr. Wayne Callaway at George Washington University in Washington, D.C., says skipping any meal can actually lower metabolism. If working breakfast into your morning schedule seems like a hassle, try the Pita Break to get started.

Pita Break
1 serving

1 pita pocket
1 tablespoon reduced-fat cream cheese (try fruit flavored)

1/2 cup fresh or dried fruit of choice
1 tablespoon chopped walnuts

1. Stuff pita pocket with cream cheese, fruit, and nuts. Place on a paper napkin and microwave on high power for 20 seconds. Pick up and eat on the go.

Calories per serving: 187 Fat: 7 g. Sodium: 154 mg.
For exchange diets, count: 1 starch, 1 fruit, 1 fat
Preparation time: 3 minutes

Menu *of the* Day

Pita Break
Vegetable Beef Soup
Diced Mango over Lemon Sherbet
Skim Milk

Nurturing Our Commitment to Healthy Changes

Never eat more than you can lift.
—from Miss Piggy's Guide to Life

Seven Strategies to Shed Seven Pounds by May Day

Strategy 2: Try eating vegetarian twice a week. A very low-saturated-fat diet can reverse atherosclerosis. That's the medical term for fatty buildup on the walls of the arteries and veins. But a very low fat intake also trims the waistline. Start by replacing meat in one meal a week. Substitute diced vegetables: eggplant, mushrooms, peppers, beans of all sorts, and lentils. And try this all-American favorite with your family or friends.

Spicy Red Beans and Rice
8 2-cup servings

1 pound red beans, washed thoroughly and drained
3 cups red wine
1 cup water
1 clove garlic, minced
1 tablespoon Worcestershire sauce

2 teaspoons Louisiana hot sauce
2 slices bacon, diced
2 medium onions, chopped
1 teaspoon salt
6 cups cooked rice

1. Marinate beans in wine, water, garlic, Worcestershire sauce, and hot sauce overnight.

2. The next day, cook bacon until crisp in heavy stockpot. Drain bacon grease. Add onions and the bean mixture to the stockpot. Cook beans on high for 6 hours in the crockpot, or for 1 1/2 hours on medium heat on the stove top, or for 30 minutes in a pressure cooker at 15 pounds of pressure. If beans begin to appear dry during cooking, add 1/2 cup water. When beans are done to desired tenderness, add salt and serve over cooked rice.

Calories per serving: 319 Fat: 2 g. Sodium: 321 mg.
For exchange diets, count: 3 starch, 1 lean meat, 1 vegetable
Preparation time: 10 minutes Cooking time: crockpot—6 hours, stove top—1 1/2 hours, pressure cooker—30 minutes

Menu *of the* Day

Spicy Red Beans and Rice
Cornmeal Muffins
with Soft Margarine
Sugar-Free Lime Gelatin with
Pears
Skim Milk

Seven Strategies to Shed Seven Pounds by May Day

Strategy 3: Be smart about fat-free foods. Americans have a huge appetite for fat-free and reduced-fat foods. Unfortunately, many of these foods have a high calorie count. The reduced-fat, fat-free label has never been a free license to eat all you want. A reasonable solution is to use the one-to-one substitution rule. When you replace regular potato chips with fat-free chips, eat the same size portion, not a bigger one. In that way, you will maximize fat and calorie savings.

Yellow Light Foods—Eat Slowly
and Stop at First Sign of Being Full

Fat-free...
pretzels
potato chips
tortilla chips
bagels
rolls and pastries
cookies

crackers
brownies
frozen desserts
waffles and pancakes
cereals
salad dressings
dips

Menu of the *Day*

Water-Packed Tuna and
Reduced-Fat Cheddar Cheese
melted on a Bun
Pickles and Lettuce on the side
Reduced-Fat Potato Chips
Raw Cauliflower with
Reduced-Fat Ranch Dip
Cranberry Juice Cocktail

Nurturing Our Commitment to Healthy Changes

He not busy being born is busy dying.
—Bob Dylan from Do It! *by John-Roger McWilliams*

Seven Strategies to Shed Seven Pounds by May Day

Strategy 4: Beware of fatty condiments. A few years ago when navy chefs offered low-fat condiments aboard ship, overweight sailors lost an average of 12 pounds over 6 months. Consider the savings from these simple low-calorie substitutions they used:

Instead of using a tablespoon of mayo on sandwiches, try

honey or sweet mustard
brown or spicy mustard
chunky salsa or hot sauce
chutney
fat-free mayo or fat-free cucumber salad dressings
fat-free western dressing
steak sauce, soy sauce, teriyaki sauce, or hot sauce
pickled peppers or roasted red peppers
fresh sliced cucumbers or alfalfa sprouts
pickled beets

Instead of flavoring vegetables with butter, try

spray butter-flavored products
dried herb blends
butter-flavored sprinkles
dots of flavored vinegar
dots of soy sauce or teriyaki sauce

Instead of flavoring potatoes with margarine, try

nonfat yogurt plus dried chives
fat-free sour cream plus dill weed
nonfat cottage cheese plus onion powder
fat-free ricotta cheese plus garlic powder
whipping in chicken broth
soft cheddar cheese spreads
herb-flavored nonfat cream cheese

Menu of the *Day*

Broiled Pork Chop
Baked Potato with Condiments
Steamed Green Vegetable with Condiments
Red Grapes
Skim Milk

Seven Strategies to Shed Seven Pounds by May Day

Strategy 5: Slow down and eat! The average American wolfs down a meal in twelve minutes. This leads to overeating because it takes almost 20 minutes for the stomach to signal the brain that the body is full. If your lunch is gone in just ten minutes, there is not enough time to register satiety, that pleasant feeling of fullness. Getting in touch with your eating style is possible. Experiment with your own feelings of fullness with vegetable meals like Make a Meal of Asparagus.

Make a Meal of Asparagus

Recipe is for a single portion. Increase accordingly.

8 ounces (or 2 cups chopped) fresh asparagus per person
1 tablespoon chicken broth per person
1 diced green onion per person

1 1/2 ounces shredded reduced-fat Swiss cheese per person
1/4 cup Caesar-flavored croutons per person

1. Wash and trim fresh asparagus.

2. Cut into bite-sized pieces, and spread in a microwave-safe casserole dish. Sprinkle with chicken broth, dot with diced green onion, cover, and microwave on high power for 4 minutes.

3. Remove cover, sprinkle with cheese and croutons, and microwave on high power for 2 more minutes.

Calories per serving: 184 Fat: 8 g. Sodium: 322 mg.
For exchange diets, count: 3 vegetable, 2 lean meat
Preparation time: 15 minutes

Menu of the **Day**

Make a Meal of Asparagus
Fresh Wheat Rolls with
Soft Margarine
Chilled Fruit Cocktail
Skim Milk

Nurturing Our Commitment to Healthy Changes

When love and skill work together, expect a masterpiece.
–John Ruskin

Seven Strategies to Shed Seven Pounds by May Day

Strategy 6: One size doesn't fit all. Rethink your average portion size. When we hit age 28 or 30, our Basal Metabolic Rate (BMR) starts to slow and we need less food to maintain a healthy weight. What's a reasonable portion? The information below helps you gauge a healthy portion size. Watching your initial portion size when coupled with slow, deliberate eating is a sure means to reduce fat and calories.

> 1/2 cup of potatoes, dried beans, fruit, or pasta is the size of a woman's fist
>
> 3 ounces of meat, fish, or poultry is the size of deck of cards or the palm of a woman's hand
>
> 1 ounce of cheese is about the size of a golf ball or a 1-square-inch cube
>
> 1 cup of fresh greens is about the size of a hand holding a tennis ball
>
> 1 teaspoon of margarine is the same as a pat of butter in a restaurant
>
> 1 teaspoon of soft margarine is about the amount that will fit on the very tip of a knife.

Menu *of the* Day

Lean Broiled Meatballs
with your favorite Pasta Sauce
over Spaghetti
Fresh Cauliflower and Broccoli
with Reduced-Fat Italian Dressing
Broiled French Bread
Grape Juice

*One doesn't discover new lands without consenting
to lose sight of the shore for a very long time.*
—André Gide

Seven Strategies to Shed Seven Pounds by May Day

Strategy 7: Stick to fruit after 7 p.m. After-dinner snacking can simply wipe out the positive effect of your best eating choices over the whole day.

How can you be hungry after you've just had dinner? Sounds like a question we might ask a preschooler who wants a dessert.

But in reality, if you're still hungry after dinner, your dinner has not provided satiety. Did it contain 2 to 3 ounces of lean meat or another protein? Did you drink your milk? Was there any fiber in the meal? Protein and fiber slow digestion and help us get the signal that we are pleasantly full.

If your stomach starts to growl in the evening, settle it down with these fruit treats:

Raspberries	Orange
Strawberries	Grapefruit
Banana	Grapes
Sliced mango	Kiwifruit
Pineapple spears	Peach
Apple	Watermelon
Pear	Cantaloupe
Nectarine	

Menu of the *Day*

Cold Roast Beef on Rye Bread
with Mustard
Sauerkraut Seasoned with
Caraway Seeds
Applesauce
Skim Milk

Nurturing Our Commitment to Healthy Changes

*One can never consent to creep
when one feels an impulse to soar.
—Helen Keller*

Orange Cream Pie
8 slices

4 cups ice milk
6 ounces frozen orange juice concentrate
3 tablespoons Grand Marnier liqueur
  or 3 teaspoons orange extract

1 reduced-fat chocolate cookie crumb crust
1 tablespoon chocolate syrup
Optional garnish: fresh mint springs

1. Slightly soften ice milk at room temperature.

2. In a large mixing bowl, combine softened ice milk, orange juice concentrate, and liqueur or extract. Blend gently until mixture is smooth.

3. Spoon mixture into the crust and drizzle with chocolate syrup.

4. Freeze for 2 hours or until firm.

5. Garnish with fresh mint sprigs.

Calories per 1-slice serving: 193 Fat: 5 g. Sodium: 169 mg.
For exchange diets, count: 1 fruit, 1 starch, 1 fat
Preparation time: 15 minutes Chilling time: 2 hours

Menu *of the* Day

Reduced-Fat Frankfurters
on a Bun with your favorite
Condiments
Carrot Sticks
Canned Baked Beans seasoned
with Green Onions
Orange Cream Pie
Herb Tea

Marinated Ham Steak

4 servings

4 3-ounce ham steaks
1/4 cup Worcestershire sauce

1/4 cup brown sugar
1/4 cup lemon juice

1. Place ham steaks in a shallow pan.

2. In a small bowl, combine remaining ingredients, then pour over meat.

3. Allow ham to marinate at least 20 minutes or up to overnight in the refrigerator.

4. Broil just until meat is warmed through, about 4 minutes on each side.

Calories per serving: 191 Fat: 4 g. Sodium: 1388 mg.
For exchange diets, count: 3 lean meat, 1/2 starch
Preparation time: 5 minutes Marinating time: 20 minutes Broiling time: 10 minutes

---

Menu *of the* Day

Marinated Ham Steak
Baked Yams sprinkled with
Cinnamon and Ginger
Cold Cauliflower Chunks with
Reduced-Fat Ranch Dressing
Strawberries
Skim Milk

Nurturing Our Commitment to Healthy Changes

From silly devotions and sour-faced saints,
good Lord deliver us. —Teresa of Avila

What You Can Learn from Your Dog

Take plenty of walks and naps

Drinks lots of water

Don't bark too much

Make friends with everyone in the neighborhood

Don't go out without your ID

Make the people you love feel welcome when they come home

Every now and then, stand out in the rain.

Wipe your feet on the rug with you come in

It's OK to leave some food in the dish.

from Iowa State University Extension *Newsletter,* March 1997.

Menu of the **Day**

Browned Ground Turkey seasoned
with Dill Weed and Garlic
stuffed in a Baked Potato and
topped with Shredded Part-Skim
Mozzarella Cheese
Radishes and Celery
Sliced Peaches and Bananas
Skim Milk

Go now with God; be not tempted to stay in the safety of known places.
Move from where you are to where God points.
—Lutheran Woman Today, *January 1996*

April 12

Seafood Marinara
4 1½-cup servings

8 ounces dry spaghetti, cooked for 8 minutes,
    drained and rinsed
8 ounces mock crab, flaked

1 cup your favorite marinara sauce
2 tablespoons chopped green chilies

1. Toss all ingredients together in a microwave casserole dish.

2. Cook on high power for 4 minutes, stopping to stir twice. Mixture will be bubbly. Do not overcook, or the crab will be tough and the spaghetti will be mushy.

> Calories per serving: 322 Fat: 4 g. Sodium: 652 mg.
> For exchange diets, count: 3 starch, 1 vegetable, 2 lean meat
> Preparation time: 15 minutes

Menu *of the* Day

Seafood Marinara
Broiled Breadsticks
sprinkled with Parmesan
Sliced Cucumbers
and Cherry Tomatoes with
Reduced-Fat Dressing
Green Grapes
Skim Milk

God relies on us to be the tangible evidence of his love for the world.
—Mayo Mathers, Today's Christian Woman, September/October 1996

Grilled Garden Sandwich
4 sandwiches

Butter-flavored spray
8 slices whole wheat bread
4 ounces reduced-fat cheddar cheese
4 slices tomato
4 mushrooms, sliced thin

4 thin slices red onion
1 teaspoon dried Italian seasoning blend
Red-wine vinegar in a shaker container
Optional garnish: fresh lettuce wedge

1. Spray non-stick griddle or skillet generously with butter-flavored spray. Preheat griddle or skillet to medium heat.

2. Lay 4 slices of bread on serving plate. Layer with cheese, tomato, mushrooms, onion, Italian seasoning blend, and drops of red-wine vinegar.

3. Place another slice of bread on top of sandwich. Spray the top of the sandwich generously with butter-flavored spray.

4. Brown sandwiches over medium heat until golden brown. Turn over gently and brown the other side. Move to serving plate; garnish with fresh lettuce wedge.

Calories per serving: 201 Fat: 5 g. Sodium: 365 mg.
For exchange diets, count: 2 starch, 1 lean meat
Preparation time: 20 minutes

Menu of the Day

Grilled Garden Sandwich
Sliced Apples
Skim Milk

A life making ourselves available to others is more rewarding
than making people and things available to ourselves.
–Juan Palomo, USA Today

April 14

Seafood Chowder
4 1½-cup servings

11-ounce can clams, shrimp, or crab with juice
1/4 cup lemon juice
1 large onion, diced fine
1 large potato, peeled and cut into 1/4-inch cubes
1 tablespoon flour

1/4 teaspoon mace
6 drops hot red pepper sauce
2 cups evaporated skim milk
1/4 teaspoon white pepper

1. In a large stockpot, combine clams, lemon juice, diced onion, and potato. Cover and cook over medium heat for 15 minutes, allowing the juice to steam the vegetables.

2. In a shaker container, combine all remaining ingredients. Add liquid to the clams and bring just to a boil, stirring constantly as the mixture thickens. Reduce heat to low, simmer for 5 minutes, and serve with soda crackers.

Calories per serving: 199 Fat: 1 g. Sodium: 162 mg.
For exchange diets, count: 1 starch, 1 vegetable, 3 very lean meat
Preparation time: 20 minutes

Menu *of the* Day
Seafood Chowder
Soda Crackers
Reduced-Fat Baking Powder
Biscuit from a tube topped
with Finely Diced Green Onions
before baking
Fresh Pear
Tomato Juice

Render therefore unto Caesar the things which are Caesar's and unto God the things that are God's. —Matthew 22:21

Apricot Chicken
4 servings

Enjoy this elegant, but oh so inexpensive entrée on income tax day.

12 small dried apricot halves
4 boneless, skinless chicken breasts
1/2 teaspoon pepper
1/2 teaspoon ginger

4 green onions, diced
1 teaspoon dried rosemary
1/4 cup pineapple or orange juice
Garnish: 1/4 cup chopped fresh parsley

1. Preheat oven to 450°.

2. Soak apricots in very hot water for 15 minutes, then dice.

3. Season chicken with pepper and ginger and place on aluminum foil. Top with diced apricots, green onion, rosemary, and pineapple or orange juice. Fold the foil up around the chicken to make it airtight.

4. Bake for 20 minutes. Carefully unwrap foil and serve on a bed of rice. Garnish with fresh parsley.

Calories per serving: 155 Fat: 2 g. Sodium: 75 mg.
For exchange diets, count: 4 very lean meat, 1 vegetable
Preparation time: 10 minutes Soaking time: 15 minutes Baking time: 20 minutes

Menu *of the* Day

Apricot Chicken
Brown Rice
Fresh Spinach
with Reduced-Fat Dressing
Fresh Melon
Skim Milk

Five Days of Spring Fruits

Discover at least one new fruit this spring. Outstanding sources of nutrients are noted.

Apricots—Choose for vitamins A and C, potassium, and fiber.

*Look for—*plump fruit with as much golden orange color as possible. Blemishes, unless they break the skin, will not affect flavor. Avoid fruit that is pale yellow, greenish yellow, very firm, shriveled, or bruised.

*Fix it tip—*Ripen apricots at room temperature until they give to gentle pressure. To hasten ripening, place fruit in a loosely closed paper bag and check it daily. Refrigerate ripe, unwashed fruit in a paper bag for up to 2 days. Fill apricot halves with reduced-fat cream cheese and sprinkle with almonds for a quick salad or dessert.

Blueberries

*Look for—*plump, firm berries with a light grayish bloom.

*Fix it tip—*Wash and serve fresh with lemon sherbet.

Cantaloupe—Choose for vitamins A and C and potassium.

*Look for—*slightly oval fruit with yellow or golden (not green) background color. Signs of sweetness include pronounced netting and a few tiny cracks near the stem end; it should be slightly soft. The melon should be noticeably strong and sweet.

*Fix it tip—*To hasten ripening place whole melon inside loosely-closed paper bag. Once cut, melon will not get any riper; refrigerate it in sealed plastic bag. For a pretty dish, cut off the top one-fourth of a cantaloupe and hollow out.

Menu *of the* **Day**

Make your own spring Fruit Salad with Low-Fat Cottage Cheese, Assorted Fresh Fruits, and Low-Fat Granola
Cinnamon Raisin Toast
Vegetable Juice Cocktail
Herb Tea

Nurturing Our Commitment to Healthy Changes

O Lord, open thou my lips;
and my mouth shall show forth thy praise.
—Psalm 51:15

Day Two of Five Days of Spring Fruits

Cherries

Look for—plump, bright-colored sweet or sour cherries. Sweet cherries with reddish brown skin promise flavor. Avoid overly soft or shriveled cherries and those with dark stems.

Fix it tip—Add sweet cherries to a chicken salad. Poach sour cherries in a small amount of grenadine and serve over vanilla frozen yogurt.

Grapes

Look for—plump grapes firmly attached to pliable green stems. Avoid soft or wrinkled fruits and those with bleached stem areas. Grapes do not sweeten or ripen after picking.

Fix it tip—Serve with wedges of reduced-fat cheese and breadsticks for a quick appetizer.

Honeydew melon—Choose for vitamin C and potassium.

Look for—melons weighing at least 5 pounds, with waxy white rind barely tinged with green. Fully ripe fruit will have a cream-colored rind.

Fix it tip—Serve melon balls drizzled with amaretto liqueur.

Kiwifruit

Look for—softness similar to a ripe peach. Choose evenly firm fruit free of mold and soft spots. Ripen very firm fruit at room temperature, uncovered, out of direct sun. Refrigerate ripe fruit in a plastic or paper bag for up to one week.

Fix it tip—Cut a peeled kiwi into thin slices; mix with pineapple and banana for a quick salad.

Menu *of the* Day

All-Day Braised Beef Roast in
Beer in the Crockpot
Pour 1 can of beer over a beef roast
and cook for 4 to 8 hours on low.

Hot Shell Pasta sprinkled with
Cavenders™ Greek seasoning
Your favorite Fresh Fruit of spring
Skim Milk

---

*Let the heaven and earth praise him,
the seas, and every thing that moveth therein.*
—Psalm 69:34

April 18

Day Three of Five Days of Spring Fruits

Lemons

Look for—firm, heavy fruit. Rough-textured lemons have thicker skins and less juice than fine-skinned varieties.

Fix it tip—Dip lemon wedges in chopped fresh parsley or in paprika for a fun garnish.

Mangoes

Look for—a fruit that gives to gentle pressure. Avoid those with shriveled or bruised skin. Ripen at room temperature, uncovered, out of direct sun.

Fix it tip—Add mangoes to a spinach and fresh vegetable salad with honey mustard dressing.

Nectarines

Look for—orange-yellow (not green) background color between areas of red. Ripe nectarines give to gentle pressure, but are not as soft as ripe peaches.

Fix it tip—Nectarines are preferred over peaches or pears for brown bag lunches, as they are less apt to bruise in transit.

Papayas

Look for—fruit with the softness of peaches, with more yellow than green in the skin. Most need to be ripened further after purchase in a closed brown bag at room temperature.

Fix it tip—Cut in half lengthwise and scoop out the seeds, or peel with a vegetable peeler and cut into slices. Sprinkle with lemon or lime juice to enhance flavor.

Menu *of the* Day

Skinless, Boneless Chicken Breast
grilled with Garlic and Dill
on a Toasted Bun
Oven-baked French Fries
Chunks of spring Fruit with
Lemon Sherbet Topping
Skim Milk

Nurturing Our Commitment to Healthy Changes

*Oh that men would praise the Lord for his goodness,
and for his wonderful works to the children of men!*
—Psalm 107:8

Day Four of Five Days of Spring Fruits

Peaches

Look for—creamy or yellow background color. Ripe peaches give to gentle pressure. Soft, ripe peaches can be used immediately. Peaches do not become sweeter after picking, but will soften and become juicier. Ripen firm fruit in a closed paper bag at room temperature. Store ripe, unwashed fruit in the refrigerator in a paper bag for up to 3 days.

Fix it tip—Serve fresh sliced peaches on cream of wheat cereal.

Pears—Choose for vitamin C and fiber.

Look for—clear fruit with firm skin. Pears gradually ripen after picking, thus are suited to quantity purchase. To ripen green fruit, store in a paper bag at room temperature until they give to firm pressure. Refrigerate ripe, unwashed pears in a bag for 3 days.

Fix it tip—Use 1 part lemon juice with 3 parts water to retard browning on cut pears. Drizzle pear slices with maple syrup, and microwave on high power for 6 to 8 minutes for a hot dessert.

Pineapple

Look for—large, plump, fresh-looking fruit with green leaves and a sweet smell. Avoid fruit with soft spots, areas of decay, or fermented odor. Ripened fruit deteriorates quickly.

Fix it tip—Cut pineapple lengthwise into quarters, cutting evenly through leaves and core. Use a curved knife to cut fruit from the rind, gently lifting it away from the core. Use the hollowed-out shell as a serving bowl for fruit salad.

Menu *of the* Day

Ham Salad made with Reduced-Fat Mayo and Diced Ham stuffed in a Pita
Reduced-Fat Potato Chips
Your favorite spring Fruit topped with Piña Colada-Flavored Yogurt
Mineral Water

Day Five of Five Days of Spring Fruits

Plums

Look for—fruit that is full colored. Ripe plums are slightly soft at the tip end and give when squeezed gently in the palm of the hand.

Fix it tip—Plums travel well in brown bag lunches. Fill the cavity of plum halves with soft strawberry-flavored cream cheese for a simple dessert.

Raspberries—Choose for fiber.

Look for—firm, plump, well-shaped berries. If soft or discolored, they are overripe. Avoid baskets that looked stained from overripe berries. Use within 1 or 2 days of purchase.

Fix it tip—Serve in a footed dessert dish with sparkling wine.

Strawberries—Choose for vitamin C and fiber.

Look for—firm, plump berries that are full colored. Chandler, Pajaro, and Douglas varieties have excellent flavor. Chandler is preferred for freezing.

Fit it tip—Slice strawberries onto pancakes or waffles.

Watermelon—Choose for vitamins C and A.

Look for—fruit heavy for its size, brightly colored, well shaped, with a brown, dry rind. Thump the melon with the knuckles; you should hear a low pitch, indicating a full, juicy interior.

Menu *of the* Day

Baked Potatoes topped with
Leftover Roast Beef or Ham
and Shredded Pepper Cheese dot-
ted with Steak Sauce
Cherry Tomatoes
Your favorite spring Fruit
marinated in a Wine Cooler
Skim Milk

April 21

Thy faith has made thee whole.
—Matthew 9:22

Health and Spirituality

Prayer. Worship. Belief in a divine being. More and more, the medical profession is agreeing that spiritual beliefs and practices enhance health and well-being.

In the 20th century, modern medicine has largely kept health and spirituality separate. But for centuries, the two were linked.

Recent studies about spirituality's importance in medicine suggest that:

> Prayer may have improved recoveries of patients who underwent heart-bypass surgery at a San Francisco hospital.

> Regular church attendance may have helped reduce hypertension in elderly men.

> Religious faith helped ease the emotional anguish of those facing a cancer diagnosis.

Medicine remains firmly anchored in science, technology, and the objective methods that have conquered many diseases. Allow your own Christian beliefs to strengthen traditional medical care you receive by praying for your doctors, nurses, and caregivers, and by openly discussing your faith with them.

Menu of the **Day**

Turkey Cold Cuts on a
Pumpernickel Bagel with Spicy
Mustard and Sweet Pickles
Chopped Broccoli, Mushrooms,
and Baby Carrots with Reduced-
Fat Parmesan Dressing
Mandarin Oranges
Skim Milk

Heal me, O Lord, and I shall be healed;
save me, and I shall be saved.
—Jeremiah 17:14

April 22

Swiss Radish Salad

4 ¾-cup servings

2 cups thinly sliced radishes
2 ounces reduced-fat Swiss cheese, shredded
2 green onions, thinly sliced
1/4 teaspoon garlic powder
1 tablespoon white wine vinegar

1/2 teaspoon Dijon mustard
1/4 teaspoon salt
1/4 teaspoon pepper
1 tablespoon olive oil

1. In a salad bowl, combine radishes, cheese, and onions.

2. In a shaker container, mix all remaining ingredients. Pour over radishes. Stir and chill for 2 hours.

Calories per serving: 78 Fat: 5 g. Sodium: 327 mg.
For exchange diets, count: 1 vegetable, 1 fat
Preparation time: 10 minutes Chilling time: 2 hours

Menu *of the* Day

Ham Slices warmed in a skillet
with Pineapple Juice
Baked Potatoes
Swiss Radish Salad
Sliced Kiwifruit with
Raspberry Yogurt topping
Skim Milk

Nurturing Our Commitment to Healthy Changes

April 23

Ask, and it shall be given you; seek, and ye shall find;
knock, and it shall be opened unto you.
—Matthew 7:7

How to Listen to God in Prayer

Prayer is your personal communication with God and must involve active listening. Centering prayer is a form of Christian contemplation in which we quiet our soul and listen for God's still small voice. Begin by finding a comfortable position. Relax your body and take several deep breaths. Fix your mind on a single word that represents God for you (such as Father or Lord). Say this word over and over silently in your mind. Use the word to bring yourself into an awareness of God's presence.

If you find your thoughts drifting toward the trivial concerns of the day, do not punish yourself, but slowly, gently use your prayer word to bring you back to God. After about 15 to 20 minutes you will emerge from your prayer time feeling calm and spiritually renewed.

Susan and Jay Trygstad, *Lutheran Woman Today,* May 1996
Used with permission.

Menu of the *Day*

Broiled Salmon Steak sprinkled
with Old Bay seasoning and
dotted with Soft Margarine
Quick Rice
Sliced Cucumbers and Red Onions
dotted with Tarragon Vinegar
Mango and Banana Slices
Skim Milk

The eyes of the Lord are over the righteous;
and his ears are open unto their prayers.
—I Peter 3:12

April 24

Easy French Dip
4 sandwiches

1/2 pound rump roast
1 large onion, cut into thin rings
1 envelope dried onion soup mix

1 can beer or beef broth
4 hoagie rolls

1. Combine all ingredients in a slow cooker. Cook over medium heat for 3 to 4 hours.

2. Slice meat and put on a hoagie bun. Serve with the juice from the slow cooker on the side, served in a short mug or custard cup.

Calories per 1-roll serving: 299 Fat: 5 g. Sodium: 1212 mg.
  (To reduce sodium, use just 1/2 packet of onion soup mix.)
For exchange diets, count: 2 lean meat, 2 starch, 1 vegetable
Preparation time: 5 minutes Cooking time: 3 hours

Menu *of the* Day

Easy French Dip
Green Beans with Dill Weed
Banana
Skim Milk

Miracles happen to those who believe in them.
—Bernard Berenson

Chicken Enchilada Casserole

4 servings

Non-stick cooking spray
11-ounce can diced white meat chicken
14-ounce can diced tomatoes
1/4 teaspoon garlic powder
1/4 cup fresh parsley

6 corn tortillas
2 ounces reduced-fat Monterey Jack cheese, shredded
3-ounce can diced green chilies

1. Preheat oven to 375°.

2. Combine chicken, tomatoes, garlic, and parsley in a bowl.

3. Spray an oblong 11- by 7-inch casserole dish with cooking spray.

4. Place 2 tortillas over the bottom of the prepared pan.

5. Spoon half of the chicken mixture over the tortillas.

6. Place 2 tortillas over the top of the chicken.

7. Spoon remaining half of chicken over the tortillas.

8. Place last 2 tortillas over the chicken.

9. Sprinkle with cheese and chilies; cover and bake for 45 minutes.

10. Remove from oven, and allow to sit for 5 minutes. Cut and serve.

Menu *of the* Day

Chicken Enchilada Casserole
Chopped Fresh Spinach with
Reduced-Fat Dressing
Pineapple Spears
Skim Milk

Calories per serving: 252 Fat: 7 g. Sodium: 335 mg.
For exchange diets, count: 1 starch, 1 vegetable, 4 very lean meat
Preparation time: 15 minutes Baking time: 45 minutes

Recipe for Popcorn Prayer

Can a prayer be as fun as a bowl of popcorn?

Try this prayer the next time you are with a group. Everyone holds hands in a circle. The leader invites everyone to participate in the prayer. The prayer can be a name, feeling, hope, sorrow, or whatever you have on your heart. The only restriction is that each time a person prays, the petition can only be one word long. This enables those who have had little experience praying aloud in public to participate fully. It's called a popcorn prayer because it seems to pop from one side of the circle to the other, and the effect is like that of corn popping on the stove. Of all corporate prayers, this may be the most participatory and most joyful!

Menu *of the* Day

Broiled Minute Steaks
with Teriyaki Seasoning
Broiled Red Skinned Potatoes
with Soft Margarine
Shredded Cabbage with
Reduced-Calorie Dressing
Golden Delicious Apple Slices
Skim Milk

Nurturing Our Commitment to Healthy Changes

The Prayer of Abandonment
For a peace that passes all human understanding,
Father, I abandon myself into your hands; Do with me what you will.
Whatever you may do, I thank you. —Brother Charles de Foucauld

Golden Cheese Sauce
8 ¼-cup servings

4 ounces reduced-fat American cheese, cut into strips or chunks
1/4 cup skim milk
1 teaspoon Worcestershire sauce

1/2 teaspoon dry mustard
1/2 teaspoon minced onion
Pinch of white pepper
1/2 cup fat-free sour cream

1. Combine all ingredients except sour cream in a medium-size microwave-safe mixing bowl.

2. Microwave on high power for 4 minutes, stirring twice with a wire whisk, until the cheese is smooth.

3. Gently fold in sour cream. Microwave 1 more minute, and serve over hot vegetables.

Calories per serving: 43 Fat: 1 g. Sodium: 250 mg.
For exchange diets, count: 1/2 skim milk
Preparation time: 10 minutes

Menu of the Day

Broiled Hamburger on a Bun
with Lettuce, Tomato, and Sprouts
Steamed head of Cauliflower
with Golden Cheese Sauce
Chilled Fruit Cocktail
Skim Milk

Praise to the Lord, the Almighty, the King of creation! O, my soul,
praise him, for he is your health and salvation! Let all who hear
now to his temple draw near, Joining in glad adoration!
—"Praise to the Lord, the Almighty" by Joachim Neander, 1650-1680

April 28

Skillet Sausage and Peppers
4 servings

4 reduced-fat sweet Italian sausages
1 green pepper, seeded and cut into 1-inch pieces

1 large onion, cut into rings
14-ounce can chunky tomatoes

1. Place sausages in a large skillet. Cook over medium-high heat, browning them evenly and pouring off any drippings.

2. Add all remaining ingredients, and cook over medium heat for 20 minutes. Serve over rice or thick slices of Italian bread.

Calories per serving: 200 Fat: 12 g. Sodium: 893 mg.
For exchange diets, count: 2 vegetable, 2 lean meat, 1 fat
Preparation time: 10 minutes Cooking time: 25 minutes

Menu *of the* Day

Skillet Sausage and Peppers
Italian Bread
Whole Kernel Corn
Honeydew Melon
Skim Milk

We give thanks unto the Lord for he is good.
—Psalm 106:1

Reinventing the Family Meal

Family mealtime provides your chance to build a family team and to forge strong relationships. As hectic summer schedules approach, it may be time to recommit to family meals. Consider these steps:

1. Decide to be together certain nights each week, then do it. You may have to ask each other, "What will be most important years from now, this meeting or activity, or having meals together?"

2. Take the phone off the hook or let the answering machine take all the calls during mealtime.

3. Prepare the meal and clean up together.

4. Eat at the table facing each other.

5. Have everyone come at the same time and remain at the table until everyone is excused.

6. Ask open-ended questions. Review the best, the worst, and the funniest events in your day.

7. Make meals a time of celebration. Occasionally bring out the good china or candles.

Susan Alexander Yates, *Today's Christian Woman,* November/December 1996

Menu *of the* Day

Pan-grilled Fillet of Sole
with Garlic, Dill Weed, and
Lemon Juice
Hot Shell Pasta dotted with White
Wine Vinegar and Dried Tarragon
Steamed Julienne Carrots
Raspberries
Skim Milk

The Johnny Appleseed Table Prayer
Oh, the Lord is good to me, and so I thank the Lord.
For giving me the things I need, the sun and the rain and the apple seed.
Oh, the Lord is good to me. Amen

April 30

Sour Cream Lemon Pie
12 slices

1 prepared reduced-fat graham cracker crust
1 cup sugar
1/4 cup cornstarch
1/8 teaspoon salt
1 cup skim milk
3 egg yolks, beaten

2 tablespoons butter-flavored soft margarine (such as I Can't Believe It's Not Butter)
1/4 cup fresh lemon juice
1 teaspoon finely grated lemon peel
1 cup nonfat sour cream
1 cup fat-free whipped topping
Optional garnish: finely grated lemon rind

1. In a medium saucepan, combine the sugar, cornstarch, and salt. Gradually stir in the milk. Bring mixture to a boil over medium heat, stirring constantly. Cook and stir for 2 minutes.

2. Beat egg yolks together in a small mixing bowl. Blend a small amount of the hot mixture into the eggs. Mix well and return all to the pan.

3. Cook over medium heat, stirring constantly for 2 more minutes. Remove from the heat; add margarine, lemon juice, and lemon peel. Mix well. Place a piece of wax paper over the top of the pudding and set aside; allow the mixture to cool at least 30 minutes.

4. Fold in sour cream, then spoon into crust. Spread with whipped topping and chill at least 2 hours. Garnish with finely grated lemon rind before serving.

Calories per 1-slice serving: 219 Fat: 6 g. Sodium: 201 mg.
For exchange diets, count: 1 1/2 fruit, 1 starch, 1 fat
Preparation time: 20 minutes Chilling time: 2 1/2 hours

Menu of the *Day*

Pork Chops on the grill
with Barbecue Sauce
Steamed Butternut Squash
with Allspice
Dinner Rolls with Soft Margarine
Green Salad with
Reduced-Fat Dressing
Sour Cream Lemon Pie
Skim Milk

Nurturing Our Commitment to Healthy Changes

Celebrating Our Connections

We have been renewed and comforted through winter. March and April were a time to gear up and take a serious look at our food choices.

May is now here. The trees have all budded, the flowers have started to bloom, and we, too, feel more alive. We now turn to invigorating our life with friends and family.

Celebrating Our Connections is a two-month focus on family and relationships. We revisit the custom of delivering May baskets. On Mother's Day, we go out to dinner and dine on especially nourishing messages for all mothers. We take a look at family behaviors and habits that encourage and support healthy choices. And by the end of May, we are thinking about our favorite graduate and Memorial Day potlucks. Family togetherness is further highlighted in favorite recipes for reunions and a selection on "How to Make a Family Cookbook."

June brings a big mouthful of summer vegetables. Take time to learn about jicama this year. Recipes for dips and cool summer desserts are sprinkled in this month. And the month ends with a food safety checklist for worry-free picnics.

However large, however colorful, however old or young your family circle is, give thanks for all your loving connections.

May Baskets

Let May Day bring out the kid in you. Celebrate the tradition by gathering a few goodies and secretly delivering them to a special friend who needs to feel like a kid again.

Ideas for May basket containers: old baskets, cardboard berry baskets, pretty paper plates, aluminum frozen dinner trays, or discarded notecard or stationery or shoe boxes.

Ideas for May basket treats: Low-Fat Rice Krispie Treats (recipe follows), boxes of raisins, whole pieces of fresh fruit, and hard candy.

Low-Fat Rice Krispie Treats
16 squares

Non-stick cooking spray
2 tablespoons reduced-fat margarine
40 large marshmallows

2 tablespoons corn syrup
6 cups crisped rice cereal

1. Spray a 13- by 9-inch baking pan with cooking spray.

2. In a large mixing bowl, microwave margarine on high for 20 seconds. Add marshmallows and corn syrup and mix well. Microwave on high for 1 1/2 minutes or until mixture is smooth when stirred. Immediately add cereal, mixing lightly until well-coated.

3. Spread mixture into baking pan, let stand for 30 minutes, then cut into squares.

> Calories per 1-square serving: 113 Fat: 1 g. Sodium: 101 mg.
> For exchange diets, count: 1 starch, 1/2 fruit
> Preparation time: 10 minutes Cooling time: 30 minutes

Menu of the Day

Pork Roast slow cooked in
Light Beer with Garlic, Oregano,
and Pepper
Mashed Potatoes
with Soft Margarine
Steamed Brussels Sprouts
dotted with Herb Vinegar
Low-Fat Rice Krispie Treats
Skim Milk

I am the vine, ye are the branches.
–John 15:5

Spring Greens

It's spring and time to give up the trusty iceberg lettuce. If you don't have access to fresh spinach or lettuce from a garden, be bold and buy a new green from the market. Here is a guide to greens:

Arugula: Mellow to bold flavor, peppery, nutty, fleshy, and tender with long medium-green leaves.

Chard: Sweet and crunchy, with spinach-flavored leaves in green or red.

Chervil: Cool licorice flavor; delicate feathery texture.

Dandelion: Bitter bite, grassy taste and texture.

Endive: Also known as whitloof chicory; slight bitter flavor. Red is sweeter than white, and curly endive is the sweetest.

Kale: Several kinds, including red and white Nagoya, red and white flowering, and red Russian. Young leaves have firm texture and cabbage flavor.

Radicchio: Red, slightly bitter, almost as firm as cabbage.

Red or Green Romaine: Tender faint beet-like flavor.

Spinach: Dark green, slightly sweet, metallic taste.

Tango: Sweet lettuce, tender soft-crisp.

Watercress: Lively heat, tender, juicy, and fleshy.

Menu *of the* Day

Toasted English Muffin broiled
with Pizza Sauce, Pepperoni,
and Shredded Mozzarella

Spring Green Salad with
Reduced-Fat Italian Dressing

Fresh Banana
and Strawberry Slices

Sugar-Free Lemonade

Genius is recognizing the uniqueness in the unimpressive.
It's looking at a homely caterpillar, an ordinary egg, and a selfish infant
and seeing a butterfly, an eagle, and a saint. —William Arthur Ward

May 3

Tarragon Radicchio
4 servings

4 ounces radicchio
1 tablespoon olive oil
1/4 teaspoon minced garlic
3 tablespoons rice vinegar (or white vinegar)

1 tablespoon finely cut fresh tarragon
  or 1 teaspoon dried tarragon
1/4 teaspoon salt
1/4 teaspoon pepper

1. Cut radicchio in half, removing core. Slice across the grain into thin slices, as if making coleslaw.

2. Wash and dry thoroughly with paper towels.

3. Heat oil in a large skillet. Add garlic, cook 1 minute, then add radicchio, stirring constantly until almost wilted. Immediately remove from heat and add vinegar, stirring well. Add tarragon, salt, and pepper. Serve hot, warm, or at room temperature.

Calories per serving: 48 Fat: 3 g. Sodium: 145 mg.
For exchange diets, count: 1 vegetable, 1/2 fat
Preparation time: 10 minutes

Menu *of the* Day

Orange Roughy grilled with
Teriyaki Sauce
Herbed Rice Side Dish from a box
Tarragon Radicchio
Orange Sherbet with
Crushed Pineapple on top
Skim Milk

May 4

And God said, "Let the earth bring forth living creatures of every kind: cattle and creeping things and wild animals of the earth of every kind," and it was so. —Genesis 1:24

May is Beef Month

Use the following Beef Cuts Cookery Guide to help you select the cut best suited for your summer grilling pleasure. The leanest, best-tasting cuts are sirloin and filet mignon.

Beef Cuts Cookery Guide

Entrée	*Suggested Cut*
Broiled Steak	T-bone, Porterhouse, Top Loin, Sirloin, Rib, Ribeye, Tri-Tip Steak, Chuck Eye, Tenderloin (Filet Mignon), Chuck Top Blade
Broiled Steak Requires Marinade	Top Round (1-inch thick), Round Tip Flank, Boneless Arm or Shoulder Steaks
London Broil	Top Round, Flank Steak
Stir-Fry	Round Tip, Sirloin, Flank, Top Round, Stir-Fry Strips
Kabobs	Sirloin Steak cut into pieces; Round Tip or Round Steak cut into strips, marinated, and woven on skewers
Fajitas	Skirt, Flank, Top Round, Sirloin Steaks

Menu *of the* Day

Your Favorite Beefsteak
Baked Potato with Fat-Free
Sour Cream and Fresh Chives
Steamed Baby Carrots dotted
with Lemon Juice and Honey
Honeydew Melon Wedge
Skim Milk

And then God said, "Let us make human kind in our image, according to our likeness; and let them have dominion over the fish of the seas, and over the birds of the air, and over cattle, and over all the wild animals of the earth and over every creeping thing that creeps upon the earth." —Genesis 1:26

May 5

All-American Beef Kabobs
8 kabobs

1/2 cup reduced-sodium soy sauce
2 tablespoons vegetable oil
1 tablespoon dark corn syrup or maple syrup
1/2 teaspoon minced garlic
1 teaspoon dry mustard
1 teaspoon ground ginger

2 pounds beef sirloin steak, cut into 1 1/2-inch pieces
3 green peppers, cut in 1-inch squares
4 small firm tomatoes, quartered
1 small yellow onion, quartered and peeled into wedges

1. In a large bowl, combine first 6 ingredients. Add sirloin and marinate in the refrigerator for 30 minutes or overnight.

2. Drain meat. Alternate meat, pepper, tomato, and onion on skewers.

3. Grill over medium-hot coals until desired doneness, allowing 15 minutes for rare.

Calories per 1-kabob serving: 318 Fat: 14 g. Sodium: 1051 mg.
  (To reduce sodium, use 1/4 cup reduced-sodium soy sauce and 1/4 cup red wine.)
For exchange diets, count: 4 lean meat, 2 vegetable, 1 fat
Preparation time: 15 minutes Marinating time: 30 minutes Grilling time: 15 minutes

---

Menu of the **Day**

All-American Beef Kabobs
White Dinner Rolls
with Soft Margarine
Watermelon
Skim Milk

May 6

Dear God, I love to eat. Thanks for all the food.
Pizza was the best idea you had. Ralph (age 7)
—from Dear God, Children's Letters to God, *by David Heller*

Memo to Mothers: Take a Day Off

As Mother's Day approaches, be kind to yourself. Throw a frozen pizza in the oven. Just for today, give yourself time to soak up all the love and attention the greeting card companies have prodded American families to share.

Consider "Life Lessons for Mothers," by Cindy Francis from the *Des Moines Register*.

The greatest gift you have to give your children is you.

Your children provide you with a second chance to do the things you loved as a youngster. Take a chance.

When you talk to your child, mostly listen.

Sometimes when your children expect punishment, give them a big hug instead.

Tell your child often, "I love you, no matter what."

Balance is the key. Balance work with play, time with the children with time alone.

Rituals like having dinner together make children feel secure.

Surprise your child with little fits of kindness.

Show your children you're on their side.

Menu *of the* Day

Frozen Pizza
with Garden Veggies added:
Diced Peppers, Onion,
Mushrooms, Carrots, Broccoli

Fresh Tangerine
Skim Milk

From your lofty abode you water the mountains;
the earth is satisfied with the fruit of your work.
—Psalm 104:13

Choose Your Fruit Cheesecake
12 slices

1 reduced-fat graham cracker crust
2 8-ounce packages 50% reduced-fat cream
  cheese, softened to room temperature
1/3 cup sugar

1 teaspoon vanilla
2 eggs or 1/2 cup liquid egg substitute
2/3 cup your favorite light fruit pie filling, such as
  blueberry, cherry, or raspberry

1. Preheat oven to 350°.

2. In a small mixing bowl, beat together cream cheese, sugar, and vanilla with an electric mixer until smooth and creamy.

3. Beat in eggs.

4. Pour in prepared crust. Spoon in small amounts of the pie filling and gently swirl with a toothpick.

5. Bake for 40 minutes until the center is set. Cool to room temperature, and then refrigerate at least 1 hour.

Calories per 1-slice serving: 192 Fat: 9 g. Sodium: 343 mg.
For exchange diets, count: 1/2 skim milk, 1 starch, 1/2 fruit, 1 fat
Preparation time: 10 minutes Baking time: 40 minutes
  Chilling time: 1 hour

Menu *of the* Day

Low-Fat Hot Dogs on the grill
served on a Bun with your
favorite Condiments
Canned Baked Beans
Reduced-Fat Potato Chips
Choose Your Fruit Cheesecake
Sugar-Free Cola

Humility means to live as close to the truth as possible: the truth about ourselves, the truth about each other, the truth about the world in which we live.
—Coming Home: A Prayer Journal, *by Richard J. Foster*

Saying Yes to Your Family

Feeling guilty about a messy house, throw-together meals, and doing everything halfway?

This Mother's Day, say yes to your family and let the rest go. Your house has to be clean enough to keep your family healthy, but "hospital clean" signals an obsession.

Children and family relationships need to take priority over possessions, committees, and meaningless rituals. If it takes you an hour every week to water your plants, you may have too many plants. Give a couple away.

Saying no to volunteer causes doesn't make you less of a human being or a mother. Choose one or two things that you have a passion for, and complete the assignments with joy.

Never immediately say yes to any request. Allow yourself just 15 seconds to be reminded of how a new commitment is going to impact those you love most.

Menu of the Day

Hamburgers from the
drive-through

Frozen Veggies steamed
in the microwave

Sliced Apples, Celery, and
Raisins tossed with Vanilla Yogurt

Iced Tea

Family Meals Cited as Key Factor in Drug-Free Behaviors

The following characteristics were recently identified among baby boomer families as making drug use among teenagers least likely:

1. Eating dinner with their families 6 to 7 nights a week.

2. Attending a drug-free school.

3. Being concerned about performing well in school.

4. Feeling that using drugs is morally wrong.

5. Not having friends who smoke cigarettes, use alcohol, or smoke marijuana.

6. Attending church regularly with parents.

Parental characteristics that place teens at higher risk for using drugs:

1. Rarely having dinner together.

2. Expecting their children to use drugs.

3. Not giving a specified curfew.

4. Not attending religious services or not taking children along.

5. Having smoked marijuana and the teen knows it.

6. Thinking marijuana is not dangerous.

7. Blaming the drug problem on the teen's friends, or on society, or on the entertainment industry, which makes light of drug use.

Menu *of the* Day

Chicken Salad *(Canned Chicken, Sweet Pickles, and Light Mayo)*
on Wheat Toast
Fresh Spinach Salad with
Reduced-Fat Dressing
Pineapple Spears in Juice
Skim Milk

Honor your father and your mother, so that your days may be long in the land that the Lord your God is giving you. —Exodus 20:12

Honey Lemon Chicken

4 servings

1/4 cup honey
1/4 cup lemon juice
1 teaspoon rosemary
1 teaspoon grated lemon peel

1/2 teaspoon salt
1/8 teaspoon pepper
4 boneless, skinless chicken breasts

1. In a shallow pan, combine all ingredients except chicken and mix well. Place chicken in marinade for at least 30 minutes or up to 24 hours.

2. Remove chicken from marinade. Broil chicken for 5 minutes; turn and broil 4 more minutes or until the juices run clear.

Calories per serving: 231 Fat: 5 g. Sodium: 331 mg.
For exchange diets, count: 3 lean meat, 1 fruit
Preparation time: 10 minutes Marinating time: 30 minutes Broiling time: 10 minutes

Menu *of the* Day

Honey Lemon Chicken
Broiled Red-Skinned Potatoes
Steamed Broccoli
Sliced Green Grapes
and Chunks of Cantaloupe
Skim Milk

Faith is a power that can take up quite insurmountable obstacles and lift them from our path, it can change the whole landscape for us, it can make possible what looks impossible.
—Lewis Maclachlan from Living Prayer *by Maxie Dunham*

May 11

Dreamy Amaretto Nectarines

4 ½-cup servings

2 tablespoons amaretto liqueur or 2 teaspoons almond extract

2 tablespoons dark brown sugar

1 cup nonfat sour cream

2 cups thinly sliced fresh nectarines

1. In a small mixing bowl, stir amaretto and brown sugar until smooth. Add sour cream and mix well.

2. Put fruit into footed glass dishes. Drizzle with cream.

Calories per serving: 103 Fat: 0 Sodium: 71 mg.
For exchange diets, count: 1/2 skim milk, 1 fruit
Preparation time: 10 minutes

Menu *of the* Day

Fresh Parmesan Cheese, Dried Basil, and Chunk Tuna tossed with Linguine
French Bread with Soft Margarine
Fresh Greens with Italian Dressing
Dreamy Amaretto Nectarines
Skim Milk

May 12

And at the end, if we are brave enough to love, and strong enough to forgive, then we achieve fulfillment no other living creature will ever know.
—Rabbi Harold S. Kushner, from How Good Do We Have To Be?

Spring Fruit Meringues
4 servings

2 egg whites, at room temperature
1 teaspoon vanilla
1/4 teaspoon cream of tartar
Dash of salt

1/2 cup sugar
1 tablespoon cocoa
2 cups fresh sliced strawberries, blueberries, or raspberries

1. Preheat oven to 275°. Line baking sheets with parchment paper or brown grocery sack paper.

2. In a mixing bowl, beat egg whites with vanilla, cream of tartar, and salt until soft peaks form. Beat in sugar a little at a time until stiff peaks form. Sprinkle cocoa over the top and gently fold in.

3. Drop by 1/4 cup portions onto parchment paper. Indent each with the back of a spoon.

4. Bake for 45 minutes or until dry to the touch. Remove meringues and cool. Fill the center of each with fruit, and serve immediately.

Calories per serving: 115 Fat: 0 Sodium: 5 mg.
For exchange diets, count: 2 fruit
Preparation time: 15 minutes Baking time: 45 minutes Cooling time: 15 minutes

Menu of the Day

Pita Bread stuffed with
Mock Crab, Onion, Celery,
and Lite Mayonnaise
Sautéed Zucchini, Green Onions,
and Tomatoes
Spring Fruit Meringues
Skim Milk

*Ours is a world where people don't know what they want
and are willing to go through hell to get it.*
—Don Marquis

May 13

Take Time for Lunch

Just for today, take time to eat a real lunch. Pressures of the modern American workplace are shortchanging us in multiple ways—one of the first is being cheated of a sit-down, chew-it-up, smoothly-digested lunch. And quite frankly, the sacrifice of skipping lunch serves no meaningful purpose.

It seems the whole world is gearing up for some massive intercontinental competition in the next century, and America had better get on the stick if it hopes to maintain its edge.

But humankind still has basic needs and must still submit to certain inalienable truths of nature, the superlative ones being that you can't take it with you, that you only go around once, and that how well you loved and were loved is about all that's left when, at last, you succumb.

Let us be reminded of what work is really all about—namely, a means to an end. This end. Home. Family. Friends. Work is the support system for the people in our lives, not the other way around.

Just today, sit down and enjoy your lunch.

Menu *of the* Day

Round Steak slow-cooked
in Barbecue Sauce
Steamed Fresh Green Beans
Broiled French Bread
Fresh Pear
Skim Milk

May 14

Let us be the first to give a friendly sign, to nod first, smile first, speak first, and, if necessary, forgive first. —Jo Petty from Apples of Gold

Seasoned Rice

Take the "plain" out of white, brown, or wild rice with these seasoning combinations.

Use the following to season 4 cups of cooked rice:

1/2 cup raisins + 1/2 teaspoon curry powder

1 cup shredded carrots + 1 green onion, diced

4-ounce can chopped green chilies + 1/4 teaspoon chopped cilantro
+ 1/8 teaspoon crushed red pepper

1/2 cup chopped dried pears or apples + 1/2 teaspoon ground cinnamon

1 cup halved or quartered cherry tomatoes + 1/4 cup chopped fresh basil

---

Menu of the *Day*

Broiled Chicken Breast
Seasoned Rice
Fresh Greens with
Reduced-Fat Dressing
Half a Cantaloupe with
Lemon Yogurt on top
Sugar-Free Soft Drink

Is Food Ruling Your Day?

Laura Pulfer, a baby boomer and commentator for National Public Radio,
asserts the current generation is putting money only where its mouth is
(from the *Cincinnati Enquirer,* December 2, 1996).

Our communities are begging people to go to symphonies, operas, and museums. And we are spending time and money on food.

We talk about pasta the way our parents' generation exchanged information about guest conductors. We read restaurant reviews the way other generations devoured critical essays about avant-garde art. Food is adored and discussed, and recipes are passed along to friends like sheet music. Food is not the thing before the performance. It is the main event.

No wonder we're fat. The National Center for Health Statistics said that for the first time overweight Americans are in the majority. We don't even grow flowers anymore. You can't eat those, for heaven's sake.

At the grocery store I see people who can't wait to start shoveling it in. They open packages of cookies and pretzels and eat them in the checkout line. Maybe the management could investigate the possibility of letting people bring buckets of chicken into the opera. Or at least Milk Duds. Maybe there's room for a pasta bar next to the coatroom at the art museum.

by Laura Pulfer, columnist for *The Cincinnati Enquirer.* Used with permission of *The Cincinnati Enquirer.*

Menu *of the* Day

Sirloin Steak on the Grill
Whole Kernel Corn
with Diced Pimientos
Fresh Baked Wheat Bread from
frozen dough with Soft Margarine
Lemon Sorbet with
Diced Fresh Apricots
Skim Milk

Men for the sake of getting a living forget to live.
—Margaret Fuller (1810-1850)

Carry Dinner Home

Growing numbers of Americans are going to restaurants and grocery stores to buy prepared food to take home to eat. The food business calls this practice "home meal replacement."

Ethnic food bars, together with soup, salad, and sandwich bars, are the most popular. Perhaps this represents the best of both worlds—having help on the preparation and still having a traditional family dinner at home. Nearly half of the consumer food dollar is spent on food prepared away from home.

So as you become pressed for time, choose one of these healthy home meal replacements:

> chicken without the skin
>
> spaghetti with lean meat or vegetable sauce
>
> oriental chicken or fish with vegetable dishes (avoid deep-fried sweet and sour dishes)
>
> vegetable pizzas
>
> sandwiches with lean roast beef, turkey, or ham filling
>
> veggie salads with clear dressings
>
> shrimp cocktail
>
> vegetable relish trays with reduced-fat dip
>
> lettuce in a bag with reduced-fat dressing
>
> fruit trays and fruit salads with clear fruit juice dressings

---

Menu *of the* Day

Lean Ham Steaks skillet-grilled
with Thyme and Marjoram
Baked Potato in the microwave
Veggie Salad from the deli
Chocolate Sundae
Sparkling Grape Juice

Peace be within your walls,
and security within your towers.
—Psalm 122:7

May 17

Chicken Curry and Rice Salad
4 1-cup servings

1 cup leftover white or brown rice
2 teaspoons curry powder
2 cups cooked chicken
1 cup seedless grapes, halved
1 large red onion, cut into thin strips

Dressing:
1/3 cup nonfat mayonnaise
1/3 cup nonfat lemon yogurt
2 teaspoons curry powder
1/4 cup all fruit orange marmalade
1 tablespoon white or cider vinegar

1. Combine ingredients for salad in a large bowl.

2. In a small bowl, combine ingredients for dressing.

3. Pour dressing over salad; mix and serve or refrigerate until serving time.

Calories per serving: 323 Fat: 2 g. Sodium: 271 mg.
For exchange diets, count: 1 starch, 2 fruit, 2 lean meat
Preparation time: 20 minutes

Menu of the Day
Chicken Curry and Rice Salad
Broiled Breadsticks
Strawberry Ice Milk
Apple Juice

Real friends are those who, when you've made a fool of yourself, don't feel that you've done a permanent job. —Jo Petty, from Apples of Gold

Breakfast Frittata
4 wedges

Non-stick cooking spray
1-pound bag refrigerated or frozen diced potatoes
   with onions
1 medium green pepper, diced
4 ounces reduced-fat smoked sausage, quartered
   lengthwise and cut into small pieces

4 large eggs or 1 cup liquid egg substitute
1/4 teaspoon pepper
2 ounces reduced-fat Monterey Jack cheese,
   shredded

1. Spray a 12-inch skillet with cooking spray and preheat over medium heat. Add potatoes and peppers and cook for 10 to 15 minutes, stirring occasionally. Add sausage and cook 5 minutes, stirring until potatoes and peppers are tender. (Frozen potatoes will require a longer cooking time.)

2. In a medium-size mixing bowl, beat eggs and pepper together. Slowly pour eggs over the potato mixture. Cook for 7 to 10 more minutes until eggs are firm. Sprinkle with shredded cheese.

3. Move skillet to the serving table and serve.

Calories per 1-wedge serving: 260 Fat: 8 g. Sodium: 1040 mg.
For exchange diets, count: 2 starch, 1 lean meat, 1 fat
Preparation time: 20 minutes

Menu *of the* Day

Breakfast Frittata
Reduced-Fat Cinnamon Rolls
from a tube
Honeydew Melon Balls
in Pineapple Juice
Skim Milk

Chocolate Raspberry Breeze
4 1-cup servings

Sit out on the deck and sip this treat.

2 cups fat-free chocolate ice milk   4 ice cubes
2 cups fresh or frozen raspberries

1. Blend ice milk and raspberries in a blender on medium speed for 1 minute. Add the ice cubes one at time, blending for an additional minute.

2. Pour into 4 chilled tall glasses.

Calories per serving: 153 Fat: 0 Sodium: 37 mg.
For exchange diets, count: 1 skim milk, 1 fruit
Preparation time: 10 minutes

Menu of the Day

Broiled Lean Hamburger on a Bun
with Fresh Leaf Lettuce
and Sliced Radishes
Steamed Cabbage and Carrots
with Dill Seed
Chocolate Raspberry Breeze

May 20

It's Graduation

Today, say a prayer for a recent graduate. Reflect on these commencement thoughts:

With this wonderful, precious commodity of a fine education, I hope you will go out into your community and find some way to give back some of what your country has given you.
　—President Clinton

Years from now if someone asks you if you remember the commencement speech given at your graduation, all I ask that you say is this: "I just remember one thing. I remember that he told me to stand up for what's right."
　—Bob Dole

I want to give some of my famous advice to the graduates. First, never give up because it "Ain't over 'til it's over."
　—Yogi Berra

Whether it be a matter of personal relations within a marriage or of political initiatives within a peace process, there is no sure-fire, do-it-yourself success kit. There is risk and truth and the world before you. And do make that world before you a better one by going into it with boldness. You are up to it and fit for it. You deserve it and if you make your own best contribution, it will become a bit more deserving of you.

—Seamus Heaney, 1995 Nobel Literature Prize Winner

Quotes reprinted from *The Des Moines Register,* May 1996

Menu *of the* Day

Lean Cold Cuts on Rye Bread
with Pickles and Mustard
Reduced-Fat Potato Chips
Baby Carrots
Angel Food Cake from
the bakery with your favorite
Pie Filling on top
Skim Milk

*Behold, how good and how pleasant it is
for brethren to dwell together in unity!*
—Psalm 133:1

May 21

Are You a Potluck Misfit?

Valerie Van Kooten reflects on summer get-togethers:

It's that time of year again: Drag out the picnic baskets and outdoor eating utensils, dust off the Thermos and schlepp food around the countryside in a bizarre ritual called a potluck dinner.

I have come to dread them. Not that I don't like lukewarm lemonade as well as the next person, but I am a potluck reject. My gelatin doesn't gel, my meatballs leak through everything else in the basket, and my Pink Perfection salad wilts to its lowest common denominator—cottage cheese.

Is there anything more painful than watching a mass of famished people pointedly spurn your potluck offering? What to do next is the true test of potluck success. Whenever you have a potluck bomb, everyone will wait to see who picks up that pathetic-looking gluck and take it home. Here's my solution: don't claim it. Bring your offering in a disposable tinfoil pan and let it sit there.

Used with permission.

Menu of the *Day*

Turkey Breast Fillets on the grill
served on Wheat Buns with
Honey Mustard
Steamed Cabbage and Carrots dotted with Honey and Caraway Seed
Potato Salad from the deli
Watermelon
Skim Milk

Whither thou goest, I will go; and where thou lodgest,
I will lodge; thy people shall be my people,
and thy God my God. —Ruth 1:16

Simple Beef Stir-Fry

4 2-cup servings

4 teaspoons cornstarch
2 cups no-added-salt beef broth
3 tablespoons lemon juice
1 teaspoon finely grated orange peel
1 tablespoon vegetable oil

12 ounces top sirloin, cut 3/4-inch thick and sliced thin crosswise
6 cups diced raw vegetables such as peppers, mushrooms, onion, celery, carrots, broccoli, and cauliflower
3 tablespoons chopped fresh cilantro

1. Measure cornstarch into a small bowl. Gradually add broth, stirring until the cornstarch dissolves. Mix in lemon juice and orange peel.

2. In a large skillet, heat oil over medium heat. Add beef and stir-fry for 3 minutes.

3. Using a slotted spoon, transfer beef to a plate. Add vegetables to the skillet and stir-fry just until they begin to turn color, about 3 minutes.

4. Stir broth mixture quickly into the skillet, add beef, and cook for 3 to 5 minutes, just until the sauce thickens. Sprinkle with cilantro and serve over rice.

Calories per serving: 169 Fat: 3 g. Sodium: 75 mg.
For exchange diets, count: 3 very lean meat, 3 vegetable
Preparation time: 20 minutes

Menu of the *Day*

Simple Beef Stir-Fry
White Rice
Fresh Blueberries
Fortune Cookie
Milk

Let there be peace on earth and let it begin with me.
Let there be peace on earth, the peace that was meant to be.
—Sy Miller (1908-1971) and Jill Jackson

May 23

Rhubarb Crunch

8 1-cup servings

6 cups chopped rhubarb (or use half rhubarb, half
   strawberries)
1 package regular or sugar-free raspberry gelatin
1/2 cup orange juice
2 teaspoons vanilla

2/3 cup flour
1/3 cup oatmeal
1/2 cup brown sugar
1 teaspoon cinnamon
1/4 cup margarine

1. Preheat oven to 350°.

2. Combine rhubarb, gelatin, orange juice, and vanilla in a 9-inch square baking dish.

3. Use a pastry blender to combine all remaining ingredients in a small mixing bowl until they are crumbly. Sprinkle crumbs over the rhubarb.

4. Bake for 45 minutes uncovered, just until bubbly. Cool and serve. Use nonfat vanilla yogurt, vanilla ice milk, or vanilla frozen yogurt as a topping.

Calories per serving 178 Fat: 7 g. Sodium: 117 mg.
For exchange diets, count: 1 starch, 1 fruit, 1 fat
Preparation time: 15 minutes Baking time: 45 minutes

Menu *of the* Day

Crab Salad from the deli on Thick
slices of French Bread
Fresh Lettuce, Radishes, and
Green Onions with
Reduced-Fat French Dressing
Rhubarb Crunch
Skim Milk

I commune with my heart in the night;
I meditate and search my spirit.
—Psalm 77:6

Spicy All-Purpose Marinade for Grilled Meats
for 1 pound of meat or 8 2-ounce servings

3 tablespoons reduced-sodium soy sauce
2 tablespoons sherry, orange juice, brandy,
 or vinegar
2 teaspoons Chinese five-spice powder
2 teaspoons honey

1/2 teaspoon minced garlic
1/2 teaspoon ginger powder
1/2 teaspoon white or black pepper
Optional seasonings: chopped green onion or
chives

1. Combine all ingredients in a shallow pan. Add beef, pork, chicken, turkey, ham, or fish.
Cover and refrigerate for at least 30 minutes or up to 24 hours.

Marinade has negligible calorie value per serving. Sodium: 236 mg. per 1/8 recipe
Preparation time: 10 minutes

Menu of the *Day*

Grilled Lean Meat soaked in
Spicy All-Purpose Marinade
Steamed Red Potatoes
Raw Cauliflower and Broccoli
with Reduced-Fat Dip
Fresh Strawberries
and Vanilla Ice Milk
Mineral Water

Almond Flan
8 slices

1/4 cup water	14-ounce can nonfat sweetened condensed milk
1/2 cup sugar	1 1/2 cups skim milk
3 large eggs or 3/4 cup liquid egg substitute	1 tablespoon almond extract

1. Preheat oven to 325°.

2. In a small heavy saucepan, bring water and sugar to a boil, stirring until sugar is dissolved. Boil syrup, without stirring, until golden in color. Pour into a 1 1/2 quart soufflé dish, tilting the dish to coat the bottom and some of the side with caramel.

3. In a large mixing bowl, beat together eggs, condensed milk, skim milk, and almond extract until smooth. Pour mixture into the soufflé dish.

4. Put the soufflé dish in a baking pan and add enough hot tap water to pan to reach halfway up the side of the soufflé dish. Bake for 1 1/4 hours or until mixture is set.

5. Remove soufflé dish from baking pan. Cool 1 hour, then refrigerate for 3 hours or up to 1 day.

6. To remove flan from dish, dip the dish in a baking pan of hot water for 4 seconds. Run a knife around the edge of the dish and invert flan onto a round serving plate. Garnish with fresh fruit.

Calories per 1-slice serving: 233 Fat: 1 g. Sodium: 100 mg.
For exchange diets, count: 1 skim milk, 2 1/2 fruit
Preparation time: 20 minutes Baking time: 1 1/4 hours
Cooling time: 4 hours

Menu *of the* Day

Broiled Bacon, Lettuce, and
Tomato on Wheat Toast
Steamed California-Blend
Vegetables
Almond Flan
with Fresh Fruit topping
Decaf Coffee

May 26

God is the love within us.
—A Course in Miracles

Roasted Red Potatoes and Asparagus
4 servings

4 small red potatoes
1 pound asparagus, trimmed and cut into 2-inch
   pieces
1 tablespoon olive oil

1 tablespoon balsamic vinegar
1/4 teaspoon salt
1/4 teaspoon black pepper

1. Preheat oven to 500°.

2. Cut potatoes into eighths; mix with asparagus, and toss with olive oil.

3. Spread vegetables in an 8- by 15-inch baking pan. Bake for 20 minutes.

4. Remove vegetables from the oven, and transfer to a serving bowl; dot with vinegar, sprinkle with salt and pepper, and serve.

   Calories per serving: 153 Fat: 3 g. Sodium: 142 mg.
   For exchange diets, count: 1 starch, 2 vegetable, 1/2 fat
   Preparation time: 10 minutes Baking time: 20 minutes

Menu *of the* Day

Broiled Ground Pork Pattie
sprinkled with Old Bay Seasoning
Roasted Red Potatoes
and Asparagus
Fresh Leaf Lettuce and Diced
Cucumber with Reduced-Fat
Ranch Dressing
Applesauce
Skim Milk

Daily Bread
154

We had two rules at our house. The first was: "Either show up for dinner or bring a note from God excusing you." The second: "Absolutely no one uses the phone while we're eating." –Erma Bombeck

May 27

Unforgettable Creamed Spinach and Sausage

4 servings

1 large onion, diced
4 reduced-fat Italian sausages, casings removed and meat diced
16-ounce package frozen spinach, thawed and squeezed dry
1 1/2 teaspoons flour

1 cup no-added-salt chicken broth
1/4 cup evaporated skim milk
1/2 teaspoon ground nutmeg
1/4 teaspoon salt
1/4 teaspoon white pepper

1. Sauté onion and diced sausage in a heavy stockpot or Dutch oven until onion is tender. Drain any fat from the pan.

2. Add spinach, cooking over medium heat until all the water evaporates, about 5 minutes.

3. In a shaker container, mix together the flour, broth, milk, and nutmeg.

4. Slowly add broth and milk mixture to the spinach, stirring constantly, and cooking over medium heat until mixture is thick and bubbly.

5. Season with salt and pepper and serve in pasta bowls.

Calories per serving: 134 Fat: 6 g. Sodium: 594 mg.
For exchange diets, count: 1 very lean meat, 1 fat, 2 vegetable
Preparation time: 15 minutes

Menu *of the* Day

Unforgettable Creamed Spinach and Sausage
Rye Bread with Soft Margarine
Sliced Mangoes
Skim Milk

May 28

To create a friendly meal time atmosphere, stick with the old but wonderful rule: treat guests like family and family like guests.
—Janice Rosenberg in Reinventing Home

Rate your Family's Togetherness

	Usually	Sometimes	Never
As a parent or caregiver, do you:			
Eat your meals as a family?	___	___	___
Serve meals and snacks on a regular schedule?	___	___	___
Give your youngster freedom to choose the foods he or she eats?	___	___	___
Respect a child's appetite when he or she has had enough?	___	___	___
Involve children in planning and preparing family meals?	___	___	___
Make an effort to keep mealtime pleasant?	___	___	___
Attempt to keep eating to a designated place(s) in the house?	___	___	___
Set a good role model with healthy food choices?	___	___	___
Avoid rewarding or punishing a child with food?	___	___	___
Give kids enough time to eat?	___	___	___
Turn off the TV during mealtime?	___	___	___
Offer foods that appeal to kids?	___	___	___
Serve a variety of meals and snacks?	___	___	___

Menu of the Day

Make Your Own Supper Night
OK, here are a few starters

Popcorn Sprinkled with Cheese

Nachos with Reduced-Fat Cheese and Salsa

Peanut Butter and Jelly Sandwiches

Cheese Crispie (shredded cheese on a tortilla, melted in the microwave)

Yogurt and Fruit

Daily Bread

Make a Family Cookbook

Foods prepared by our mothers and grandmothers form an important part of family heritage. These recipes are precious heirlooms and deserve to be collected and passed on through family cookbooks.

How do you get started with the project?

Tell grandmas, aunts, and cousins your idea and ask them to start hunting for family recipes that are already recorded. Also ask them to make a list of family favorites that have no written recipe. Summertime family reunions or holiday gatherings are a perfect time to put the recipes together. Next, assign three or four people to work together as the family cookbook committee. Select individuals representing all sides of the family that have a sincere interest in cooking and the conviction to see the project through to completion.

The committee makes the following decisions:

Which recipes will require testing, or do we trust the author's record?

What recipe format will be easiest for all family members to understand? You can simply adapt the one I've used in this book. Keep directions short, complete, and clear.

Select an editor whose job it is to make sure all recipes are typewritten in the selected style and to assign recipe testing as needed.

Keep track of phone calls, postage, and photocopy expenses so all family members can contribute to the cost.

Consider including the family history, a family tree, or a personal introduction at the beginning of the collection.

Menu *of the* Day

Grandma's Favorite Main Dish
Grandpa's Favorite Side Dish
Uncle's Favorite Salad
Aunt's Favorite Dessert

I have been reminded of your sincere faith, which first lived in your grandmother and in your mother and I am persuaded now lives in you also.
–2 Timothy 1:5

Herb Vinegar

Herb vinegar is a low-fat, low-cost way to flavor salads, vegetables, and even starch-based side dishes such as couscous, rice, and wheat pilaf. Vinegars are preferred over homemade herbed oils, as vinegar is too acidic for dangerous bacteria to grow.

This is all there is to it:

1. Collect several old wine, salad dressing, or olive oil bottles. Soak off the label.

2. Sterilize the bottle, washing the cap thoroughly and obtaining a clean cork if needed.

3. Insert a combination of fresh herbs (the stems and the leaves) and spices into the bottle. Fill it quite full.

4. Fill the bottle with vinegar. You can use any vinegar as the base: white, red wine, cider, or rice vinegar.

5. Put on the cap or insert the cork, and store in a cool dark place for at least 2 weeks for the flavor to develop.

Try these combinations for starters:

fresh tarragon in cider vinegar

garlic cloves, rosemary or sage, and lemon peel in white wine vinegar

fresh mint and orange peel in cider vinegar

Menu of the Day

Pork Chops on the grill
Potato Salad
Steamed Fresh Spinach
dotted with Herb Vinegar
Chocolate Chip Cookies from a bag
Skim Milk

In recalling her own childhood dinner hour: "We argued.
We sulked. We laughed. We pitched for favors. We shouted.
We listened. It is still our family's finest hour." —Erma Bombeck

May 31

Strawberry Shortcake
4 servings

1 pint strawberries, sliced
1/4 cup sugar
1 cup + 3 tablespoons reduced-fat baking mix
1/4 cup skim milk

1 tablespoon sugar
2 tablespoons soft margarine
Garnish: fat-free whipped topping

1. Sprinkle strawberries with sugar and let stand covered in the refrigerator for 1 hour.

2. Preheat oven to 425°.

3. In a medium mixing bowl, stir all remaining ingredients together until a soft dough forms.

4. Gently smooth the dough into a ball on a wooden board lightly dusted with flour or baking mix. Knead the dough 12 times, then roll out 1/2-inch thick.

5. Cut dough with a 3-inch round cutter (or just use the edge of a short drinking glass).

6. Place shortcakes on a baking sheet and bake for 12 minutes or until golden brown.

7. Cool shortcakes on a rack for at least 15 minutes, then split in half. Layer the cake and berries sandwich-style on individual dessert plates, and garnish with whipped topping.

Calories per serving: 161 Fat: 7 g. Sodium: 282 mg.
For exchange diets, count: 1 starch, 1/2 fruit, 1 fat
Preparation time: 20 minutes Resting time: 1 hour
Baking time: 12 minutes Cooling time: 15 minutes

Menu *of the* Day

Hard Shell Tacos filled
with Browned and Seasoned
Ground Turkey
Fresh Tomatoes, Lettuce, and
Reduced-Fat Cheddar Cheese
Strawberry Shortcake
Skim Milk

A happy home is one in which each spouse grants the possibility that the other may be right, though neither believes it.
—Don Fraser from Quotable Quotes

Beer-Grilled Sirloin
4 4-ounce servings

1 pound sirloin, well trimmed and portioned into 4
   steaks
Marinade:
1/4 cup reduced-sodium soy sauce

1 cup beer
2 tablespoons brown sugar
1 teaspoon ground ginger

1. Combine marinade ingredients in a shallow bowl or pan. Add sirloin.

2. Cover and refrigerate for at least 30 minutes or up to 24 hours.

3. Grill over medium-hot flame for 4 minutes per side, turning once.

Calories per serving: 213 Fat: 6 g. Sodium: 547 mg.
For exchange diets, count: 4 lean meat
Preparation time: 5 minutes Chilling time: 30 minutes Grilling time: 8 minutes

---

Menu of the Day

Beer-Grilled Sirloin
Baked Potato with Soft Margarine
Sautéed Zucchini,
Peppers, and Onions
Chilled Fruit Cocktail
on Angel Food Cake
Skim Milk

Strawberry Surprise Muffins
12 muffins

1 package light or reduced-fat bran muffin mix   3/4 cup strawberry preserves

1. Preheat oven as directed on muffin mix.

2. In a small mixing bowl, mix bran muffin mix as directed.

3. Spoon half of batter into prepared muffin cups. Top with 1 tablespoon strawberry preserves. Spoon remaining batter over preserves.

4. Bake as directed.

Calories per serving: 112 Fat: 4 g. Sodium: 122 mg.
For exchange diets, count: 1 starch, 1 fat
Preparation time: 10 minutes Baking time: 15 to 20 minutes

Menu of the Day

Chicken Salad from the deli
Strawberry Surprise Muffins
Fresh Vegetable Relishes
Skim Milk

June 3

From *Handbook of Health*, 1922

Fruits and vegetables are the Kindling foods, which help the Coal foods to burn, and supply certain stuffs and elements which the body needs and which the Coal foods do not contain.

Fruits and vegetables contain the priceless vitamins and mineral salts, which are not present in sufficient proportions in the meats, starches, and fats. The products of their digestion and burning in the body help to neutralize or render harmless, the waste products from meats, starches, and fats.

They have a very beneficial effect upon the blood, the kidneys, and the skin. In fact, the reputation of fruits and fresh vegetables for "purifying the blood" and "clearing the complexion" is really well deserved. The special longing for greens and sour things in the spring after their scarcity in our diet all winter, is a true sign of their wholesomeness.

—Woods Hutchinson

Menu *of the* Day

Tender Vegetable Pasta tossed with your favorite Fresh Vegetables and Parmesan Cheese and Oregano

Breadsticks baked with sprinkles of Basil

Fresh Nectarine

Skim Milk

Jump-Start your Vegetable Quota

What is considered a serving of vegetables?

1 cup of raw leafy greens, easily fitting on a small salad plate

1/2 cup of other kinds of vegetables, like half of a broccoli spear

3/4 cup pure vegetable juice, just enough to fill a short glass

1. Drink vegetable juice cocktail instead of a soft drink when you dine out.

2. Add another vegetable (such as frozen broccoli) to a can of reduced-sodium soups (such as chicken noodle soup).

3. Add a vegetable (such as frozen peas) to traditional casseroles (like tuna and noodle).

4. Bolster nutritional goodness of packaged rice mixes by adding a bag of California blend vegetables to it.

5. Dilute your beer with tomato juice.

6. Shun "naked sandwiches" and insist on added crunch—like sliced radishes or cucumbers, spinach, or shredded cabbage.

7. Load frozen pizza with fresh mushrooms, peppers, and onions.

8. Extend chili with a second or third variety of beans.

9. Stock the fridge with clear containers of raw carrots, celery, and radishes.

10. Throw your favorite vegetables into some aluminum foil with a little reduced-fat margarine, and grill alongside the burgers.

continued tomorrow…

Menu of the Day

Grilled Skinless Chicken Breast
with Barbecue Sauce
Shredded Broccoli Slaw from a bag
with Diced Red Onion and
Reduced-Fat Coleslaw Dressing
Broiled French Bread
Honeydew Melon
Skim Milk

*Discipline is like broccoli. We may not care for it ourselves,
but feel sure it would be good for everybody else.
—Bill Vaughan*

Day 2 of Jump-Start Your Vegetable Quota

11. Add a vegetable (like chunky tomatoes) to omelets or scrambled eggs.

12. Serve vegetables before putting meat on the plate.

13. Offer at least two servings of vegetables at the main meal of the day.

14. Lace lasagna with spinach or shredded carrots.

15. Add fresh peppers, mushrooms, or onions to boxed potato mixes.

16. Focus on the vegetables that you already enjoy, eating two spoonfuls instead of one.

17. Enjoy sweet corn season, but never add salt to the boiling water, as the corn will become tough. Unsalted water will also reach a boil faster than salted water.

18. Soup on the stove is good anyday. For bean soup from dried beans, cook them uncovered for a firm texture. Cover the pot to produce softer beans.

19. No time to dice all those veggies for stir-fry? Go ahead and buy the frozen stirfry blend.

20. Don't feel guilty about plain old canned green beans for the kids' lunch. It's a start.

21. Add one of those dry packaged vegetable soup mixes to 1 cup reduced-fat mayonnaise and 1 cup nonfat sour cream for a party dip.

Menu *of the* Day

Vegetable Burgers on a Bun
Go wild with fresh slices of jicama.

Baked Beans from a can
Sliced Kiwifruit
Skim Milk

22. Need entertainment for a picnic? Kids of all ages love to spit watermelon seeds.

23. Extend your favorite brand of salsa during the tomato season by adding 1 cup of chopped seeded fresh tomatoes to a 12-ounce jar.

24. It's OK to add bits of leftover bacon to asparagus or Brussels sprouts.

Ten Days of Vegetables from Artichokes to Zucchini

Discover at least two new vegetables this summer.
Outstanding sources of vitamins and minerals are noted.

Artichokes

Look for—tight compact heads that feel heavy for their size. Surface brown spots do not affect quality.

Fix it tip—Clean just before cooking. Using a stainless steel knife, slice off the stem. Remove and discard coarse outer leaves, then cut off the top third of artichoke. Snip off thorny tips of remaining leaves with kitchen shears. Rinse well and plunge immediately into a solution of 1 part lemon juice to 3 parts water to prevent browning. In a large deep pan, boil 1 gallon water, 1/4 cup vinegar, 1 tablespoon salad oil, 10 peppercorns, and 2 bay leaves. Add 5 artichokes and return to a boil. Cover and boil for 30 minutes or until the stem end is tender when pierced; drain and serve with a dipping sauce. Melt 3 parts reduced-fat margarine with 1 part lemon juice and 1 part fresh chives or parsley; or dip in fresh Parmesan cheese.

Asparagus

Look for—firm, brittle spears that are bright green almost their entire length, with tightly closed tips. Wrap ends in a damp paper towel and refrigerate unwashed for up to three days.

Fix it tip—Add chopped asparagus to omelets or serve cooked, chilled asparagus with your favorite oil and vinegar or Italian salad dressing.

Menu *of the* Day

Chunk Chicken from a can
with Diced Fresh Vegetables
(Carrots, Radishes, Peppers) and
Reduced-Fat Ranch Dressing
Broiled Bagel
Tomato Juice
Red Grapes
Skim Milk

June 7

Day 2 of 10 Days of Vegetables from Artichokes to Zucchini

Beans

Look for—slender, crisp beans that are bright and blemish-free. Avoid mature beans with large seeds and swollen pods. Refrigerate unwashed beans in a plastic bag for up to 4 days.

Fix it tip—Dress up cooked green beans with dill weed and crumbled bacon.

Beets

Look for—firm, smooth-skinned, small to medium beets. Leaves should be deep green and fresh looking. Cut off the tops, leaving 1 inch of stem attached. Refrigerate for up to a week.

Fix it tip—Scrub before cooking, but do not peel. Leave roots, stems, and skin intact. Try wrapping beets in foil and baking in the oven for 1 hour at 400°; then peel, slice, and serve with grated orange peel and nonfat sour cream.

Bok Choy

Look for—heads with bright white stalks and glossy dark leaves. Avoid heads with slippery brown spots on the leaves. Use as soon as possible after purchase.

Fix it tip—Cut leaves from the stalks, slice the stalks crosswise, and coarsely shred the leaves for steaming. Drizzle with reduced-sodium teriyaki sauce as a side dish with grilled meats.

Menu *of the* Day

Vegetable Taco with Diced Fresh Vegetables, Kidney Beans, and Shredded Reduced-Fat Monterey Jack Cheese in a Hard Shell Taco
Fresh Peach
Skim Milk

Day 3 of 10 Days of Vegetables from Artichokes to Zucchini

Broccoli—Choose for vitamins A and C, folate, and fiber.

Look for—compact clusters of tightly closed dark green florets. Avoid heads with yellow florets or thick, woody stems.

Fix it tip—Rinse and cut off base of stalk. Microwave covered, on high power with 2 tablespoons of orange juice and 1 teaspoon of rosemary for 3 to 5 minutes or until tender-crisp.

Brussels Sprouts

Look for—firm, compact, and fresh looking sprouts with a bright green color. They should feel heavy for their size. Discard limp leaves, then refrigerate, unwashed, for up to 3 days.

Fix it tip—To ensure even cooking, cut a shallow "X" in the stem end of the sprout. Steam, then season with basil and finely grated lemon rind.

Cabbage

Look for—firm heads that feel heavy for their size. Outer leaves should have good color and be free of blemishes. Refrigerate unwashed cabbage for up to 10 days.

Fix it tip—Add shredded cabbage to any fresh salad; or cut it into chunks, steam, and season with caraway seed and brown sugar.

Carrots—Choose for vitamin A and fiber.

Look for—firm, clean, well-shaped carrots with bright orange-gold color. Carrots with their tops still attached are likely to be freshest.

Fix it tip—Cut into coins, steam, and season with nutmeg.

Menu of the Day

Pan-Grilled Cod Fillet in Soft Margarine with Dill Weed and Fresh-Squeezed Lime Juice

Quick Rice with Soft Margarine and Old Bay Seasoning

Steamed Baby Carrots

Fresh Pear

Skim Milk

*In the elderly and in children, the soul is bigger than
the body. It's only the rest of us who let our bodies outgrow our souls.
–Elisabeth Kubler-Ross*

Day 4 of 10 Days of Vegetables from Artichokes to Zucchini

Cauliflower

Look for—firm, compact, creamy white heads with florets pressed tightly together. A yellow tinge and spreading florets indicate over-maturity.

Fix it tip—Remove and discard outer leaves, and cut out the core. Place whole head, stem side down in a microwave-safe bowl, add 2 tablespoons of water, and microwave on high power for 10 minutes. Sprinkle reduced-fat cheese over the top and garnish with paprika.

Celery

Look for—crisp, rigid green stalks with fresh-looking leaves. Avoid celery with limp stalks. Refrigerate, unwashed, for up to 2 weeks.

Fix it tip—Add chopped celery to almost any other vegetable to extend it. Try tarragon for a complementary seasoning.

Corn

Look for—fresh-looking ears with green husks, moist stems, and silk ends free of decay or worm injury. Tough skins indicate over-maturity. Wrap unhusked ears in damp paper towels and refrigerate in a plastic bag for up to 2 days.

Fix it tip—Peel the husk back and remove silk, then replace husk to enclose the kernels completely. Place in the center of the microwave and cook on high power for 2 minutes per ear. Rearrange ears halfway through cooking. Let stand for 3 minutes, then peel husks and serve with chili powder.

Menu *of the* Day

Baked Potato stuffed with Chopped
Tomatoes, Sliced Mushrooms,
Green Onions, and Diced Green
Pepper and topped with Fat-Free
Sour Cream

Open-Faced Toasted Cheese
on Rye Bread

Mandarin Oranges

Skim Milk

What doth the Lord thy God require of thee, but to fear the Lord thy God, to walk in all his ways, and to love him, and to serve the Lord thy God with all thy heart and with all thy soul. —Deuteronomy 10:12

June 10

Day 5 of 10 Days of Vegetables from Artichokes to Zucchini

Cucumbers

Look for—firm, dark green slicing, pickling, or greenhouse cucumbers that are slender but well shaped. Soft or yellow cukes are over-mature. Refrigerate whole or cut cucumbers in a plastic bag for up to 1 week.

Fix it tip—Cucumbers are waxed to preserve moisture. Peel waxed cucumbers with a vegetable peeler. Use sliced cukes instead of lettuce to add crunch to a sandwich.

Eggplant

Look for—firm eggplant that is heavy for its size, with taut, glassy, deeply-colored skin. Refrigerate, unwashed in a plastic bag for up to 5 days.

Fix it tip—Cut off stem, peel, and then cut eggplant into 1/2-inch thick slices. Arrange slices on a baking sheet, brush all sides with reduced-fat Italian salad dressing, and bake in 450° oven for 15 minutes or until tender.

Greens—choose for vitamin A.

Look for—Dark leafy greens have a pronounced flavor and include beet greens, collards, dandelion greens, kale, mustard, and turnip greens. Avoid bunches with thick, coarse-veined leaves.

Fix it tip—Tear out and discard tough stems and center ribs. Cover coarsely chopped leaves with water and boil for 10 minutes or until tender to bite. Serve with oregano, wine vinegar, and crumbled bacon.

Menu of the Day

Veggie Meatloaf made with
Shredded Carrots, Celery, and
Onion
Mashed Potatoes from a box
with Soft Margarine
Radishes
Lime Sherbet with
Crushed Pineapple on top
Skim Milk

June 11

Day 6 of 10 Days of Vegetables from Artichokes to Zucchini

Jicama—sometimes known as a Mexican potato.

Look for—firm, well-formed tubers, free of blemishes. Store whole unwashed jicama in a cool, dark, dry place for up to 3 weeks. Wrap cut pieces in plastic and refrigerate for up to 1 week.

Fix it tip—Scrub well and peel with a knife. Dice into julienne strips and serve with a dip or add to green salads.

Kohlrabi

Look for—young tender bulbs with fresh green leaves. The smaller the bulb, the more delicate the flavor and texture. Cut off leaves and stems. Refrigerate unwashed for up to a week.

Fix it tip—Scrub well and peel. Serve raw on a relish plate or cut into chunks and add to stews and soups during the last 20 minutes of cooking.

Leeks

Look for—leeks with clean, white bottoms and crisp, fresh-looking green tops. Refrigerate, unwashed, in a plastic bag for up to 1 week.

Fix it tip—Cut off and discard root ends. Trim the tops, leaving about 3 inches of green leaves. Strip away and discard coarse outer leaves. Wash and trim under cold running water, separating layers carefully to rinse out any dirt. Add sliced leeks to chicken soups and stews, or cook with carrots or peas for variety. Tarragon is a complementary seasoning.

Menu *of the* Day

Crockpot Beef and Chunky
Potatoes, Carrots, and Turnips
Fresh Baking Powder Biscuits
from a tube with Soft Margarine
Leftover Fresh Fruits marinated in
Sugar-Free Lemon-Lime Soda
Skim Milk

The peace of God, which passeth all understanding,
keep your hearts and minds in Christ Jesus.
—Philippians 4:7

June 12

Day 7 of 10 Days of Vegetables from Artichokes to Zucchini

Mushrooms

Look for—blemish-free mushrooms without slimy spots or signs of decay. Wrap in paper towels; refrigerate unwashed in plastic bags for up to 5 days.

Fix it tip—Wipe mushrooms with a damp cloth to remove dirty residue. Slice thin and add to the top of grilled meats during the last several minutes of cooking.

Okra

Look for—small to medium-size pods that are deep green and free of blemishes. Refrigerate unwashed okra in a bag for up to 5 days.

Fix it tip—Avoid cooking okra in iron, tin, copper, or brass pans, as these metals cause discoloration. Add to gumbo dishes during the last 20 minutes of cooking.

Onions

Look for—green onions (also commonly known as scallions) with crisp, bright green tops and clean white bottoms. Store green onions unwashed in the refrigerator in a plastic bag for 10 days. Store dry onions unwrapped in a dry, cool, dark place with good ventilation for up to 2 months. Wrap cut pieces in plastic wrap and refrigerate for up to 4 days.

Fix it tip—Peel medium-size dry onions and stand upright in a baking dish. Bake uncovered in a 350° oven and baste with reduced-fat margarine and finely-grated orange rind. (Light a candle while you peel onions to keep from crying.)

Menu *of the* Day

Grilled Turkey Breast
with Barbecue Sauce
Corn on the Cob
with Soft Margarine
Lettuce and Fresh Vegetable Salad
with Reduced-Fat Blue Cheese
Dressing
Cantaloupe
Skim Milk

June 13

Love your enemy —it'll drive him nuts.
—Anonymous

Day 8 of 10 Days of Vegetables from Artichokes to Zucchini

Parsnips

Look for—small to medium-size parsnips that are smooth, firm, and well shaped. Avoid large roots. Store unwashed in the refrigerator in a plastic bag for up to 2 weeks.

Fix it tip—Trim and discard the tops and root ends. Peel with a vegetable peeler, then rinse. Bake chopped parsnips with sliced apple in brown sugar and apple juice.

Peas—*choose for vitamin C, folate, potassium, and fiber.*

Look for—small, plump, bright green pods that are firm, crisp, and well filled. Store unwashed in a plastic bag in the refrigerator for up to 5 days.

Fix it tip—Top steamed peas with finely shredded fresh mint.

Peppers—*choose for vitamin C.*

Look for—bright, glossy peppers that are firm and well shaped. Refrigerate, unwashed, in a plastic bag for up to a week.

Fix it tip—Add sautéed yellow peppers to rice, barley, or pasta.

Potatoes—*Choose for vitamin C, potassium, and fiber.*

Look for—firm smooth potatoes with no wrinkles, sprouts, cracks, bruises, decay or bitter green areas. Store in a cool, dark, well-ventilated area. Try the new Yukon Gold variety.

Fix it tip—To preserve whiteness, cover peeled potatoes with cold water for a short time before cooking. Try baked potato toppings such as cottage cheese, ham or turkey, reduced-fat cheeses, or salsa

---

Menu of the **Day**

Homemade Veggie Pizza using
a packaged crust mix
Marinara Sauce, Fresh Veggies,
and Part-Skim Mozzarella
Green Salad with Reduced-Fat
Italian Dressing
Rainbow Sherbet
Grape Juice

Daily Bread

Freedom is more than a pound of sausage.
—A Soviet Russian Lieutenant, speaking about the food shortage
on 60 Minutes after the fall of communism. February 1990

June 14
Flag Day

Day 9 of 10 Days of Vegetables from Artichokes to Zucchini

Rutabagas

Look for—small to medium-size rutabagas that are smooth, firm, and heavy for their size. Store unwrapped in a cool, dry, dark place with good ventilation for up to 2 months.

Fix it tip—Rinse and peel with a vegetable peeler. Leave whole or slice for cooking; mash cooked rutabagas and season with brown sugar and cinnamon.

Salad greens—Choose darker greens for vitamin A.

Look for—crisp, fresh-looking, deeply colored leaves, free of brown spots, yellowed leaves, and decay. Heads of lettuce should give a little under pressure. Choose from arugula, Belgian endive, butterhead lettuce, chicory, escarole, iceberg lettuce, loose-leaf lettuce, radicchio, romaine lettuce, spinach, and watercress for salad variety. Rinse greens with cold water; shake and dry well. Wrap in paper towels and refrigerate up to a week. Tear salad greens into bite-size pieces.

Fix it tip—Combine greens with leftover cooked vegetables and meat, add a reduced-fat dressing, and you have a main dish salad.

Sweet Potatoes and Yams—Choose for vitamins A and C, potassium, and fiber.

Look for—firm, well-shaped vegetables with bright uniformly-colored skin. Store in a cool, dry, dark, well-ventilated place for 2 months.

Fix it tip—Bake sweet potatoes and top with brown sugar and grated orange peel.

Menu of the Day

Chef Salad with Endive, Lean Ham, Turkey, and Feta Cheese with Reduced-Fat Red Wine Vinegar Dressing
Wheat Crackers
Lemon Yogurt over Fresh Fruit
Iced Tea

And what is so rare as a day in June?
Then, if ever, come perfect days.
—J.R. Lowell, The Vision of Sir Launfal I

Day 10 of 10 Days of Vegetables from Artichokes to Zucchini

Summer Squash

Look for—yellow squash and zucchini of medium size with firm, smooth, glossy, tender skin. Refrigerate, unwashed in a plastic bag, for up to 5 days.

Fix it tip—Place slices of squash on a baking pan, brush with oil and vinegar dressing, sprinkle with grated Parmesan, and broil for 5 minutes or until tender.

Winter squash—Choose for vitamins A and C, potassium, and fiber.

Look for—hard, thick-shelled squash. Store whole squash unwrapped in a cool, dry, dark place with good ventilation for up to 2 months.

Fix it tip—Season cooked acorn or butternut squash with allspice, cardamom, cinnamon, or nutmeg.

Tomatoes—Choose for vitamins A and C, potassium, and fiber.

Look for—smooth, well-formed tomatoes that are firm, but not hard. Store, unwashed, at room temperature, stem end down, until slightly soft.

Fix it tip—To peel, submerge in boiling water for 30 seconds, then plunge into cold water.

Turnips

Look for—firm, smooth, small to medium-size turnips that feel heavy. Refrigerate, unwashed, in a plastic bag for up to a week.

Fix it tip—Rinse and peel, then leave whole, cube, slice, or quarter. If desired, cook tops separately.

Menu of the Day

Spaghetti with Chunky
Vegetable Marinara Sauce
Lettuce Salad with Reduced-Fat
Creamy Italian Dressing
Broiled French Bread
Fresh Banana
Skim Milk

Daily Bread

Every good tree bringeth forth good fruit;
but a corrupt tree bringeth forth evil fruit.
—Matthew 7:17

June 16

Red and Green Pea Salad
4 1-cup servings

1/2 cup nonfat mayonnaise (such as Kraft Free)
1/4 cup reduced-fat Italian salad dressing
16-ounce package frozen peas, thawed and drained

1 cup chopped celery
2 slices bacon, cooked and crumbled
1/4 cup chopped red onion

1. Combine mayonnaise and Italian salad dressing in a salad bowl.

2. Add remaining ingredients and mix lightly. Serve.

Calories per serving: 110 Fat: 4 g. Sodium: 189 mg.
For exchange diets, count: 1 starch, 1 fat
Preparation time: 15 minutes

Menu *of the* Day

Cold Roast Beef Sandwich
on an Onion Bagel with Lettuce
and Spicy Mustard
Red and Green Pea Salad
Fresh Plums
Skim Milk

June 17

That best portion of a good man's life,
His little, nameless, unremembered acts of kindness
and of love. —William Wordsworth

A Sensible Trip to the Soup and Salad Bar

The deluxe soup and salad bars in large markets offer plenty of healthy choices. Stop on your way home and load up!

Broth, vegetable, or tomato-based soups are better choices than creamy varieties.

Dark greens, especially spinach and watercress, are great sources of fiber, iron, folate, and calcium.

Choose low-fat cottage cheese, lean sliced ham, chicken breast, tuna, or turkey for a protein source on your salad.

Add rice, croutons, or breadsticks for chewiness.

Then pile on all the fresh vegetables you have room for.

Select a second plate for a round of fresh fruit.

Watch carefully as you add dressing. Try the reduced-fat variety, and if it doesn't suit you, then carefully dot on the full-fat stuff.

Menu *of the* Day

Hit the Soup and Salad Bar
at the Supermarket
Assorted Crackers
Skim Milk

Orange Burst Fruit Dip
10 ¼-cup servings

1/4 cup sugar
1/4 cup frozen orange juice concentrate

2 cups nonfat sour cream
1 tablespoon finely grated orange peel

1. In a small bowl, stir together all ingredients. Cover and refrigerate at least 30 minutes.

2. Serve with grapes, chunks of banana, apple slices, pear slices, pineapple spears, or mango wedges.

Calories per serving: 64 Fat: 0 Sodium: 40 mg.
For exchange diets, count: 1 fruit
Preparation time: 5 minutes Chilling time: 30 minutes

Menu of the *Day*

Pork Chops on the Grill
Corn on the Cob
Fresh Fruits and
Orange Burst Fruit Dip
Skim Milk

June 19

Salsa Ranch Dip
10 ¼-cup servings

1-ounce packet Original Ranch Party Dip Mix   1/2 cup thick and chunky medium-hot salsa
2 cups nonfat sour cream

1. Mix all ingredients together in a small mixing bowl. Refrigerate at least 30 minutes for flavors to blend.

2. Serve with raw vegetable dippers or reduced-fat tortilla chips.

Calories per serving: 55 Fat: 0 Sodium: 330 mg.
For exchange diets, count: 1 fruit
Preparation time: 5 minutes Chilling time: 30 minutes

Menu of the Day

Celebrate Father's Day
Salsa Ranch Dip
with Low-Fat Tortilla Chips
and Vegetable Dippers
Steak on the Grill
His Favorite Salad from the deli
White Dinner Rolls
Vanilla Ice Milk
with Crushed Oreos on top
Beer or Sparkling Grape Juice

Fresh Vegetable Relish
4 ¾-cup servings

1 cup shredded carrots	3 tablespoons cider vinegar
1 cup chopped cucumber	1 teaspoon sugar
1/2 cup chopped red pepper	1/4 teaspoon salt
1/4 cup finely chopped red onion	1 tablespoon vegetable oil

1. Combine carrot, cucumber, pepper, and onion in a medium bowl. Set aside.

2. Stir together vinegar, sugar, and salt. Whisk in oil. Pour over vegetables and toss to coat.

3. Cover and refrigerate at least 1 hour before serving. This is a great accompaniment to meat, poultry, or fish.

Calories per serving: 84 Fat: 4 g. Sodium: 162 mg.
For exchange diets, count: 2 vegetable, 1 fat
Preparation time: 15 minutes Chilling time: 1 hour

Menu *of the* Day

Meat Loaf
with Fresh Vegetable Relish
Squash with Cinnamon
and Brown Sugar
Blueberries
Skim Milk

*All that is worth cherishing begins in the heart,
not the head. —Suzanne Chapin*

Lemon Pudding Dessert Cake
16 servings

1 prepared 10-inch angel food cake from the bakery
3-ounce package instant lemon pudding mix

1 1/2 cups buttermilk
1 cup nonfat sour cream

1. Tear the angel food cake into bite-size pieces and line the bottom of a 13- by 9-inch pan with the pieces.

2. In a mixing bowl, combine pudding mix, buttermilk, and sour cream. Beat until thick, about 2 minutes.

3. Spread over the cake and chill at least 1 hour or until serving. Top cake with fresh pineapple or strawberries. Cut into 16 squares.

Calories per square: 101 Fat: 1 g. Sodium: 252 mg.
For exchange diets, count: 1 fruit, 1/2 skim milk
Preparation time: 15 minutes Chilling time: 1 hour

Menu *of the* Day

Veggie Toppings on your favorite
Frozen Cheese Pizza
Fresh Pineapple over Lemon
Pudding Dessert Cake
Sugar-Free Soft Drink

Lettuce with Extra Crunch
8 servings

2 tablespoons sliced almonds
1/4 cup chow mein noodles
1 tablespoon vegetable oil
2 tablespoons sugar
2 tablespoons white wine vinegar

1/4 teaspoon salt
1/4 teaspoon pepper
8 cups torn romaine lettuce
2 green onions, diced fine
2 strips bacon, broiled and crumbled

1. Preheat oven to 350°.

2. Combine almonds and noodles on a baking sheet. Bake, uncovered, for 8 minutes, then set aside.

3. In a shaker container, combine oil, sugar, vinegar, salt, and pepper. Shake well.

4. In a salad bowl, combine lettuce, onions, and bacon. Just before serving, add almond mixture and dressing, and toss.

Calories per serving: 45 Fat: 3 g. Sodium: 98 mg.
For exchange diets, count: 1 vegetable, 1/2 fat
Preparation time: 15 minutes

Menu of the Day

Cold Tuna or Salmon with
Fat-Free Mayo on a Sub Bun
Lettuce with Extra Crunch
Fresh Banana
Skim Milk

The sun does not shine for a few trees and flowers,
but for the wide world's joy. —Henry Ward Beecher

A Clean and Safe Summer Kitchen

First Things First

Keep food clean. Keep everything that comes in contact with food clean. Wash your hands frequently while you cook. Use only clean towels, sponges, and cooking dishes.

Keep hot food hot. Cook and hold cooked foods at temperatures higher than 140°. High temperatures kill most bacteria. Temperatures between 140° and 159° prevent their growth, but may allow bacteria to survive. Never allow cooked foods with protein (meat, poultry, fish, eggs, milk, or milk products) to sit at room temperature for longer than 2 hours.

Keep cold food cold. Rapidly cool any cooked foods that are to be served cold or refrigerated to 40° or below. At this temperature, bacteria that spoil food grow slowly. Below 32° is where bacteria survive, but do not reproduce.

Menu *of the* Day

Clean the Fridge Day
Leftover Lean Meat
Stir-Fried with bits of Broccoli,
Mushrooms, Carrots, Onions,
Water Chestnuts, and Teriyaki
Sauce Over Quick Rice
Leftover Fresh Fruits marinated in
Orange Juice and Mineral Water
Skim Milk

Just Say No to the Top Ten Food Safety Sins

Countertop thawing

Leftovers left out of the refrigerator

Unclean cutting boards

Room temperature marinating

Grocery store to the refrigerator lag time

Re-using platters or plates for raw and grilled meats

Stirring and tasting from the same spoon

Shared knife for meats and other foods

Undercooked high risk foods such as eggs, meat, poultry, and fish

Doggie bag delayed getting to the fridge

Menu of the Day

Reduced-Fat Bratwurst on the grill
on a Dark Bun with Spicy Mustard
Shredded Cabbage and Carrots
from a bag with Reduced-Fat
Coleslaw Dressing
Mandarin Oranges
and Sliced Bananas
Skim Milk

*Do all the good you can, and make as little fuss
about it as possible. —Charles Dickens*

Grilled to Perfect Doneness

For safe food and the best flavor, cook meat and poultry to the right internal temperature.
To check, use a meat or "instant-read" thermometer.

Meat, Fish, or Poultry	Internal Cooked Temp
Fresh Beef, Veal, Lamb	160
Ground products	or cook until no longer pink,
such as hamburger	and juices clear
Non-ground products, roasts, steaks	
Medium rare	145
Medium	160
Well done	170
Fresh Pork	
all cuts including ground pork	
Medium	160
Well done	170
Ham	
Fresh, raw	160
Fully cooked, to reheat	140
Fish	145
Poultry	
Ground chicken, turkey	165
Whole chicken, turkey	180
Stuffing	165
Poultry breasts, roasts, thighs	170
	or until juice is clear
Duck, goose	180

Menu *of the* Day

Ribeye Rubbed with
Fresh Basil and Minced Garlic
Grilled to Perfect Doneness
Grilled Potato Wedges
Lettuce Salad
with Reduced-Fat Dressing
Honeydew Melon
Skim Milk

Pack a Safe Picnic

For perishables, use clean, insulated coolers chilled with ice or chemical cold packs. Use a 75 percent food, 25 percent ice ratio. Keep the cooler closed.

Store nonperishable foods in a clean picnic or laundry basket.

Seal all foods tightly in bags, jars, or plastic containers to keep bugs out.

Pack foods that are cold or frozen already. Coolers do not chill room temperature foods.

Pack uncooked meat, poultry, or fish in well-sealed containers. Make sure the juices do not leak.

Keep your cooler in the coolest spot of the picnic grounds.

Return perishable foods to the cooler immediately after serving.

Wrap hot dishes in several layers of newspaper, then in an insulated container.

After the meal, toss perishable leftovers.

Menu of the *Day*

Pack a Picnic for the Park!
Chicken from the Deli
without the skin
Low-Fat Potato Chips
Cabbage Salad with Clear Dressing
Chunks of Fresh Fruit
Lemonade

---

*Your only treasures are those
which you carry in your heart.
–Demophilus*

Orange Glazed Sugar Snap Peas

4 1-cup servings

1 pound sugar snap peas, fresh or frozen
1 tablespoon water
1 tablespoon brown sugar

2 tablespoons orange juice concentrate, thawed
1 tablespoon margarine

1. Place peas with water in a microwave dish. Cover and cook on high power for 4 minutes. Drain liquid.

2. Combine brown sugar, orange juice concentrate, and margarine in a small cup. Microwave on high power for 30 seconds.

3. Drizzle over peas and serve.

Calories per serving: 89 Fat: 1 g. Sodium: 16 mg.
For exchange diets, count: 2 vegetable, 1/2 fruit
Preparation time: 10 minutes

Menu of the Day

Assorted Reduced-Fat Cold Cuts
Reduced-Fat Cheeses
on Fresh Hard Rolls
Orange Glazed Sugar Snap Peas
Raspberries
Skim Milk

Dilled Cucumber Soup
8 ¾-cup servings

1 cup skim milk
1 cup nonfat sour cream
1 cup nonfat plain yogurt
2 cucumbers, peeled, seeded, and chopped
1 green onion, chopped

1 tablespoon dill weed
1 tablespoon lemon juice
1/2 teaspoon salt
1/2 teaspoon white pepper
2 drops hot sauce

1. Combine all ingredients in a blender or food processor.

2. Cover and process just until smooth.

3. Chill at least 30 minutes. Stir before serving.

Calories per serving: 67 Fat: 1 g. Sodium: 201 mg.
For exchange diets, count: 1 vegetable, 1/2 skim milk
Preparation time: 20 minutes Chilling time: 30 minutes

Menu *of the* Day

Dilled Cucumber Soup
Tuna Salad Sandwich
Tomato Juice
Fresh Apple
Skim Milk

June 29

Mexican Stuffed Peppers
8 peppers

8 large, firm green peppers
2 cups cooked rice (follow package directions)
16-ounce can pinto beans, well drained
1 cup mild salsa

Topping: 4 ounces shredded reduced-fat Monterey Jack cheese

1. Preheat oven to 375°.

2. Slice tops off peppers and remove seeds.

3. Mix rice, beans, and salsa in a mixing bowl.

4. Carefully stuff peppers. Place on a baking sheet and sprinkle with cheese.

5. Bake for 45 minutes. Peppers should be tender crisp, yet retain their shape for serving.

Calories per 1-pepper serving: 195 Fat: 3 g. Sodium: 655 mg.
For exchange diets, count: 1 lean meat, 1 vegetable, 1 1/2 starch
Preparation time: 15 minutes Baking time: 45 minutes

Menu of the Day

Mexican Stuffed Peppers
Reduced-Fat Tortilla Chips
Fresh Nectarine
Skim Milk

And now abideth faith, hope, love these three;
but the greatest of these is love.
–I Corinthians 13:13

June 30

Pineapple Margaritas
4 12-ounce servings

2 1/2 cups coarsely crushed ice
1 3/4 cups chilled pineapple juice
1/2 cup orange juice concentrate

1/3 cup lime juice
1 tablespoon super fine sugar
Garnish: pineapple spear

1. Chill 4 glasses in the freezer.

2. Blend crushed ice with remaining ingredients until frothy.

3. Pour into chilled glasses, garnish, and serve.

Calories per serving: 127 Fat: 0 Sodium: 2 mg.
For exchange diets, count: 2 fruit
Preparation time: 15 minutes

Menu *of the* Day

Pineapple Margaritas
Barbecued Chicken on the grill
Pasta Salad from a box
Watermelon
Skim Milk

Taking a Full Breath of God's World

I know it's hard to say good-bye to June. But greet July with a spirit of fire-works, and enjoy summer in big gulps.

This two-month section breathes in the countless blessings from the earth: home grown tomatoes, cooking perfect sweet corn, making homemade ice cream, discovering a new salad green, slicing up peach salsa, turning off the stove and dining on a main dish salad, blending up a fruit soup, trying a low-fat BLT (It can't be!), drying fresh herbs in the microwave, and getting hungry for apples by the time August is over.

These last two months of summer see us on the road for family vacations (traveler's eating hints) and then hurrying home to get ready for school.

This time of year stirs memories of having our feet measured and stepping into new shoes for the first day of school; of having perfectly sharpened pencils with clean, flat erasers; and a full notebook with clean pages to be filled.

Allow summer's end to take you back to that time of new beginnings. Fall can be the start of something wonderful for you. Approach it with the excitement of meeting your new teacher on the first day.

The slate is blank. Ask God how you should fill it.

"That's the man that ate the bugs," a small boy said when he
saw Air Force Captain Scott O'Grady, who survived for six days
on grass, rain water, and bugs after being shot down in Bosnia.

July 1

Carrot and Spinach Dip
10 ¼-cup servings

10-ounce package frozen chopped spinach, thawed
  and squeezed dry
2 large carrots, coarsely grated
1 small onion, diced
2 cups nonfat ricotta cheese

1/4 cup shredded Parmesan cheese
1 tablespoon dried red pepper
1 tablespoon dried basil
1 teaspoon minced garlic

1. Combine all ingredients in a mixing bowl. Stir well.

2. Cover and refrigerate at least 2 hours for flavors to blend. This dip lasts 5 days.

Calories per serving: 65 Fat: 1 g. Sodium: 95 mg.
For exchange diets, count: 1 vegetable, 1/2 skim milk
Preparation time: 15 minutes Chilling time: 2 hours

Menu *of the* Day
Carrot and Spinach Dip
Reduced-Fat Summer Sausage
Reduced-Fat White and Wheat
Crackers
Choice of Melon
Skim Milk

Taking a Full Breath of God's World

He that cometh to me shall never hunger;
and he that believeth on me shall never thirst.
—John 6:35

Beef Rollups
4 rollups

4 large (10-inch) flour tortillas
3-ounce container garden-vegetable-flavored
  reduced-fat cream cheese
1 cup shredded carrots

1/2 cup reduced-fat pepper jack cheese, shredded
1/2 pound well-trimmed deli roast beef, thinly
  sliced

1. Spread cream cheese evenly over one side of each tortilla; top each with shredded carrots and shredded cheese. Layer roast beef over the cheese, then roll up tightly.

2. Wrap in plastic wrap. Refrigerate at least 30 minutes before serving. These may be prepared ahead and keep for 3 days in the refrigerator.

Calories per 1-rollup serving: 398 Fat: 10 g. Sodium: 524 mg.
For exchange diets, count: 2 1/2 starch, 1 vegetable, 3 lean meat
Preparation time: 15 minutes Chilling time: 30 minutes

Menu *of the* Day

Beef Rollups
Fresh Lettuce and Tomato
on the side
Fresh Strawberry
and Ice Milk Sundaes
Skim Milk

The rainbow never tells me / That gust and storm are by;
Yet she is more convincing / Than philosophy.
—Emily Dickinson

July 3

Grilled Vegetables
8 servings

4 medium bell peppers (green, yellow, orange, red),
   cut in half lengthwise, with seeds removed
4 small zucchini, cut in half lengthwise
8 small onions, cut in half lengthwise

8 ounces fresh mushrooms
1 tablespoon olive oil
2 tablespoons red wine vinegar

1. Place prepared vegetables on a platter or shallow dish.

2. Combine oil and vinegar in a shaker container with a sprinkle cap. Sprinkle the surfaces of the vegetables with oil and vinegar mixture.

3. Preheat grill to medium-hot (375°).

4. Grill vegetables 4 inches from the heat source for 15 minutes, turning once during cooking.

5. Cover and refrigerate leftovers and eat them cold for lunch.

Calories per serving: 47 Fat: 2 g. Sodium: 4 mg.
For exchange diets, count: 2 vegetable
Preparation time: 15 minutes Grilling time: 15 minutes

Menu of the Day

Hamburgers on the Grill
with Lettuce, Tomato,
Cucumbers, and Sprouts
Grilled Vegetables
Cucumber Salad from the deli
Reduced-Fat Tortilla Chips
Rainbow Sherbet
with Fresh Fruit on top
Skim Milk

Taking a Full Breath of God's World

In the beauty of the lilies Christ was born across the sea,
With a glory in his bosom that transfigures you and me;
as he died to make men holy, let us die to make men free,
While God is marching on. —Julia Ward Howe, "Battle Hymn of the Republic"

Homemade Ice Cream for the Whole Gang
24 ½-cup servings or 12 1-cup servings

5 eggs, beaten
3 tablespoons flour
1/4 teaspoon salt
2 cups sugar
1 1/4 cups whole milk

2 tablespoons vanilla
1 1/2 quarts whole milk
1 pint half and half
Crushed ice and rock salt

1. In a medium saucepan, combine beaten eggs, flour, salt, and sugar. Whisk in 1 1/4 cups whole milk. Cook over medium heat, stirring constantly, until mixture is thickened and clear.

2. Pour cooked mixture into the freezing container of a manual or electric ice cream freezer. Stir in vanilla, 1 1/2 quarts whole milk, and half and half.

3. Layer crushed ice and rock salt around freezing container. Manually turn or process electrically until ice cream is semi-solid.

Calories per 1/2-cup serving: 140 Fat: 3 g. Sodium: 81 mg.
For exchange diets, count: 1 skim milk, 1 1/2 fat
Preparation time: 15 minutes Freezing time: 30 minutes

Menu of the Day

Grilled Skinless Boneless
Chicken Breasts with your
favorite Barbecue Sauce
Corn on the Cob dotted with
Soft Margarine and
Sprinkled with Fresh Chives
Cabbage Salad with Clear Dressing
from the deli
Homemade Ice Cream for the
Whole Gang
Lemonade

When thou makest a feast, call the poor, the maimed, the lame, the blind.
And thou shalt be blessed; for they cannot recompense thee.
–Luke 14:13-14

July 5

American Cancer Society Guidelines on Diet, Nutrition, and Cancer Prevention. December 1996

1. Choose most of the foods you eat from plant sources. Eat five or more servings of fruits and vegetables each day. Eat other foods from plant sources, such as breads, cereals, grain products, rice, pasta, or beans several times each day.

2. Limit intake of high-fat foods, particularly fatty animal foods. Choose foods low in fat. Limit consumption of high-fat meats and cheese.

3. Be physically active: Achieve and maintain a healthy weight. Be at least moderately active for 30 minutes or more on most days of the week. Stay within your healthy weight range.

4. Limit consumption of alcoholic beverages.

Menu *of the* Day

Fresh Vegetable Chef Salad
with Lean Ham and
Reduced-Fat Cheese
Reduced-Fat Salad Dressing
Broiled French Bread
Fresh Blueberries
over Lemon Yogurt
Skim Milk

Taking a Full Breath of God's World

God made the country and man made the town.
—Cowper, The Task

Common Questions about Diet, Nutrition, and Cancer

What are antioxidants? Certain nutrients in fruits and vegetables appear to protect the body against the oxygen-induced damage to tissues that occurs constantly as a result of normal metabolism. Because such damage is associated with increased cancer risk, antioxidant nutrients are thought to protect against cancer. Antioxidant nutrients include vitamin C, vitamin E, selenium, and carotenoids.

Do artificial sweeteners cause cancer? Several years ago, experiments on rats suggested saccharin may cause cancer. Since then, however, studies of primates and humans have shown no increased risk of cancer from either saccharin or aspartame. Physicians may recommend pregnant women limit consumption of artificial sweeteners.

Does beta carotene reduce cancer risk? Because beta carotene, an antioxidant, is found in fruits and vegetables and because eating fruits and vegetables is clearly associated with a reduced risk of cancer, it seemed possible that taking high doses of beta carotene supplements might reduce cancer risk. However, studies have proven no benefit from supplements and two studies associate beta carotene supplements with a *higher* risk of lung cancer.

Questions about cancer continue tomorrow...

Menu *of the* Day

Broiled Cod Sprinkled with Old
Bay or Mrs. Dash's Seasoning
Steamed Fresh Broccoli and
Baby Carrots seasoned with
Lemon Juice and Dill Seed
Wheat Rolls with Soft Margarine
Pineapple Chunks
with Sliced Bananas
Reduced-Fat Sandwich Cookies
Skim Milk

Day 2 of Common Questions about Diet, Nutrition, and Cancer

What is folic acid and can it prevent cancer? Folic acid (also known as folate or folacin) is a B vitamin found in many vegetables, beans, fruits, whole grains, and fortified breakfast cereals. Folic acids reduce the risk of some cancers.

Does olive oil affect cancer risk? Olive oil, like all fats, is high in calories, but its fat is mostly monounsaturated and is most likely neutral with respect to cancer risk.

Do pesticides and herbicides on fruits and vegetables cause cancer? Pesticides and herbicides can be toxic when consumed in high doses. Current evidence is insufficient to link pesticides in foods with an increased risk of cancer.

What is selenium and can it reduce cancer risk? Selenium is a mineral antioxidant. Animal studies suggest that selenium protects against cancer. Selenium supplements are not recommended, as there is only a narrow margin between safe and toxic doses. Grain foods are good sources of selenium.

Can soybeans reduce cancer risk? Soybeans are an excellent source of protein and a good alternative to meat. Human studies have failed to prove soy to be cancer-protective.

Menu of the Day

Ground Pork Tacos
with Fresh Tomatoes, Lettuce,
Peppers, Green Onions, and
Reduced-Fat Cheese
Fresh Pear
Skim Milk

Taking a Full Breath of God's World

Lord of the far horizons / Give us the eyes to see
Over the verge of the sundown / The beauty that is to be.
—Bliss Carman, Lord of the Far Horizons

Sweet and Sour Cabbage Salad
8 1-cup servings

1 bag (6 cups) shredded cabbage and carrots
1 red or green bell pepper, chopped
2 green onions, thinly sliced, including tops
1/2 teaspoon celery seed

1/2 teaspoon mustard seed
1/4 cup sugar
1/2 cup vinegar
3 large ice cubes

1. Combine vegetables and seeds in a large salad bowl.

2. In a small saucepan over high heat, combine sugar and vinegar. Bring to a boil and cook for 2 minutes. Remove from heat and stir in ice cubes.

3. Stir liquid into vegetables; cover and refrigerate at least 30 minutes or until serving. This salad will be tasty for a week when kept refrigerated.

Calories per serving: 80 Fat: 0 Sodium: 34 mg.
For exchange diets, count: 2 vegetable, 1/2 fruit
Preparation time: 15 minutes Chilling time: 30 minutes

Menu *of the* Day

Minute Steaks on the grill
Pasta Salad from a box
Sweet and Sour Cabbage Salad
Chilled Fruit Cocktail
with Fresh Bananas
Skim Milk

Best Bets for Vitamin C

The Recommended Daily Allowance (RDA) is 60 mg.

Food	*mg. Vitamin C*
Guava, 1 medium	165
Red bell pepper, 1/2 cup	95
Papaya, 1/2	95
Orange juice, 3/4 cup	75
Orange, 1	60
Broccoli, 1/2 cup	60
Green bell pepper, 1/2 cup	45
Kohlrabi, 1/2 cup	45
Strawberries, 1/2 cup	45
Grapefruit, 1/2	40
Cantaloupe, 1/2 cup	35
Tomato juice, 3/4 cup	35
Mango, 1/2	30
Tangerine, 1	25
Potato, 1 baked with skin	25
Cabbage, 1/2 cup	25
Tomato, 1 medium	25
Spinach, 1 cup raw	15

Menu of the Day

Broiled Lamb Chops rubbed with
Garlic and Fresh or Dried Mint
Quick Rice
Sliced Fresh Tomatoes and
Cucumbers with
Reduced-Fat Ranch Dressing
Tangerine
Skim Milk

Taking a Full Breath of God's World

A thing of beauty is a joy for ever;
Its loveliness increases; it will never pass into nothingness
—Keats, from Endymion

Fresh Corn in the Skillet

4 ¾-cup servings

2 slices bacon, diced
1 green pepper, diced
1 onion, diced

3 large ears sweet corn, kernels sliced off
1/4 teaspoon salt
1/2 teaspoon pepper

1. In a skillet over medium heat, cook diced bacon until crisp. Remove bacon from pan to a paper towel to drain. Drain fat from pan.

2. Add all remaining ingredients to the pan and cook uncovered over medium heat for 15 minutes, stirring occasionally. Add bacon, toss and serve.

Calories per serving: 72 Fat: 2 g. Sodium: 185 mg.
For exchange diets, count: 1 starch
Preparation time: 20 minutes

Menu of the Day

Turkey Breast on the grill
Fresh Corn in the Skillet
Hard Rolls
Bing Cherries
Skim Milk

In some sense, life leaves us all wounded forever. To be human is to face that and laugh anyway. —Leonard Pitts, Jr., columnist for the Miami Herald, in a February 3, 1997, reflection on the tragic death of Ennis Cosby.

July 11

Best Bets for Vitamin A
The RDA is 1000 Retinol Equivalents (RE)

Food	*RE Vitamin A*
Sweet potato, 1/2 cup	2800
Carrot, 1 medium	2025
Kale, 1/2 cup	480
Mango, 1/2 medium	405
Turnip greens, 1/2 cup	395
Spinach, 1 cup	375
Papaya, 1/2	305
Red bell pepper, 1/2 cup	285
Apricot, 3	275
Cantaloupe, 1/2 cup	260
Romaine lettuce, 1 cup	145
Tomato, 1	75
Broccoli, 1/2 cup	70

Menu of the *Day*

Goulash
Lean Browned Ground Beef with tender cooked Elbow Macaroni Noodles, Fresh Onions, Red Peppers, and Tomatoes

Cornbread from a box
Cold Cucumbers in Vinegar and Sugar Substitute
Fresh Cantaloupe
Skim Milk

As the earth becomes more crowded, there is no longer any "away."
One person's trash basket is another's living space.
—American Academy of Sciences, 1966

Gazpacho

8 ¾-cup servings

3 cloves fresh garlic, minced
3 tablespoons white vinegar
1/2 teaspoon salt
1 teaspoon vegetable oil
1 teaspoon tarragon
1 teaspoon sugar

24-ounce can vegetable juice cocktail, divided
1 large green pepper, halved and seeded
1 large cucumber, pared
2 ribs celery
2 medium tomatoes, peeled and quartered

1. Combine minced garlic, vinegar, salt, oil, tarragon, sugar, and 2 cups of vegetable juice cocktail in a large bowl.

2. In a blender or food processor, process pepper, cucumber, celery, tomatoes, and 1 cup of the vegetable juice cocktail until finely chopped. Add to garlic and vinegar mixture.

3. Chill at least 30 minutes.

Calories per serving: 44 Fat: 0 Sodium: 424 mg.
For exchange diets, count: 2 vegetable
Preparation time: 15 minutes Chilling time: 30 minutes

Menu of the Day

Gazpacho
Broiled Onion Bagels broiled with
Part-Skim Mozzarella Cheese
Fresh Peaches over
Angel Food Cake
Skim Milk

Consider the lilies of the field, how they grow; they toil not, neither do they spin:
And yet I say unto you, That even Solomon in all his glory was not
arrayed like one of these. —Matthew 6:28-29

July 13

Mile High Raspberry Pie
8 slices

2 large egg whites
1 teaspoon lemon juice
1 teaspoon vanilla
2/3 cup sugar

10-ounce package frozen raspberries, thawed
1 1/2 cups fat-free whipped topping
1 reduced-fat graham cracker crust

1. Beat first four ingredients for 15 minutes in a large bowl at high speed.

2. Fold in thawed berries and whipped topping, pour into the crust, and freeze for at least 3 hours.

Calories per 1-slice serving: 209 Fat: 3 g. Sodium: 170 mg.
For exchange diets, count: 1 starch, 2 fruit
Preparation time: 20 minutes Freezing time: 3 hours

Menu *of the* Day

Tuna Salad with Reduced-Fat
Mayo and Diced Cucumber
on a Kaiser Roll
Steamed Stirfry Veggies
Mile High Raspberry Pie
Skim Milk

If you are all wrapped up in yourself,
you are overdressed. –Kate Halverson

Grilled Chicken with Peach Salsa

4 servings

4 skinless boneless chicken breasts
1 cup no-added-salt chunky salsa

1 ripe peach, peeled and chopped fine

1. Preheat grill or broiler to medium heat.

2. Meanwhile, combine salsa and peaches in a small mixing bowl

3. Broil chicken breasts 3 inches from heat for 4 minutes. Turn and baste with peach salsa. Cook for 4 more minutes or until juice runs clear. Transfer to a serving platter.

Calories per serving: 176 Fat: 3 g. Sodium: 80 mg.
For exchange diets, count: 4 very lean meat, 1/2 fruit
Preparation time: 5 minutes Cooking time: 8 minutes

Menu *of the* Day

Grilled Chicken with Peach Salsa
Cornbread Muffin from a box
Spinach Salad with Reduced-Fat
Ranch Dressing
Sugar-Free Vanilla Pudding
Bing Cherries
Mineral Water

Are You Full Yet?

Today's menu is high in vegetable fiber and you'll feel full long after dinner.

Researchers at the University of Sidney have devised a Satiety Index based on how full volunteers felt after eating 240 calories worth of different foods. Calorie for calorie, bulky, high-fiber foods such as fruits and vegetables rated high. High-fat foods ranked low, since 240 calories worth is a small portion.

Interesting Facts from the Satiety Index:

Potatoes ranked highest—seven times higher than the least filling food, croissants.

Whole grain bread is 50 percent more filling than white bread.

Cakes, donuts, and cookies were among the least filling.

Oranges and apples outscored bananas.

Fish is more satisfying per calorie than lean beef or chicken.

Popcorn is twice as filling as a candy bar or peanuts.

Published by Iowa State University Extension Service, January 1997.

Menu *of the* Day

Fresh Pasta and Sauce
from the refrigerator section
of the supermarket
Broiled Fresh Bread
with Fresh Parmesan on top
Sautéed Zucchini and Onions
seasoned with Fennel and Garlic
Green Grapes and
Diced Cantaloupe
Skim Milk

July 16

If you get simple beauty and naught else,
You get about the best thing God invents.
—R. Browning, from "Fra Lippo Lippi"

Quick Crab Soup

6 1½-cup servings

14-ounce can no-added-salt chicken broth
2 cans Pepper Pot soup
1 cup water

14-ounce can evaporated skim milk
6-ounce can crabmeat, drained
1/2 teaspoon curry powder

1. Combine all ingredients in a large stockpot. Heat to boiling, simmer for just 15 minutes, and serve hot.

Calories per serving: 181 Fat: 5 g. Sodium: 1138 mg.
For exchange diets, count: 1 skim milk, 1/2 starch, 1 lean meat
Preparation time: 5 minutes Cooking time: 15 minutes

Menu of the Day

Quick Crab Soup
Toasted English Muffins
Fresh Cucumber Slices
Apple Slices
Skim Milk

Flowers always make people better, happier and more helpful.
They are sunshine, food and medicine to the soul.
—Luther Burbank

July 17

Garlic Potatoes Baked in Foil
4 ½-cup servings

2 large potatoes, scrubbed, quartered, and cut into wedges
1 teaspoon minced garlic
1 tablespoon olive oil

1/2 teaspoon salt
1/2 teaspoon rosemary
2 tablespoons wine vinegar
1/2 teaspoon pepper

1. Combine all ingredients in a mixing bowl, stirring potatoes to coat with seasonings.

2. Wrap potatoes in two 12-inch square foil pouches, carefully sealing all edges.

3. Grill over medium flame for 15 to 18 minutes or until potatoes are tender.

Calories per serving: 87 Fat: 3 g. Sodium: 272 mg.
For exchange diets, count: 1 starch
Preparation time: 10 minutes Grilling time: 15 minutes

Menu *of the* Day

Turkey Breasts on the Grill
with Barbecue Sauce
Garlic Potatoes Baked in Foil
Kohlrabi Slices
Watermelon
Skim Milk

Taking a Full Breath of God's World

The grass withereth and the flower thereof falleth away;
But the word of the Lord endureth forever.
—I Peter 1:24-25

California Dip Italiano
12 3-tablespoon servings

1 envelope dry onion soup mix   2 tablespoons dried Italian seasoning blend
16-ounce container fat-free sour cream

1. Combine all ingredients in a bowl. Cover and chill at least 2 hours for flavors to blend.

Calories per serving: 49 Fat: 0 Sodium: 344 mg.
For exchange diets, count: 1/2 skim milk
Preparation time: 5 minutes Chilling time: 2 hours

Menu *of the* Day

Spaghetti with Lean Ground Pork
and your favorite Sauce
Fresh Cauliflower,
Broccoli, and Carrots with
California Dip Italiano
Reduced-Fat Fudgesicle
Orange-Pineapple Juice

Our deepest fear is not that we are inadequate.
Our deepest fear is that we are powerful beyond measure.
It is our light, not our darkness that most frightens us.
—Nelson Mandela, 1994

July 19

Brown Rice Chicken Salad
4 1½-cup servings

3/4 cup instant brown rice
3/4 cup no-added-salt chicken broth
1/2 cup reduced-fat mayonnaise
1 Granny Smith apple, cored, seeded, and diced

1 tablespoon lemon juice
6-ounce can white meat chicken
2 ribs celery, diced
1 small bunch seedless red grapes, cut in half

1. Combine rice and broth in a microwave-safe casserole dish. Cover and microwave according to package directions. Cool to room temperature. To speed cooling, transfer the rice to a chilled shallow salad bowl.

2. Mix all remaining ingredients with cooled rice. Cover and chill at least 30 minutes or until serving time.

Calories per serving: 224 Fat: 9 g. Sodium: 200 mg.
   (To reduce fat, use fat-free mayonnaise or salad dressing.)
For exchange diets, count: 1 starch, 1 vegetable, 2 lean meat, 1/2 fat
Preparation time: 10 minutes Chilling time: 30 minutes

Menu of the Day
Brown Rice Chicken Salad
Reduced-Fat Wheat Crackers
Radishes
Fresh Nectarine
Skim Milk

Taking a Full Breath of God's World

Walk gently, breathe peacefully, and laugh hysterically.
—Author unknown

Peppery Barley Salad

8 ¾-cup servings

1 cup quick cooking barley	2 tablespoons water
2 cups no-added-salt chicken broth	1/2 teaspoon salt
8 ounces fresh mushrooms, sliced thin	1 teaspoon dry mustard
4 carrots, scrubbed and grated	1 teaspoon dried tarragon
4 green onions, diced	1/2 teaspoon fresh ground black pepper
1 tablespoon olive oil	1/4 teaspoon garlic powder
1/4 cup lemon juice	

1. Cook barley in broth according to package directions. Drain well.

2. Meanwhile, in a salad bowl, combine mushrooms, carrots, and green onions. Add barley.

3. In a shaker container, mix remaining ingredients. Pour over barley and vegetables, stirring to mix. Cover and refrigerate at least 30 minutes. This salad keeps for 3 days.

Calories per serving: 83 Fat: 2 g. Sodium: 147 mg.
For exchange diets, count: 1 starch
Preparation time: 20 minutes Chilling time: 30 minutes

Menu *of the* Day

Lean Sliced Ham from the deli
on a Hard Roll with Spicy Mustard
Peppery Barley Salad
Fresh Peaches
Skim Milk

One morning while I was praying, God pointed out to me that my insecurities were rooted in self-centeredness. "I created you in my image," he reminded me. "Quit concentrating on your inabilities and look instead to my abilities." —Mayo Mathers in "Being True to His Image." Today's Christian Woman., *January/February 1997.*

July 21

Pears and Berries Soup

8 ¾-cup servings

This recipe is a favorite of mine
from the *American Institute for Cancer Research Newsletter*

6 pears, peeled, seeded and chopped
1 1/3 cups fresh or frozen raspberries (reserve 8 whole berries for garnish)

1/2 teaspoon cinnamon
3 cups cran-raspberry beverage

1. Puree the pears, berries, and cinnamon in a blender or food processor. Add the cran-raspberry beverage and blend again.

2. Chill at least 30 minutes or until serving time. Garnish each bowl with a fresh raspberry.

Calories per serving: 138 Fat: 0 Sodium: 2 mg.
For exchange diets, count: 2 1/2 fruit
Preparation time: 15 minutes Chilling time: 30 minutes

Menu *of the* Day

Pears and Berries Soup
Reduced-Fat Gouda Cheese
Broiled on a Bagel
Fresh Cauliflower and
Cherry Tomato Relishes
Skim Milk

Taking a Full Breath of God's World

July 22

In everybody's garden a little rain must fall
Or life's sweetest fairest flowers wouldn't grow and bloom at all.
—From a service conducted by Pastor Barb Ilten
of St. Paul's ELCA, December 1996

Quick and Sassy Turkey Kabobs Olé

4 servings

12 large cherry tomatoes, stemmed
6-ounce jar marinated artichoke hearts, drained
8 large pitted black olives
8 large pimiento-stuffed green olives

4 mushrooms, quartered
1/2 pound smoked turkey, cut into cubes
2 tablespoons red wine vinegar

1. Preheat grill or broiler.

2. Thread ingredients onto skewers. Sprinkle with red wine vinegar.

3. Grill or broil 3 inches from heat for 8 to 10 minutes, turning once during cooking.

Calories per serving: 142 Fat: 6 g. Sodium: 716 mg.
For exchange diets, count: 2 very lean meat, 1 vegetable, 1 fat
Preparation time: 10 minutes Grilling time: 10 minutes

Menu *of the* Day

Quick and Sassy
Turkey Kabobs Olé
Pasta Salad from a box
Strawberries
Skim Milk

---

*The ultimate lesson all of us have to learn is unconditional love,
which includes not only others but ourselves as well.*
–Elisabeth Kubler-Ross

July 23

Honey Mustard Chicken or Fish
4 4-ounce servings

1 envelope honey mustard salad dressing mix
1/3 cup orange juice

1/4 cup white wine
1 pound boneless skinless chicken pieces or firm
   white fish fillets

1. Mix first three ingredients together in an 8 by 11-inch glass baking dish. Place chicken or fish fillets in the pan, turning to coat. Cover and refrigerate for at least 30 minutes.

2. Grill chicken 3 inches from medium heat source for 3 minutes on each side. Grill fish 5 inches from medium heat source for 3 minutes on each side.

Calories per serving: 177 Fat: 3 g. Sodium: 584 mg.
For exchange diets, count: 4 very lean meat, 1/2 fruit
Preparation time: 10 minutes Marinating time: 30 minutes Grilling time: 6 minutes

---

Menu *of the* Day

Honey Mustard Chicken or Fish
Steamed Squash
Tender Brussels Sprouts
with Margarine
Bing Cherries
Skim Milk

Taking a Full Breath of God's World

*A real friend is one who overlooks your broken-down gate
and admires the flowers in your garden.
—Author unknown*

Colorful Jicama Salad

8 ³/₄-cup servings

1/4 cup white wine vinegar
2 tablespoons lime juice
1 tablespoon chopped fresh parsley
1/2 teaspoon minced garlic

10-ounce package frozen peas, thawed
10-ounce package frozen corn, thawed
1 small cucumber, peeled, seeded, and diced
1 small jicama, peeled and diced

1. Combine first four ingredients in a salad bowl, stirring to blend.

2. Add vegetables. Stir to blend, cover, and refrigerate at least 1 hour or until serving. This salad lasts 3 or 4 days.

Calories per serving: 63 Fat: 0 Sodium: 30 mg.
For exchange diets, count: 2 vegetable
Preparation time: 15 minutes Chilling time: 1 hour

Menu *of the* Day

Roast Beef from the deli
on a Hard Roll
Colorful Jicama Salad
Orange Sherbet over
Honeydew Melon
Skim Milk

Kitchen Wisdom

Test your kitchen wisdom with these questions from daily quizzes
given at the New York Cooking School:

1. What are the temperatures for meats cooked to rare, medium, and well-done?

2. How does the taste of fresh squeezed lemon juice differ from that in the bottles?

3. What are four rules for successful sautéing?

4. What does reducing do to a liquid, and how is it done?

5. What is the difference between the zest and pith of an orange?

6. How long should cheese sit at room temperature before being served?

7. What are two tricks to flaming?

Answers:

1. 120, 145, and 170 degrees

2. Fresh squeezed lemon juice is less bitter and richer in flavor.

3. Make sure the pan is very hot. Lubricate the pan lightly with oil. Never crowd the pan. Never cover the pan.

4. A reduction thickens a liquid and concentrates its flavors by boiling uncovered.

5. The zest is the outermost layer of skin on an orange; the pith is the spongy, fibrous white skin around the fruit itself.

6. Cheese should be removed from the refrigerator at least a half hour before being served.

7. Use spirits with a high percentage of alcohol. Both the food and the liqueur should be warmed.

Menu of the Day

BLTs made with Broiled Canadian
Bacon with Lettuce and Tomato on
Toast with Light Mayonnaise
Steamed Sugar Snap Peas
Mango Slices
Skim Milk

Taking a Full Breath of God's World

July 26

Caviar Olé

8 ½-cup servings

4-ounce can chopped ripe olives
2 4-ounce cans chopped green chilies
14-ounce can chopped tomatoes, drained well
3 green onions, diced

1/2 teaspoon minced garlic
1 teaspoon olive oil
1 tablespoon red wine vinegar
1 teaspoon seasoned pepper

1. Combine all ingredients in a glass bowl. (Drink or discard the tomato juice.)

2. Cover and chill at least 2 hours. Serve with reduced-fat corn chips.

Calories per serving: 25 Fat: 2 g. Sodium: 347 mg.
For exchange diets, count: 1 vegetable
Preparation time: 10 minutes Chilling time: 2 hours

Menu of the Day

Grilled Chicken Breast
Baked Corn Chips
with Caviar Olé
Granny Smith Apple
Skim Milk

Southwestern Couscous and Ham
4 2-cup servings

2 cups no-added-salt chicken broth
1/2 teaspoon turmeric
1 cup couscous
1 cup cooked black beans, drained and rinsed
8 ounces cooked lean ham, chopped
1 fresh tomato, chopped

1 green onion, diced
2 tablespoons chopped fresh parsley
1 large jalapeño pepper, seeded and diced
1 tablespoon lemon juice
1/4 teaspoon cumin

1. Bring broth and turmeric to boiling in a medium saucepan. Stir in couscous.

2. Remove from heat, cover, and let stand for 5 minutes.

3. Meanwhile, combine all remaining ingredients in a casserole dish. Add couscous, mix lightly with a fork, and serve.

Calories per serving: 269 Fat: 5 g. Sodium: 889 mg.
   (To reduce sodium, substitute cooked chicken for the ham.)
For exchange diets, count: 2 lean meat, 2 starch
Preparation time: 20 minutes

Menu *of the* Day

Southwestern Couscous and Ham
Corn Muffin from a box
Fresh Green Salad with
Reduced-Fat Dressing
Red Grapes
Skim Milk

Behind every flower stands God.
—Japanese Proverb

Savory Salmon on the Grill
4 servings

1/3 cup lime juice
1/2 teaspoon salt
1/2 teaspoon celery seeds
1/4 teaspoon black pepper
4 drops liquid red pepper seasoning

4 4-ounce salmon steaks
1 green onion, finely chopped
1 tablespoon water
1 tablespoon honey

1. Combine first five ingredients in an 8- by 11-inch glass baking dish.

2. Place salmon steaks in the dish to marinate, turning them once to coat. Cover and refrigerate at least 30 minutes.

3. Grill steaks 6 inches from medium heat element about 3 minutes per side.

4. Meanwhile, combine onion, water, and honey in a small mixing bowl. Pour over the steaks during the last 2 minutes of grilling.

Calories per serving: 244 Fat: 11 g. Sodium: 336 mg.
For exchange diets, count: 4 lean meat, 1 vegetable
Preparation time: 10 minutes Marinating time: 30 minutes Grilling time: 6 minutes

---

Menu *of the* Day

Savory Salmon on the Grill
Corn on the Cob
with Soft Margarine
Coleslaw from the deli
Chilled Fruit Cocktail
Skim Milk

Lemon Rice
4 ³/₄-cup servings

1 large lemon
1/4 teaspoon salt
1/4 teaspoon ground turmeric

2 1/4 cups water
1 cup white rice

1. Grate lemon peel onto wax paper.

2. Squeeze lemon juice into a 2-quart saucepan. Add salt, turmeric, and water.

3. Bring mixture to a boil; stir in rice and reduce heat to low. Cover and simmer for 20 minutes. *Do not stir* or rice will become sticky.

4. Add grated lemon rind. Fluff with a fork and serve.

Calories per serving: 175 Fat: 0 Sodium: 133 mg.
For exchange diets, count: 2 starch
Preparation time: 10 minutes Cooking time: 20 minutes

Menu *of the* Day

Grilled Turkey Breast
seasoned with Dried Tarragon
Lemon Rice
Steamed Asparagus
Fresh Tangerine
Skim Milk

Taking a Full Breath of God's World

*A man who could make one rose would be accounted most wonderful,
yet God scatters countless such flowers around us.* —Martin Luther

Herb Lore

Summer is the best time to experiment with the fresh flavor and power of herbs and spices. Consider the conventional wisdom attributed to these common herbs:

Bergamot—named for a 16th century Spanish herbalist, was used by Native Americans to treat mild fevers, headaches, colds, and sore throats. Also known as bea balm, used to make Oswego tea at the time of the Boston Tea Party.

Caraway—Two chemicals, carvol and carvene, are thought to soothe the smooth muscle tissue of the digestive tract and help expel gas. It is also a possible remedy for menstrual cramps (smooth muscle tenseness). It has been found in remains of Stone Age meals.

Cinnamon—may help regulate blood sugar and appetite by increasing the efficiency of insulin.

Chives—allium compound thought to enhance immune function and block carcinogenic action. Recorded 4000 years ago in China. May stimulate appetite and promote digestion.

Garlic—may act to lower blood cholesterol and decrease blood clotting, providing protection against heart disease, cancer, and strokes. Use 1/4 teaspoon minced garlic to replace 1 clove.

Ginger—One gram of fresh gingerroot (or about 1/2 teaspoon) taken 30 minutes before travel could prevent motion sickness. Soothes the stomach and reduces nausea.

Menu *of the* Day

Pizza Submarine Sandwich:
*Browned Ground Pork with Pizza
Sauce and your favorite Fresh
Herbs on a Submarine Roll
Broiled with Part-Skim
Mozzarella Cheese*

Lettuce and Reduced-Fat Dressing
Fresh Pineapple
Skim Milk

*Until you have heard the whippoorwill, either nearby or
in the faint distance, you have not experienced summer night.*
—Henry Beetle Hough from the Vineyard Gazette, *Edgartown, Mass.*

July 31

Drying Herbs

To preserve home-grown or farmer's market herbs for year-round use,
dry them by one of the following methods:

Air-dry herbs by hanging them on laundry racks in a dark, dry room. After a few weeks,
test for dryness.

To oven-dry herbs, place them on metal screens and dry in a conventional oven at 150°
for 12 to 24 hours.

To dry herbs in the microwave, lay them in a single layer between two paper towels and
microwave on high power for 1 minute. If they are still soft, continue heating for 20 seconds.

When the leaves are dry and crisp, remove them from the stems, crush lightly between two
pieces of waxed paper, and pour into an old spice container. Date and label.

Fresh herbs may also be frozen. Remove the leaves and lay them flat on a baking sheet.
After several hours in the freezer, place them in airtight bags and
store them in the freezer.

Menu *of the* Day

Green Pepper stuffed with
Lean Browned Ground Beef,
Dried Herbs, Quick Rice, and
Tomato Sauce
Cold Cucumbers with
Reduced-Fat Ranch Dressing
French Bread
Sliced Kiwifruit marinated
in Sugar-Free Soft Drink
Skim Milk

Taking a Full Breath of God's World

Avoid Traveler's Diarrhea

August is family vacation month. If you're venturing to some exciting locale follow these tips to avoid the visitor's most common health problem.

Safe Food Choices:

Freshly prepared dishes served steaming hot
Meats cooked to order, rather than rewarmed
Fruits you peel yourself
Breads and baked goods

Hot tea and coffee
Bottled water
Bottled soft drinks and fruit juices

Be Wary Of:

Tap water and ice
Uncooked vegetables or peeled fruits
Cold salads

Buffet lines
Food sold on the street
All foods that are rewarmed

Menu *of the* Day

Minute Steaks braised in
the skillet with Fresh Tomatoes,
Zucchini, and Onion, and
dotted with Worcestershire Sauce
Broiled Onion Bagel
Sliced Fresh Peaches
Skim Milk

*If we really want to love,
we must first learn how to forgive.
—Mother Teresa*

"Lasts Three Days" Tomato Salad

8 ½-cup servings

1 tablespoon olive oil
2 tablespoons lemon juice
1 teaspoon minced garlic
1/4 teaspoon salt

1 teaspoon oregano leaves
1/2 teaspoon basil leaves
4 large, firm, ripe tomatoes, sliced 1/2-inch thick
   (or may substitute cherry tomatoes, sliced in
   half)

1. Combine first 6 ingredients in a shallow salad bowl. Mix well. Add sliced tomatoes and spoon marinade over the top.

2. Cover and chill at least 30 minutes. Salad lasts for 3 days.

Calories per serving: 28 Fat: 2 g. Sodium: 72 mg.
For exchange diets, count: 1 vegetable
Preparation time: 5 minutes Marinating time: 30 minutes

Menu of the *Day*

Grilled Hamburger on a Bun
"Lasts Three Days" Tomato Salad
Steamed Broccoli Spears
Fresh Yellow Cherries
Skim Milk

Taking a Full Breath of God's World

August 3

Recipe to Preserve Children
*Take one large grassy field, one half dozen children, two or three
small dogs, a pinch of brook and some pebbles.*

Lime Melon Medley

4 1-cup servings

1/2 honeydew melon, cut into chunks
1/2 cantaloupe, cut into chunks

Juice squeezed from 1 fresh lime

Combine ingredients in a salad bowl. Mix, cover, and chill for 1 hour.

Calories per serving: 81 Fat: 0 Sodium: 22 mg.
For exchange diets, count: 1 1/2 fruit
Preparation time: 10 minutes Chilling time: 1 hour

Menu *of the* Day

Soft Flour Tortilla
microwaved with drained Kidney
Beans, Salsa, and shredded
Reduced-Fat Pepper Cheese
Shredded Lettuce and Tomato
on the side
Lime Melon Medley
Skim Milk

Orange Coconut Salad
4 ³/₄-cup servings

2 11-ounce cans mandarin oranges, drained well
1/4 cup coconut

1/2 cup nonfat sour cream
1 teaspoon orange juice

1. Combine drained oranges and coconut in a small salad bowl.

2. Spoon sour cream into a glass measuring cup. Stir in orange juice and then fold into salad. This salad is best chilled for 30 minutes before serving.

Calories per serving: 98 Fat: 1 g. Sodium: 51 mg.
For exchange diets, count: 1 1/2 fruit
Preparation time: 10 minutes Chilling time: 30 minutes

Menu *of the* Day

Sloppy Joe on a Bun
Steamed Green Beans
Orange Coconut Salad
Skim Milk

You never really leave a place you love.
Part of it you take with you—leaving part of you behind.
—Anonymous

Perfect Corn on the Cob

Select corn with fresh-looking, bright green husks and moist, plump, juicy-looking yellow or white kernels.

To microwave: Remove silk, but leave corn in the husk. Microwave 3 minutes for 1 large ear, or 2 minutes per ear if cooking more than one.

To boil: Remove husks and silk before cooking. Drop corn into a large pot of boiling water. Cover, let the water return to boiling, then turn off the heat and keep the pot covered. Remove enough ears for the first serving after 5 minutes. Remove all of the ears after 15 minutes, to ensure tenderness.

To foil-roast: Preheat conventional oven to 400° or preheat grill to medium heat. Husk the corn and wrap each ear in aluminum foil, with 1 teaspoon of reduced-fat margarine in each packet. Roast in the oven or in a covered grill for 25 minutes.

Menu *of the* Day

Grilled Reduced-Fat Bratwurst on
a Bun with Mustard and Pickles
Perfect Corn on the Cob
with Soft Margarine
Fresh Raspberries
over Vanilla Ice Milk
Cranberry Juice mixed with
Sugar-Free Lemon-Lime
Soft Drink

Veggie Corn Bread
12 squares

Non-stick cooking spray
10-ounce package mixed vegetables, thawed and
  drained very dry

1 green onion, diced
12-ounce package corn muffin mix

1. Preheat oven to 425°.

2. Spray a 9-inch baking pan generously with cooking spray.

3. Spread drained vegetables over the bottom of the pan. Sprinkle green onion over the vegetables.

4. Prepare corn muffin batter according to package directions.

5. Pour corn muffin batter over the vegetables and bake for 20 to 25 minutes. Remove from the oven, let stand for 3 minutes, then invert onto a serving plate. Cut into squares and serve.

Calories per square: 101 Fat: 3 g. Sodium: 244 mg.
For exchange diets, count: 1 starch, 1/2 fat
Preparation time: 10 minutes Baking time: 25 minutes

Menu of the Day

Sirloin Steak on the grill
Veggie Corn Bread
Green Vegetable Salad
with Reduced-Fat Dressing
Chocolate Ice Milk
Decaf Coffee

*I feel sorry for Moses. He spent 40 years wandering the desert,
eating nothing but bread off the ground and the occasional bird, and every
day a million people would come up to him and ask, "Are we there yet?"*
–Robert G. Lee

School is Just Around the Corner

As school shopping begins, don't forget school breakfast supplies.

These are some yummy ideas that kids can make on their own in the morning. Be sure to add juice and milk!

Cheese slices on toast, English muffins, or bagels

Cereal with banana slices

Peanut butter on a toaster waffle

Strawberries in instant oatmeal

Cold pizza

Leftover spaghetti

Apple and cheese slices on wheat crackers

Frozen yogurt with granola on top

Raisin toast with reduced-fat strawberry cream cheese

Menu of the Day

Spaghetti Noodles with your
favorite Pasta Sauce
Green Salad
with Reduced-Fat Dressing
French Bread broiled with
Reduced-Fat Mozzarella Cheese
Sugar-Free Lemonade

No-Bake Fudge Clusters
24 cookies

1/3 cup cocoa
1 1/2 cups sugar
1/2 teaspoon salt
1/2 cup milk
1/4 cup white corn syrup

1/4 cup margarine
1 teaspoon vanilla
2 cups quick cooking oats
1 cup coconut

1. Combine first three ingredients in a deep microwave-safe bowl. Use a whisk to stir in milk and syrup.

2. Microwave the mixture for 5 minutes, stopping the cooking two times to stir. Stir in margarine, vanilla, oats, and coconut.

3. Drop by spoonfuls onto waxed paper. Cool and store in an air-tight container.

Calories per cookie: 88 Fat: 3 g. Sodium: 125 mg.
For exchange diets, count: 1 starch
Preparation time: 15 minutes

Menu *of the* Day

Sub Sandwich with Smoked
Turkey, Reduced-Fat Cheese,
Honey Mustard, and Fresh
Cucumber Slices
Reduced-Fat Potato Chips
Baby Carrots
No-Bake Fudge Clusters
Skim Milk

Taking a Full Breath of God's World

August 9

*Last year my son and I planted tomatoes in our backyard.
A few months later he was so amazed they actually grew,
he said we must have a "gardening angel." –Robert G. Lee*

Sauerkraut Supreme
4 2-cup servings

1 quart sauerkraut, rinsed and drained
1 medium apple, peeled, cored, and diced
2 large potatoes, peeled and cubed

1 small onion, diced
1/2 teaspoon fennel seed
8 ounces lean ham, diced

Combine all ingredients in a Crockpot, and cook on low for 2 to 4 hours.

Calories per serving: 252 Fat: 3 g. Sodium: 1990 mg.
For exchange diets, count: 2 very lean meat, 1 starch, 4 vegetable
Preparation time: 10 minutes Cooking time: 2 to 4 hours

Menu of the Day

Sauerkraut Supreme
Rye Bread and Soft Margarine
Fresh Pear
Skim Milk

Minister: *Do you know what's in the Bible?* Little girl: *Yes. I think I know everything that's in it.* Minister: *You do? Tell me.* Little girl: *OK. There's a picture of my brother's girlfriend, a ticket from the dry cleaners, one of my curls, and a Pizza Hut coupon.* —Mark Brown

August 10

Minted Carrots
4 servings

4 large carrots, peeled and sliced into coins
1 tablespoon brown sugar

1 tablespoon water
1 tablespoon finely chopped fresh mint leaves

1. Layer carrots in the bottom of a microwave-safe casserole dish. Sprinkle with brown sugar, water, and mint.

2. Cover and microwave on high power for 4 minutes. Remove cover and serve.

Calories per serving: 44 Fat: 0 Sodium: 26 mg.
For exchange diets, count: 2 vegetable
Preparation time: 10 minutes

Menu *of the* Day

Chicken Breast rolled in Baking
Mix, dotted with Margarine,
sprinkled with Italian Seasoning,
and baked until tender
Brown Rice seasoned
with Dried Thyme
Minted Carrots
Fresh Pineapple Chunks
Skim Milk

Taking a Full Breath of God's World

A sure test of character is what we do when no one else is watching. —Anonymous

Family Reunion Potato Casserole
16 1-cup servings

1 pound lean ground beef
1-ounce envelope taco seasoning mix
24-ounce bag frozen hash browns with pepper and onion, thawed

13-ounce can cream of cheddar cheese soup
4-ounce can green chilies, drained
1 cup skim milk
1/2 cup chunky salsa

1. Preheat oven to 375°.

2. Brown ground beef in a skillet and drain well. If the meat appears fatty, place it in a colander over a bowl and rinse it with 1 cup of boiling water, then drain for 5 more minutes.

3. Place drained meat in the bottom of a 9- by 13-inch baking pan. Sprinkle taco seasoning over the browned meat. Sprinkle potatoes over the taco seasoning.

4. In a mixing bowl, mix cheese soup, green chilies, and skim milk together until smooth. Pour over potatoes.

5. Bake for 1 hour or until potatoes are tender. Garnish the casserole with chunky salsa before serving.

Calories per serving: 181 Fat: 7 g. Sodium: 722 mg.
For exchange diets, count: 1 starch, 1 lean meat, 1 fat
Preparation time: 20 minutes Baking time: 1 hour

Menu *of the* Day

Family Reunion Potato Casserole
Wheat Rolls
Sweet and Sour Bean Salad
from the deli
Watermelon
Sugar-Free Lemonade

Polynesian Pork Chops
4 4-ounce servings

4 4-ounce center-cut pork chops, trimmed well of
  all visible fat
1/4 cup reduced-sodium soy sauce
2 tablespoons water

1/4 teaspoon minced garlic
1 bell pepper, seeded and diced
1 green onion, diced

1. Preheat large skillet over medium heat. Brown pork chops for about 5 minutes on each side.

2. Meanwhile, combine remaining ingredients in a small mixing bowl. Pour sauce over the chops and simmer uncovered over medium-high heat for 10 to 15 minutes or until pork is cooked through.

Calories per serving: 214 Fat: 9 g. Sodium: 580 mg.
For exchange diets, count: 4 lean meat
Preparation time: 10 minutes Cooking time: 20 minutes

Menu of the *Day*

Polynesian Pork Chops
Quick Rice seasoned with Soft
Margarine and Dried Chives
Cherry Tomatoes
Honeydew Melon
Skim Milk

Taking a Full Breath of God's World

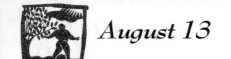

August 13

*The pillars of the earth are the Lord's,
and he hath set the world upon them.
—I Samuel 2:8*

Ginger Apricot Sauce
1 cup of sauce or 8 2-tablespoon servings

8-ounce jar all-fruit apricot spread
1/2 teaspoon ginger
1/4 cup catsup

2 tablespoons lemon juice
1 tablespoon soy sauce
1/4 teaspoon rum extract

1. Combine all ingredients in a medium saucepan. Bring to a boil, stirring occasionally. Reduce heat and simmer 15 minutes.

2. Use as a basting agent over grilled poultry during the last 5 minutes of cooking or pass at the table as a side sauce.

Calories per serving: 43 Fat: 0 Sodium: 245 mg.
For exchange diets, count: 1/2 starch
Preparation time: 5 minutes Cooking time: 20 minutes

Menu *of the* Day

Turkey Breast on the Grill with
Ginger Apricot Sauce
Sliced Red Potatoes cooked in
aluminum foil on the grill with
Fresh Parsley and Soft Margarine
Fresh Romaine Lettuce with
Reduced-Fat Dressing
Lowfat Strawberry Frozen Yogurt
Skim Milk

The worst sin toward our fellow creatures is not to hate them, but to be indifferent to them; that's the essence of inhumanity. —George Bernard Shaw

August 14

Love Those School Lunches!

Kid complaints about school lunch are as universal as chewing gum stuck under the bus seat! But for more than 50 years, school lunch has provided a third of the daily nutritional needs for America's children. Many schools are working continually to reduce total fat and saturated fat in the lunches. For example, 1% and skim milk are now being offered. Here are some tips for parents to support school lunch:

Go over the posted menu with your children—especially if there is a new food item. Explain what you think it might taste like.

Get involved in school lunch. There are parent advisory committees in many school food service programs.

Visit school and have lunch with your children.

Get to know the school cooks. Let them know that you care about your child's lunch. And pass on compliments about their favorites.

If kids want to brown bag it, be sure to get them involved in the shopping and planning. They will probably eat every bite if they have packed the lunch.

Menu *of the* Day

Broiled Salmon Seasoned with
Garlic and Lemon Juice
Steamed Cabbage and Carrots
Wheat Rolls with Soft Margarine
Sliced Tomatoes
Watermelon
Skim Milk

Taking a Full Breath of God's World

We should have a way of telling people they have bad breath without
hurting their feelings. "Well, I'm bored...let's go brush our teeth."
Or, "I've got to make a phone call, hold this gum in your mouth."
—Anonymous

Stuffed Tomato Supper

4 servings

4 large, firm ripe tomatoes
1/2 green pepper, diced
1 green onion, diced

2 cups low-fat cottage cheese
1/4 teaspoon seasoned salt

1. Slice top from tomato and scoop out the inside flesh, juice, and seeds. Reserve for use in chili, meatloaf, or spaghetti sauce.

2. In a small mixing bowl, combine remaining ingredients.

3. Stuff each tomato with one-fourth of mixture. Cover and chill until serving time.

Calories per serving: 111 Fat: 1 g. Sodium: 603 mg.
For exchange diets, count: 2 vegetable, 2 very lean meat
Preparation time: 10 minutes

Menu *of the* Day

Stuffed Tomato Supper
Broiled Garlic Bagel with
Reduced-Fat Cheddar Cheese
Fresh Apricots
Skim Milk

*It is a wholesome and necessary thing for us to turn
again to the earth and in the contemplation of her beauties
to know a sense of wonder and humility. —Rachel Carson*

August 16

Popovers
6 servings

Non-stick cooking spray
2 eggs
1 cup evaporated skimmed milk

1 tablespoon cooking oil
1 cup flour
1/4 teaspoon salt

1. Preheat oven to 400°. Spray muffin tins very generously with cooking spray.

2. Combine all ingredients in a blender and process for 30 seconds or until smooth. Scrape sides of blender often.

3. Pour batter into prepared muffin tins. Bake for 40 minutes. Turn oven off, and remove popovers from the oven.

4. Immediately after removal from the oven, prick each popover with a fork to let steam escape. If crisper popovers are desired, return popovers to the oven (it's still turned off) for 5 to 7 minutes. Serve warm.

Calories per serving: 150 Fat: 4 g. Sodium: 153 mg.
For exchange diets, count: 2 starch
Preparation time: 10 minutes Baking time: 50 minutes

Menu *of the* Day

Chef Salad with Fresh Vegetables
*Leftover Lean Meat with
Reduced-Fat Cheese and
Reduced-Fat Salad Dressing*

Popovers with Soft Margarine
Green Grapes
Skim Milk

The tree of the field is man's life.
—Deuteronomy 20:19

Pull Apart Orange Rolls
12 servings

1 fresh orange, rind grated and juice squeezed out
1/2 cup sugar

1/4 cup margarine, melted
2 cans country style refrigerated biscuits

1. Preheat oven to 350°.

2. In a small bowl, mix grated rind from orange with sugar.

3. In another small bowl, mix melted margarine with juice squeezed from orange.

4. Dip biscuits in margarine mixture, then in sugar mixture and place in Bundt pan.

5. Pour any remaining margarine and sugar over the biscuits. Bake for 30 minutes. Turn onto a platter and serve.

Calories per serving: 118 Fat: 5 g. Sodium: 220 mg.
For exchange diets, count: 1 starch, 1 fat
Preparation time: 10 minutes Baking time: 30 minutes

Menu *of the* Day

Tuna and Noodle Casserole using
Water-Pack Tuna, Reduced-Fat
Cream of Mushroom Soup, and
Spiral Pasta
Pull Apart Orange Rolls
Fresh Green Salad
with Reduced-Fat Dressing
Fresh Pear
Skim Milk

Oh, the summer night has a smile of light, and she sits on a sapphire throne.
—B.W. Procter from Quotable Quotes

August 18

Peachy Ham Steak
4 4-ounce servings

4 4-ounce ham steaks
4 peach halves

4 pitted dates
1 teaspoon soy sauce

1. Place meat in the broiler, 3 inches from heat, and broil 10 minutes on each side, turning meat only once.

2. Five minutes before the end of cooking, stuff each date in center of a peach half. Place peach halves on the ham steaks, dot with soy sauce, and finish broiling.

Calories per serving: 272 Fat: 14 g. Sodium: 1653 mg.
For exchange diets, count: 4 lean meat, 1 fruit
Preparation time: 20 minutes

Menu *of the* Day

Peachy Ham Steak
Baked Potato with
Soft Margarine and Chives
Wheat Roll
Fresh Strawberries
Skim Milk

Taking a Full Breath of God's World

The first time non-Scandinavians eat at a Scandinavian-American's house, they have the lingering suspicion that if they hadn't arrived so early, the cook would have had time to finish seasoning the food.
—John Louis Anderson, from Scandinavian Humor

The National State of Mealtime Grace

A recent survey by *USA Today* (April 21, 1997) reports 63% of American families take time to say a table grace. A similar poll in 1947 showed that fewer than half of families, just 43%, said grace.

Nearly all cultures embrace the giver of life, the provider of food at mealtime. Saying grace may be humanity's universal act of worship.

Consider this thoughtful Hindu prayer:

> Let us live together, eat together
> Together, let us do noble deeds and share the fruits
> Let us understand each other, casting aside jealousy and ill-will
> Let us all work for peace and peace alone.

from *Bless This Food* by Delacorte Press

Menu *of the* Day

All-White Menu that Pays Homage to the Scandinavian Arctic Homeland

Egg Salad on White Bread
Pasta in Cheese Sauce
Peeled Apple Slices
Rice Pudding
Milk

Speak to the earth, and it shall teach thee,
and the fishes of the sea shall declare unto thee.
—Job 12:8

August 20

Golden Angel Cake
12 servings

18-ounce package angel food cake mix
1 tablespoon orange juice concentrate

1 teaspoon grated orange rind

1. Prepare angel food cake according to package directions, but add orange juice concentrate with the water, and add the orange rind with the final flour packet.

2. Bake and cool according to package instructions.

Calories per serving: 140 Fat: 0 Sodium: 255 mg.
For exchange diets, count: 1 starch, 1 fruit
Preparation time: 15 minutes Baking time: 40 minutes Cooling time: 1 hour

---

Menu of the Day

Grilled Salmon or Halibut Steaks
seasoned with Teriyaki Sauce
Bowtie Pasta sprinkled
with Crushed Thyme
Fresh Tomato Slices
Sorbet over Golden Angel Cake
Skim Milk

Taking a Full Breath of God's World

> The sun, with all those planets revolving around it and dependent on it,
> can still ripen a bunch of grapes as if it had nothing else in the universe to do.
> —Galileo

Brown Bags Packed with Love

Think of the children you know in August. Surprise them with an assortment of good-for-you brown bag goodies.

小 small boxes of raisins

yogurt-covered raisins

juice boxes

dried apricots

dried apples

fruit leather

dried pineapple

dried pears

banana chips

individual cans of Mexican-flavored vegetable juice cocktail

Menu of the *Day*

Barbecued Chicken on the grill
Corn on the Cob
Cabbage Salad from the deli
Half a Cantaloupe stuffed
with Nonfat Lemon Yogurt
Sugar-Free Soft Drink

Fall Garden Casserole
8 1-cup servings

1/4 cup slivered almonds
4 slices bacon, diced
4 medium zucchini, sliced thin
1 large onion, cut in wedges
2 large fresh tomatoes, seeded and chopped
1 tablespoon flour

1 teaspoon garlic, minced
1 teaspoon basil
1/4 teaspoon salt
1/4 teaspoon pepper
2 ounces reduced-fat Swiss cheese, shredded

1. Preheat oven to 400°.

2. In a large skillet, sauté almonds with diced bacon. When bacon is cooked crisp, drain grease, and remove almonds and bacon to a small bowl lined with paper towels.

3. In a 3-quart baking dish, layer zucchini, onion, and tomatoes.

4. In a small mixing bowl, combine flour, garlic, basil, salt, and pepper. Fold this mixture into the vegetables.

5. Spread cheese over top of vegetables; sprinkle with reserved almonds and bacon. Bake for 20 minutes or microwave on high for 12 to 15 minutes.

Calories per serving: 98 Fat: 6 g. Sodium: 211 mg.
For exchange diets, count: 2 vegetable, 1 fat
Preparation time: 15 minutes Baking time: 20 minutes

Menu *of the* Day

Fall Garden Casserole
Hot Wheat Rolls
with Soft Margarine
Celery Sticks
Fresh Blueberries
Skim Milk

Taking a Full Breath of God's World

One of the very nicest things about life is the way we must regularly stop whatever we are doing and devote our attention to eating.
—Luciano Pavarotti from My Own Story

Cinnamon Spice Zucchini Bread
24 1-slice servings

Non-stick cooking spray
3 cups flour
1 1/2 teaspoons salt
1 tablespoon ground cinnamon
1 teaspoon baking soda
1/2 teaspoon baking powder
1 cup sugar

1/2 cup vegetable oil
1/2 cup nonfat sour cream
3 eggs or 3/4 cup liquid egg substitute
1 teaspoon vanilla
1 teaspoon finely grated orange rind
3 cups shredded zucchini

1. Preheat oven to 350°.

2. Spray 2 loaf pans with cooking spray.

3. In a large mixing bowl, combine first 5 ingredients.

4. In another medium bowl, whisk together sugar, oil, sour cream, eggs, vanilla, and rind. Stir into flour mixture. Fold in zucchini. Pour into prepared pans and bake for 45 to 50 minutes or until breads test done (insert wooden pick—it should come out clean).

5. Remove from pans to wire rack to cool.

Menu of the Day

No-Added-Salt Tomato Soup from a can with Chunks of Fresh Tomato and Basil
Cinnamon Spice Zucchini Bread
Reduced-Fat Sliced Cheddar Cheese
Leftover Fresh Fruits in Juice
Skim Milk

Calories per serving: 140 Fat: 1 g. Sodium: 206 mg.
For exchange diets, count: 1 starch, 1/2 fruit, 1 fat
Preparation time: 15 minutes Baking time: 50 minutes

Experience "Back to School" for Yourself

Autumn and back-to-school rituals nudge all of us to make a fresh start. Consider these tips for starting and exercise program:

1. Ask yourself why you're starting something new. To succeed, do it for yourself.

2. Expand your view of your options: choose an activity you enjoy. If it's square dancing, then do it!

3. Make people who encourage your change part of your support network.

4. Accept that you may need help to overcome serious problems such as depression or compulsive behavior.

5. Redefine success not as your ultimate goal, but as each small victory along the way.

6. The longer we stick with our changes the more likely they are to become permanent. To make a behavior a habit takes a minimum of four weeks. To get to the point where you don't think about it—you just get out of bed in the morning and do it—that takes six months.

Menu *of the* Day

Green Peppers stuffed and baked
with Browned Lean Ground Beef,
No-Added-Salt Tomato Sauce,
and Quick Rice
Sliced Cucumbers with
Reduced-Fat Italian Dressing
Wheat Roll and Soft Margarine
Red Grapes
Skim Milk

Taking a Full Breath of God's World

God gives birds their food, but they must fly for it.
—Dutch Proverb

Stuffed Butternut Squash
8 ½-squash servings

4 acorn squash, washed, seeded, and cut in half
2 green onions, chopped
1 teaspoon dried thyme

1 teaspoon marjoram
1/3 cup fat-free Parmesan cheese
1 cup nonfat sour cream

1. Preheat oven to 375°.

2. Place squash halves in the microwave oven and cook on high power for 10 minutes.

3. Combine all remaining ingredients in a small mixing bowl.

4. Place precooked squash on a baking pan, stuff with cheese and vegetable mixture, and bake for 30 minutes or until the squash is tender.

Calories per serving: 145 Fat: 1 g. Sodium: 76 mg.
For exchange diets, count: 1 vegetable, 1 1/2 starch
Preparation time: 20 minutes Baking time: 30 minutes

Menu of the *Day*

Chicken from the deli
Stuffed Butternut Squash
Radishes and Celery Sticks
Frozen Banana
Skim Milk

But the eyes of the Lord will roam the earth
to strengthen those who are fully committed to him.
—II Chronicles 16:9

August 26

It's Time for Apples

The height of the apple season is late summer and early fall.

Whatever the variety, look for firm, unblemished, bright fruit. Green does not necessarily mean sour. Greenings and Granny Smith apples are tart, keep well, and are suited for eating fresh or using in cooking.

Fresh sliced apples (Red and Yellow Delicious, Cortland, Jonathans) are especially good when paired with soft and firm cheeses.

To bake an apple (choose Delicious, Rome, or Cortland) in the microwave: peel, then remove the center core section. Place apple in a microwave-safe custard cup or cereal bowl. Spoon 1 teaspoon of brown sugar or maple syrup into the core section, sprinkle with 1 teaspoon of orange or lemon juice, cover, and microwave on high power for 3 minutes. This simple dessert is completed with a dab of vanilla ice milk.

Menu *of the* Day

Sirloin Tips marinated in
Soy Sauce and grilled
Tender cooked Shell Pasta tossed
with fresh Minced Garlic
Cabbage Salad from the Deli
Fresh Apple
Skim Milk

Taking a Full Breath of God's World

August 27

Dear God, Was there really a Garden of Eden? My family has a garden too. But it is small and crummy. It just has a few rotten vegetables. Don't tell my mother I said this please. Larry (age 10)
—from Dear God, Children's Letters to God, by David Heller

Cinnamon Applesauce Salad
4 ½-cup servings

1 package sugar-free cherry gelatin	1 cup boiling water
1 teaspoon cinnamon	1 1/2 cups applesauce

Combine gelatin powder and cinnamon in a small mixing bowl. Add boiling water and stir until completely dissolved. Add applesauce and chill for 3 hours or until gelatin is set.

Calories per serving: 47 Fat: 0 Sodium: 6 mg.
For exchange diets, count: 1 fruit
Preparation time: 10 minutes Chilling time: 3 hours

Menu *of the* Day

Reduced-Fat Breaded Fish Square
on a Bun
San Francisco Blend Vegetables
seasoned with Dill
Cinnamon Applesauce Salad
Skim Milk

Daily Bread

Believe in the Lord your God, so shall ye be established;
believe his prophets, so shall ye prosper.
–2 Chronicles 20:20

August 28

After School Strawberry Banana Freeze
4 ¾-cup servings

For Zach and Tyler

1 cup strawberries
1 banana, cut into chunks

1/2 cup low-fat berry-flavored yogurt
8 ice cubes

Add all ingredients to blender container. Blend on medium speed for 2 minutes or until ice is crushed fine.

Calories per serving: 71 Fat: 0 Sodium: 18 mg.
For exchange diets, count: 1 fruit
Preparation time: 10 minutes

Menu *of the* Day

Broiled Pork Chops
Acorn Squash stuffed and baked
with Raisins and Brown Sugar
Cold Cauliflower and
Broccoli Chunks with
Reduced-Fat Ranch Dressing
Fresh Peaches topped with Fat-
Free Whipped Topping
After School Strawberry
Banana Freeze
Skim Milk

Taking a Full Breath of God's World

August 29

Dear God, I saw the Grand Canyon last summer.
Nice piece of work. Love, Alan (age 9)
—from Dear God, Children's Letters to God, *by David Heller*

Packing a Safe School Lunch—Review the Rules with your Kids!

1. Never leave a school lunch with perishable food at room temperature for more than two hours.

2. Use a clean insulated bag or lunch box. Tuck small, refreezable ice packs around food to keep it cold. Or freeze a juice box and use it for safe cooling.

3. Refrigerate an insulated vacuum bottle ahead of time.

4. Assemble the lunch the night before and chill it well. It will stay cold (and safe) longer.

5. Keep food away from sunlit window sills, radiators, and warm vehicles.

6. Keep your lunch bag or box clean after every use.

Menu of the *Day*

Crab Salad from the deli
French Rolls
Baby Carrots
Melon Cubes from
the Produce Section
Reduced-Fat Chocolate
Sandwich Cookies
Soft Drink

He shall be like a tree planted by the rivers of water,
that bringeth forth his fruit in his season.
—Psalms 1:3

August 30

5-Hour Oven Beef Stew
8 1-cup servings

Give yourself and your family a welcome home treat with this oven dinner recipe.

1 pound stewing beef, cubed
2 large carrots, peeled and sliced into coins
2 potatoes, peeled and cut into cubes
2 ribs celery, diced
1 onion, diced
1 teaspoon salt

1/2 teaspoon thyme
1/2 teaspoon pepper
1 teaspoon sugar
2 tablespoons tapioca
2 14-ounce cans chunky tomatoes, drained well

Mix ingredients in order given in a large casserole dish. Cover and bake for 5 hours at 250°. You may remove cover during last hour of baking to brown the top of the stew.

Calories per serving: 157 Fat: 3 g. Sodium: 249 mg.
For exchange diets, count: 2 lean meat, 1/2 starch
Preparation time: 15 minutes Baking time: 5 hours

Menu *of the* Day

5-Hour Oven Beef Stew
French Bread from the Bakery
Sweet Pickle Slices
Nonfat Yogurt with
Crushed Pineapple stirred in
Iced Tea

Taking a Full Breath of God's World

Indian summer fades too soon; / but tenderly above the sea
Hangs, white and calm, the hunters moon.
—from "Indian Summer," by John Greenleaf Whittier

Allspice Apple Crunch
8 squares

1 cup quick oats
3 tablespoons brown sugar or 3 tablespoons Sugar
  Twin brown sugar substitute
2 tablespoons margarine, melted
1/2 teaspoon allspice (may substitute cinnamon)
6 medium baking apples, peeled and sliced thin

1/4 cup water
1/4 cup brown sugar or 1/4 cup Sugar Twin
  brown sugar substitute
2 tablespoons flour
1/2 teaspoon allspice (may substitute cinnamon)

1. Preheat oven to 350°.

2. Combine oats, 3 tablespoons brown sugar or substitute, margarine, and allspice in a small mixing bowl, and mix well.

3. In an 8-inch square baking dish, mix sliced apples and water with remaining brown sugar or substitute, flour, and allspice. Top with reserved oat mixture and bake for 30 minutes.

Calories per square: 139 Fat: 2 g. Sodium: 30 mg.
For exchange diets, count: 1 starch, 1 fruit (with sugar)
Preparation time: 20 minutes Baking time: 30 minutes

Menu of the Day

Lean Pork Cubes stir-fried with
Minced Garlic, Strips of Zucchini,
Yellow Squash, Scallions, and
Fresh Pea Pods, seasoned with
Teriyaki Sauce
Quick Rice
Allspice Apple Crunch
Skim Milk

Gathering a Harvest

The vibrant and abundant life of summer is changing. Vines are beginning to dry in the garden, and a hint of color is coming into the leaves. The sky is a deeper blue. The wind is still our friend, but we have a jacket on for our evening walk.

In the Midwest, harvest time is the sound of a combine, the stubble of cornstalks on the landscape, and the gathering in of all kinds of plant life. Regardless of the size or kind of yield, there is an urgency in making way for winter. To get next to nature, September and October call us to go on leaf tours and orchard visits. We watch football games in down coats, sitting on wool blankets and sipping on hot chocolate. As days continue to get colder, we resist the urge to comfort ourselves with food. Instead, we laugh out loud at Christian humor or begin planning for the holidays.

Oven dinners fill the house with delicious smells. Squash and onions and apples find their way into dinner menus. Baking seems to be fun again as we warm up the house with the heat of bread baking. We say good-bye to those quick summer meals on the go and take time to think about and enjoy breakfast and lunch.

All Hallow's Eve ends this two-month section with the taste of pumpkin, a candle in the jack-o-lantern, and the smell of a bonfire.

Nature is the living, visible garment of God.
—Goethe

September 1

Sticky Buns
12 servings

1/4 cup soft margarine
1/2 cup brown sugar
1/4 cup chopped nuts
1 tablespoon water

1/2 cup white sugar
1 1/2 teaspoons cinnamon
2 11-ounce cans refrigerated buttermilk biscuits

1. Preheat oven to 400°.

2. Microwave margarine 30 seconds in a very small glass mixing bowl. Pour half (2 tablespoons) of the melted margarine into a Bundt pan. Add the brown sugar, nuts, and water to the pan, mixing well. Use a spatula to spread mixture evenly over the bottom of the pan.

3. Mix white sugar and cinnamon together in a shallow dish. Dip each biscuit very lightly in the remaining melted margarine, then into the cinnamon and sugar.

4. Carefully fold biscuits in half with sticky side to the outside, gently pinching the sides together. Place the folded biscuits side by side around the Bundt pan. Bake for 20-25 minutes.

5. Turn buns out onto a plate, sticky or coated side up. Cool for 15 minutes and serve. Use a knife to cut wedges.

6. Buns may be frozen and reheated in the microwave.

Calories per serving: 188 Fat: 6 g. Sodium: 306 mg.
For exchange diets, count: 1 starch, 1 fruit, 1 fat
Preparation time: 10 minutes Baking time: 20 minutes
    Cooling time: 15 minutes

Menu *of the* Day

Chunky Chicken Salad
with Celery, Onion, and Light
Mayonnaise
Carrot Sticks
Watermelon
Sticky Buns
Skim Milk

Oven Fries
4 servings

4 small potatoes, scrubbed and sliced into wedges
2 teaspoons olive oil

1 teaspoon dried rosemary
1 teaspoon dried thyme

1. Preheat oven to 425°.

2. Combine all ingredients in a gallon-size zippered plastic bag. Shake to coat potatoes with oil and herbs.

3. Turn potatoes out onto a non-stick baking sheet.

4. Bake for 30 minutes.

Calories per serving: 109 Fat: 2 g. Sodium: 4 mg.
For exchange diets, count: 1 1/2 starch
Preparation time: 10 minutes Baking time: 30 minutes

Menu of the *Day*

Turkey Frank on a Bun
Oven Fries
Radishes
Grapefruit Sections
sprinkled with Cinnamon
Skim Milk

---

*If you're not movin' over, making room and livin'
on the edge of this world—then you're taking up
too much space. —Anonymous*

September 3

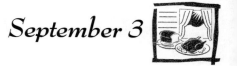

All About Baking with Oil

Using vegetable oil to replace margarine or shortening in recipes for baked goods
can save fat grams and calories. Use this chart to help get started:

Replace butter, margarine, or shortening	*With oil*
1 teaspoon	3/4 teaspoon
1 tablespoon	2 1/4 teaspoons
2 tablespoons	1 1/2 tablespoons
1/4 cup	3 tablespoons
1/3 cup	1/4 cup
1/2 cup	1/4 cup + 2 tablespoons
2/3 cup	1/2 cup
3/4 cup	1/2 cup + 1 tablespoon
1 cup	3/4 cup

Menu *of the* Day

Crockpot Beef Rump Roast
with Potatoes, Celery, Onions,
Carrots, 1 can of Beef Broth,
and 1 can of Beer
Green Salad with Reduced-Fat
Buttermilk Dressing
Wheat Toast
Bing Cherries
Skim Milk

September 4

I like trees because they seem more resigned to the way they have to live than other things do.
—Willa Cather

Three Kinds of Olive Oil: What's the Difference?

	Extra Virgin	Regular	Extra Light Taste
Flavor:	rich, fruity	mild, classic	subtle
Color:	dark green	golden	pale yellow
Use:	full flavor for salads marinades vegetable dishes basting	all purpose for sautéing and dressings	to get started in using olive oil

Olive oil, rich in monounsaturated fat and a staple of the Mediterranean diet, may be kept for up to two years if stored in a tightly sealed container, away from heat and light. During hot months, olive oil can be refrigerated to retain freshness. However, this may cause clouding. The oil's flavor is not changed by clouding. Bring the oil to room temperature to clear the clouding.

Menu *of the* Day

Grilled Pork Chops basted
with Worcestershire Sauce and
Brown Sugar

Grilled Zucchini, Tomato,
and Onion Kabobs brushed with
Olive Oil

Pumpernickel Bread with
Soft Margarine

Green Grapes

Skim Milk

Church Bulletin Bloopers: *Reminder: Children who are causing disruptions or incidents in class hinder the learning of others. Please do not hesitate to send a child out until he or she can be composted.* —Trinity Lutheran, Yankton, South Dakota

September 5

Real Cuban Black Bean Soup

12 1-cup servings

1 pound black beans, washed
6 cups water
Water
1 bay leaf
6 whole allspice
1 medium onion, chopped
1 green pepper, chopped

4 cloves garlic, minced
1 tablespoon olive oil
1/8 teaspoon oregano
1/8 teaspoon cumin
1/4 cup dry white wine
Optional: salt and pepper to taste

1. Soak beans overnight in a stockpot filled with water.

2. Add additional water until the water level is 2 inches above the beans.

3. Add bay leaf and allspice and bring the mixture to a boil. Reduce heat to simmer until the beans are soft, about 1 1/2 hours.

4. Sauté onion, green pepper, and garlic in the olive oil in a skillet until tender. Add vegetable mixture, oregano, and cumin to the beans and continue cooking until they are creamy, about 1 hour. Add salt and pepper to taste before serving.

Calories per serving: 59 Fat: 1 g. Sodium: 15 mg.
For exchange diets, count: 2 vegetable
Soaking time: overnight Preparation time: 20 minutes
Cooking time: 2 1/2 hours

Menu of the **Day**

Real Cuban Black Bean Soup
Turkey Breast on the grill
with Barbecue Sauce
Sliced Cucumber Salad
from the deli
Sliced Mangos
Sparkling Grape Juice

Church Bulletin Bloopers:
Electric chair available for the asking from Jeri O.
It is looking for a good home.
—Holy Cross Lutheran, Houston, Texas

More Than Garlic Bread
4 servings

1 tablespoon olive oil
1 teaspoon minced garlic
1 teaspoon dried oregano

1/2 teaspoon ground pepper
8-ounce French baguette (French bread)
1/4 cup grated Parmesan cheese

1. Preheat oven to 375°.

2. Mix oil, garlic, oregano, and pepper in a small bowl.

3. Cut bread in half lengthwise. Brush cut surfaces with oil and spice mixture. Sprinkle with cheese.

4. Place loaves, cheese side up, on a large baking sheet. Bake for 10 minutes. Cut and serve.

Calories per serving: 195 Fat: 7 g. Sodium: 417 mg.
For exchange diets, count: 2 starch, 1 fat
Preparation time: 10 minutes Baking time: 10 minutes

Menu of the Day

Low-Fat Lasagna Frozen
Dinner, garnished with Fresh
Chopped Parsley
More Than Garlic Bread
Fresh Lettuce Salad with Dressing
from a bag
Cantaloupe
Skim Milk

Church Bulletin Bloopers: *The sound system has been installed and the property committee is looking for feedback. The State of Michigan tested our water. It is good except for the taste.* —St. Paul Lutheran, Au Gres, Michigan

September 7

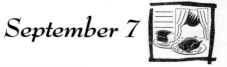

Maple Mustard Canadian Bacon

4 servings

1 1/2 tablespoons Dijon mustard
1 tablespoon maple syrup

1 dash Tabasco sauce
1/2 pound sliced Canadian bacon

1. Preheat broiler.

2. In a small bowl, stir together mustard, syrup, and hot sauce.

3. Arrange bacon in one layer on the rack of the broiler pan.

4. Brush bacon with maple and mustard mixture. Broil for 3 minutes, turn slices, and brush again. Broil 2 more minutes.

Calories per serving: 100 Fat: 4 g. Sodium: 846 mg.
For exchange diets, count: 2 lean meat
Preparation time: 10 minutes Broiling time: 5 minutes

Menu of the Day

Pancakes made from
Reduced-Fat Biscuit Mix
All Fruit Spread and Vanilla
Yogurt topping
Maple Mustard Canadian Bacon
Vegetable Juice Cocktail

No one's head aches when he is comforting another.
—Indian Proverb

Vegetable Pizza Squares
24 servings

Non-stick cooking spray
8-roll tube reduced-fat crescent dinner rolls
3 ounces nonfat cream cheese, softened
1/2 cup reduced-fat ranch-type buttermilk salad dressing

4 cups assorted raw vegetables, cut in 1/2-inch pieces (recommend cauliflower, green and red pepper, carrots, broccoli)
Garnish: chopped fresh chives

1. Preheat oven to 375°.

2. Remove rolls from the tube and press flat into a 15 by 8-inch jelly roll pan that has been sprayed with cooking spray. Pat out to form a crust. Bake for 8 to 10 minutes or until lightly browned. Cool crust for 20 minutes.

3. Meanwhile, combine softened cream cheese with salad dressing, and spread over cooled crust. Spread chopped vegetables over dressing, and garnish with chives. Refrigerate at least 30 minutes or until serving.

Calories per serving: 52 Fat: 2 g. Sodium: 166 mg.
For exchange diets, count: 1 vegetable, 1 starch

Preparation time: 20 minutes Baking time: 10 minutes
Cooling time: 20 minutes Chilling time: 30 minutes

Menu *of the* Day

Pre-Game or Post-Game Menu for Fall Football Weekend
Vegetable Pizza Squares
Carryout Chili from the deli
Sliced Apples and
Fat-Free Caramel Dip
Hot Chocolate

Au Gratin Microwave Vegetables
8 ¾-cup servings

16-ounce package frozen vegetables (suggest California blend, mixed vegetables, or stirfry blend)
11-ounce can reduced-fat cheddar cheese soup

1 teaspoon Worcestershire sauce
1/4 cup chicken broth
2 tablespoons dried parsley

1. Place frozen vegetables in a 2-quart microwave-safe baking dish.

2. In a small mixing bowl, use a whisk to combine cheese soup, Worcestershire sauce, and broth; stir until smooth.

3. Pour cheese sauce over vegetables, blending well. Sprinkle with parsley, cover with plastic wrap, and microwave on high power for 15 minutes.

Calories per serving: 32 Fat: 1 g. Sodium: 195 mg.
For exchange diets, count: 1 vegetable
Preparation time: 5 minutes Cooking time: 15 minutes

Menu of the **Day**

Sliced Deli Turkey on a
Hard Roll with Light Mayo
Au Gratin Microwave Vegetables
Leftover Fresh Fruits
marinated in Pineapple Juice
Skim Milk

Truth has no special time of its own.
Its hour is now—always. —Albert Schweitzer

Unleavened Bread in the Machine
16 wedges

I have used this method for communion bread.

3/4 cup water
1/4 cup honey
2 cups wheat flour
1/2 cup bread flour

1 teaspoon salt
1 teaspoon baking powder
1 tablespoon oil for brushing loaves

1. Combine first six ingredients in order listed in 1 1/2 pound bread machine bowl. Select "dough" option. Dough will be prepared in about 1 1/2 hours.

2. Remove dough from pan and shape into 4 1-inch thick round circles.

3. Place on a baking sheet, and bake for 20 minutes at 350°.

4. Remove loaves from oven and brush lightly with oil or spray with non-stick cooking spray. Bake 10 more minutes.

5. Cool on a rack and break each circle into 4 wedges.

Calories per 1-wedge serving: 95 Fat: 1 g. Sodium: 156 mg.
For exchange diets, count: 1 starch
Preparation time: 20 minutes Bread machine time: 1 1/2 hours Baking time: 30 minutes

Menu *of the* Day

Reduced-Fat Cheese
and Reduced-Fat Cold Cuts
Unleavened Bread in the Machine
Fresh Apples
Grape Juice

Life was meant to be lived and curiosity kept alive.
One must never, for whatever reason,
turn his back on life. —Eleanor Roosevelt

September 11

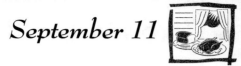

Why School Breakfast?

The National School Breakfast program was established in 1975 to make a morning meal available to all children nationwide. The United States is the only major industrialized nation that does not include breakfast for all students as an integral part of the school day. Currently 6.4 million children are being served.

Over 70 percent of American families with school-age children are headed by either a single parent who works or by two parents who both work. This leaves little time in the morning for fixing breakfast.

Studies continue to show that children who eat breakfast at home or at school perform better. Children who eat breakfast score significantly higher on standardized achievement tests, work faster, are more creative, and make fewer mistakes.

Children who eat breakfast are more likely to obtain the 40-plus daily nutrients essential for growth and development, particularly calcium.

Does your school offer breakfast? If not, introduce the idea to your school administrator.

Menu *of the* Day

Broiled Halibut with Lemon
Juice, Dill Weed, and Thyme
Boiled Red Potatoes
with Soft Margarine
Shredded Cabbage
with Reduced-Fat Dressing
Honeydew Melon
Skim Milk

*Friendship multiplies the good of life and divides the evil.
'Tis the sole remedy against misfortune,
the very ventilation of the soul.* —Baltasar Gracian

Breakfast Taco
4 servings

1 strip bacon, cooked crisp, drained, and crumbled
4 eggs, beaten well

4 small flour tortillas, warmed 30 seconds in the microwave
2 ounces reduced-fat cheddar cheese, shredded

1. Mix crumbled bacon with beaten eggs. Scramble eggs in a skillet over medium-low heat until firm.

2. Spoon cooked egg over warmed tortillas. Sprinkle with cheese. Roll up and serve with salsa on the side.

Calories per serving: 205 Fat: 12 g. (To reduce fat, substitute diced lean ham for the bacon.)
Sodium: 281 mg.
For exchange diets, count: 1 1/2 lean meat, 1 starch, 1 fat
Preparation time: 15 minutes

Menu of the *Day*

Breakfast Taco
with Salsa on the side
Green Salad
with Reduced-Fat Dressing
Fresh Banana
Skim Milk

Banana Rockets
4 servings

A wonderful breakfast or after-school or dessert treat
from my friends at the National Dairy Council.

1/2 cup vanilla yogurt
1 tablespoon reduced-fat peanut butter
1 teaspoon sugar

2 cups banana-flavored wheat cereal
4 small bananas

1. Combine yogurt, peanut butter, and sugar in a small bowl.

2. Cut four large squares of plastic wrap. Put 1/4 cup cereal on each square.

3. Peel banana. Insert a popsicle stick in one end of each banana. Spread each banana with yogurt mixture and lay on cereal. Turn to coat evenly and wrap each banana in the plastic wrap. Twist ends to hold. Freeze or refrigerate for at least 30 minutes or until ready to eat.

Calories per serving: 225 Fat: 5 g. Sodium: 196 mg.
For exchange diets, count: 1 1/2 starch, 1 fruit, 1 fat
Preparation time: 10 minutes Chilling time: 30 minutes

Menu *of the* Day

Tender Cooked Wheat Spaghetti
with Chopped Zucchini, Pepper,
Scallions, Pasta Sauce, and
Parmesan Cheese
Baby Carrots
Banana Rockets
Skim Milk

I think if you have a talent, then you must absolutely give it to people as long as you can. —Ingrid Bergman

Pineapple Upside Down Cake
8 wedges

Non-stick cooking spray
1 tablespoon soft margarine
1/4 cup brown sugar
8-ounce can pineapple tidbits in juice, drained well,
  juice reserved

12-ounce package caramel or lemon muffin mix
1 egg
Reserved juice from pineapple tidbits

1. Preheat oven to 350°.

2. Spray an 8-inch round baking pan with cooking spray.

3. Measure margarine into the pan and place into preheated oven to melt the margarine.

4. Measure brown sugar into the pan and mix well with melted margarine, covering surface of the pan.

5. Arrange pineapple over the brown sugar and margarine.

6. In a small mixing bowl, combine caramel or lemon muffin mix, egg, and reserved pineapple juice, mixing just until moist. Spread batter over the pineapple, and bake for 20 to 25 minutes.

7. Cool for 10 minutes, then turn out onto a round serving plate.

Calories per 1-wedge serving: 164 Fat: 5 g. Sodium: 312 mg.
For exchange diets, count: 1 starch, 1 1/2 fruit
Preparation time: 15 minutes Baking time: 25 minutes
  Cooling time: 10 minutes

Menu *of the* Day

Broiled Hamburger on a Bun
Steamed Cauliflower and Carrots
Pineapple Upside Down Cake
Skim Milk

Spaghetti Squash Salad
8 ¾-cup servings

Spaghetti squash is a football shaped squash with a pale to dark yellow shell and pale, yellow flesh that resembles spaghetti. It has a bland, crisp, and lightly sweet flavor.

1 spaghetti squash
2 tomatoes, seeded and chopped
1 cucumber, peeled and chopped
1 green onion, chopped

1 green pepper, seeded and diced
1 yellow pepper, seeded and diced
1/2 cup reduced-fat Italian salad dressing

1. Cut squash lengthwise and remove the seeds.

2. Place squash, cut side down, in a Dutch oven with 2 inches of water. Cover and bring to a boil; reduce heat and simmer for 20 minutes or until tender.

3. Drain and cool squash at least 15 minutes.

4. Remove spaghetti-like strands using a fork, and transfer to a large salad bowl.

5. Add vegetables and mix lightly.

6. Add dressing, and toss.

Calories per serving: 63 Fat: 2 g. Sodium: 123 mg.
For exchange diets, count: 1 vegetable, 1/2 starch
Preparation time: 15 minutes Cooking time: 20 minutes Cooling time: 15 minutes

Menu *of the* Day

Grilled Chicken Breast Sandwich
Spaghetti Squash Salad
Fresh Blueberries
Skim Milk

*I know God will not give me anything I can't handle.
I just wish that He didn't trust me so much.
—Mother Teresa*

Carrot and Snow Pea Salad

4 1-cup servings

3 medium carrots, cut into julienne strips
1/4 pound snow peas, trimmed and cut into
    julienne strips
1/4 cup white wine vinegar

1 teaspoon Dijon mustard
1 teaspoon honey
1 green onion, diced

1. Combine carrots and peas in a 2-quart microwave-safe dish.

2. Sprinkle with 1 tablespoon of water. Cover and microwave on high power for 4 minutes.

3. Immediately remove cover and drain in a colander.

4. Mix remaining ingredients together in the bottom of a large salad bowl. Add cooled vegetables; toss and serve.

Calories per serving: 52 Fat: 1 g. Sodium: 20 mg.
For exchange diets, count: 2 vegetable
Preparation time: 10 minutes

Menu *of the* Day

Your Favorite Meatloaf
Steamed Pasta with Soft Margarine
Carrot and Snow Pea Salad
Fresh Banana
Skim Milk

*To laugh often and much; to win the respect of intelligent people
and the affection of children... This is to have succeeded.*
—Ralph Waldo Emerson

September 17

Handling Poultry Safely

When you shop for fresh chicken, look for one that is clean, plump, and not discolored, with skin that is not shriveled or spotted.

Refrigerate chicken right in the wrapping it came in. It will keep for two days after purchase. To store in the freezer for up to 6 months, overwrap the unopened package in freezer wrap or aluminum foil.

Handle raw chicken with caution:

Wash your hands before and after handling.

Thoroughly clean cutting board and other work surfaces that chicken has touched, using scouring powder.

Wash the sink, knives, and other utensils that have been in contact with chicken in hot sudsy water before reusing.

After handling chicken, wash your hands before handling the kitchen towel or washcloth.

Defrost frozen chicken in the refrigerator for 12 hours or use your microwave, following manufacturer's instructions.

Marinate raw chicken, covered, in the refrigerator. Do not use leftover marinade.

Refrigerate leftover cooked chicken right after cooking.

Menu of the Day

Old Fashioned Roast Chicken
in the oven
*Just rub with garlic powder and
roast for 2 hours at 350°.*

Corn on the Cob
with Soft Margarine
Cabbage Salad from the deli
Ice Milk with Cocoa and
Almonds sprinkled on top
Cranberry Juice

God's garden is a place you can go during rain, sleet, ice, or snow.
—Andrea Eiken, age 11, Christ the King Lutheran Church,
Birmingham, Alabama

Honey Crunch Chicken Breasts
4 servings

4 4-ounce boneless skinless chicken breasts
1/4 cup steak sauce

1/2 cup honey-crunch wheat germ

1. Preheat oven to 375°.

2. Measure steak sauce into a shallow bowl. Roll each chicken breast in the sauce.

3. Measure wheat germ into a clean plastic bag. Shake the chicken breasts in the wheat germ and place on a baking sheet.

4. Bake for 25 minutes or until chicken is crisp and golden brown and the juices run clear.

Calories per serving: 207 Fat: 4 g. Sodium: 178 mg.
For exchange diets, count: 5 very lean meat, 1/2 starch
Preparation time: 10 minutes Baking time: 25 minutes

Menu *of the* Day

Honey Crunch Chicken Breasts
Hot Spiral Pasta
seasoned with Rosemary
Green Salad
with Reduced-Fat Dressing
Applesauce
Skim Milk

You know it's going to be a boring service when the ushers ask for your espresso order as they hand you a bulletin. –Christian Comedian Bill Jones

September 19

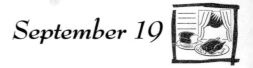

The Science of Taste

Have you ever wondered why nothing tastes good when you have a cold? Blame your nose, because detecting flavor depends more on your ability to smell than taste. There are 6 million olfactory nerves and they are nearly 10 thousand times more sensitive than taste buds.

The nose can distinguish thousands of different odors, while the taste buds just sense sweet, salty, bitter, and sour.

Because smell dulls with age, so does taste. This is the cumulative damage of nasal membranes from years of colds, sinus infections, or allergies.

Make up for taste deprivation with these tips:

Vary your diet. Eating the same foods eventually dulls your ability to taste them. If you've been having oatmeal for breakfast for the last month, switch to toaster waffles or fruit bread.

Cook with more herbs and spices. Add small amounts of dried herbs to vegetables, starches, and meats just before serving.

Take time to consider color and texture with every menu.

Eat foods at moderate temperatures. Very hot and very cold foods are more difficult to taste.

Menu *of the* Day

Roast Beef from the deli on a Sub
Bun with your favorite Condiments
Reduced-Fat Potato Chips
Cold Cauliflower Chunks
with Reduced-Fat Salad Dressing
Nectarine
Skim Milk

September 20

Even if Mom can't cook like Aunt Bea, a home-cooked meal has a certain quality that no Boston Market can ever replace.
William Mattox Jr., USA Today contributing writer

Quick Bean Tostadas
4 servings

4 large flour tortillas
16-ounce can refried beans
4 ounces reduced-fat cheddar cheese

1/2 cup chunky salsa
2 green onions, diced

1. Preheat oven to 400°.

2. Lay tortillas out on 2 large baking sheets.

3. Layer ingredients on top of tortillas in order given. Do not fold or roll tortillas, leave flat.

4. Bake for 15 minutes and serve.

Calories per serving: 237 Fat: 7 g. Sodium: 1131 mg.
For exchange diets, count: 1 1/2 starch, 1 lean meat, 1 fat, 1 vegetable
Preparation time: 10 minutes Baking time: 15 minutes

Menu *of the* Day

Quick Bean Tostadas
Lettuce and Tomato
Pineapple Chunks
Skim Milk

*To every thing there is a season,
and a time to every purpose under the heaven.*
—Ecclesiastes 3:1

September 21

Cheeseburger Rice Skillet Dinner

4 servings

1/2 pound lean ground beef
1 medium onion, diced
1 1/2 cups water
1/2 cup catsup

1 tablespoon prepared mustard
1/4 teaspoon pepper
1 1/2 cups instant rice
2 ounces reduced-fat cheddar cheese, shredded

1. Brown ground beef and onion in a large skillet on medium-high heat; drain fat into a colander. Pour 1 cup hot tap water over the meat and allow to drain for 5 minutes.

2. Return drained meat to the pan. Stir in water, catsup, mustard, and pepper. Bring the mixture to a boil.

3. Stir in rice and cover. Remove from the heat and allow to stand for 5 minutes. Fluff the mixture with a fork. Sprinkle with cheese, and cover for 3 more minutes.

Calories per serving: 302 Fat: 40 g. Sodium: 213 mg.
For exchange diets, count: 2 1/2 lean meat, 2 starch
Preparation time: 10 minutes Cooking time: 10 minutes

Menu *of the* Day

Cheeseburger Rice Skillet Dinner
Corn Muffin from a mix
Lettuce Salad with Reduced-Fat
Buttermilk Dressing
Strawberries
Skim Milk

No man also having drunk old wine
straightway desireth new. —Luke 5:39

Pumpkin Bread in the Machine
24 ½-slice servings

1 1/3 cups water
1/4 cup orange juice
1/2 cup canned pumpkin
1 egg
3 cups bread flour
1/2 cup whole wheat flour
1 teaspoon salt

1 teaspoon pumpkin pie spice (or may substitute
  3/4 teaspoon cinnamon, 1/8 teaspoon allspice,
  and a pinch each of ginger, nutmeg, and cloves)
3 tablespoons brown sugar
1 1/2 teaspoons dry yeast
2 tablespoons margarine

1. Recipe is meant for large (3 cup flour) loaf. Add ingredients to pan in order listed (recipe tested with Hitachi Automatic Home Bakery). If your machine calls for dry ingredients first, then invert the order of ingredients. Program for "Bread" or regular setting.

2. Push "Start," and remove bread from machine approximately 4 hours later.

Calories per serving: 130 Fat: 1 g. Sodium: 100 mg.
For exchange diets, count: 1 starch, 1 fruit
Preparation time: 10 minutes Baking time: 4 hours

Menu *of the* Day

Cold Sliced Turkey
Reduced-Fat Mozzarella Cheese
Pumpkin Bread in the Machine
Sparkling Apple Juice

A time to be born, and a time to die; a time to plant,
and a time to pluck up that which is planted.
—Ecclesiastes 3:2

September 23

Pineapple Shrimp Pizza
4 2-slice servings

12-inch self–rising crust frozen cheese pizza
1/2 pound shrimp, thawed, shells and tails removed

1/2 cup well drained pineapple tidbits
1/4 cup shredded Parmesan cheese

1. Place frozen pizza on a pizza stone or baking sheet and place in cold oven.

2. Preheat oven to 425°.

3. When oven reaches 425°, begin timing and bake for 15 minutes.

4. Remove pizza from oven; sprinkle with shrimp, pineapple, and cheese.

5. Reduce heat to 375° and bake for 15 more minutes. Slice into 8 wedges.

Calories per serving: 191 Fat: 7 g. Sodium: 290 mg.
For exchange diets, count: 1 starch, 2 lean meat
Preparation time: 5 minutes Baking time: 35 to 40 minutes

Menu *of the* Day

Pineapple Shrimp Pizza
Lettuce Salad with Reduced-
Calorie Ranch Dressing
Green Grapes
Skim Milk

Use a little wine for thy stomach's sake.
–I Timothy 5:23

Spinach Salad with Feta Cheese and Smoked Turkey

4 servings

1 pound fresh spinach, washed and torn into small
   pieces
8 ounces fresh mushrooms, sliced thin
1 small red onion, sliced thin
8 ounces smoked turkey, cut into strips
2 ounces feta cheese, crumbled

Dressing:
3 tablespoons lemon juice
1/2 teaspoon salt
1/4 teaspoon pepper
1 tablespoon olive oil

1. Combine ingredients for the salad in a large bowl.

2. Combine ingredients for the dressing in a shaker container. Shake to mix, and pour over dressing just before serving.

Calories per serving: 164 Fat: 7 g. Sodium: 495 mg.
For exchange diets, count: 2 lean meat, 2 vegetable
Preparation time: 15 minutes

Menu *of the* Day

Spinach Salad with Feta Cheese
and Smoked Turkey
Broiled Sesame Seed Bagel
with Soft Margarine
Fresh Pear
Sparkling White Wine mixed
with Cran-Raspberry Juice

Southwestern Potato Salad
4 servings

4 medium red potatoes
1 tablespoon water
1 teaspoon cumin
1/4 teaspoon minced garlic
2 tablespoons lime juice

1 teaspoon grated lime peel
1/2 teaspoon ground pepper
1/2 cup nonfat sour cream
1 green onion, chopped

1. Scrub potatoes and slice into wedges. Place in 1-quart microwave-safe casserole dish.

2. Sprinkle with 1 tablespoon of water; cover and microwave for 6 to 8 minutes, until potatoes are tender. Remove cover; drain well and allow to cool for 15 minutes.

3. Meanwhile, combine all remaining ingredients in a small mixing bowl.

4. Transfer cooked potatoes to a salad bowl, toss with dressing, and serve. May refrigerate for up to 24 hours.

> Calories per serving: 75 Fat: 0 Sodium: 7 mg.
> For exchange diets, count: 1 starch
> Preparation time: 15 minutes Cooling time: 15 minutes

Menu *of the* Day

Broiled Pork Chops
brushed with Steak Sauce

Southwestern Potato Salad

Steamed Green Beans
with Dried Fennel

Crushed Pineapple
over Raspberry Sherbet

Skim Milk

The New Biology of Weight Control

"She can eat anything she wants and never gains weight."
"He puts on five pounds just walking through the bakery."

Nutritionists are beginning to unlock some of the mysteries that we have observed for decades. Why is weight loss so often followed by weight gain? Why do most people return to a "set point" weight despite rigorous efforts to exercise?

The most recent discovery concerns the role of lepton, a hormone secreted by fat cells in proportion to the amount of body fat. Lepton is thought to regulate feeding behavior (or appetite) through the hypothalamus. These hormone levels vary significantly in individuals and may explain why two people who eat the same diet may not weigh the same.

This is an oversimplification of what lepton does: As body fat is lost through caloric and fat restriction and/or exercise, lepton levels decrease because body fat is lost. But at the same time, the hypothalamus senses the lepton deficiency and works to counteract it. The hypothalamus begins producing more neuropeptide Y (NPY). NPY stimulates food intake, reduces energy expenditure, and promotes weight gain.

Thus, most forms of obesity are likely to result not from an uncontrolled lust for food or lack of discipline but from biochemical defects at one or more points in a complicated, highly individual system. Insulin, the famous diabetes hormone, is also implicated in the science of weight regulation. See tomorrow's reading.

Menu *of the* Day

Reduced-Fat Fish Square
on a Bun
Steamed Green Beans
Vanilla Yogurt with
Chopped Dried Apricots
Herb Tea

The grass withereth, the flower fadeth:
but the word of our God shall stand forever.
—Isaiah 40:8

September 27

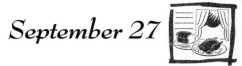

Insulin is More Than a Diabetes Hormone

In contrast to the recent discovery of lepton, the hormone insulin has been studied in relation to obesity for more than a decade.

The theory is that insulin is secreted from the pancreas in direct proportion to body fatness. And it provides a type of negative feedback to the brain when food restriction occurs.

This means that it behaves in a manner similar to lepton (see reading from Sept. 26). Insulin seems to inhibit hypothalamic neuropeptide Y (NPY). NPY is the part of the hypothalamus that stimulates food intake, reduces energy expenditure, and promotes weight gain.

As body fatness decreases (such as during weight loss diets), insulin levels decrease, hypothalamic NPY is no longer inhibited, and increased food intake occurs, leading to weight gain.

Hope for successful obesity treatment lies in our ability to understand these and other factors that regulate how we eat. For instance, lepton analogues may be developed to counteract the NPY response to weight loss.

Menu of the Day

Round Steak
Marinate overnight in Red Wine
and Italian Dressing, then broil
to desired doneness
Wheat Toast
Steamed Italian Vegetable Blend
Chilled Tropical Fruit from a can
Skim Milk

Whatever befalls the Earth befalls the children of the Earth.
We did not weave the web of life; we are merely a strand in it.
Whatever we do to the web, we do to ourselves.
—Chief Seattle of the Duwamish people, 1853

Lemon Carrots with Rice

4 1-cup servings

1 1/2 cups sliced fresh carrots
2 tablespoons water
1/4 cup lemon juice
3/4 cup water

1/2 cup raisins
1 cup Original Minute Rice®
1/2 teaspoon grated lemon rind

1. Place carrots in microwave-safe dish with 2 tablespoons water. Cover and microwave on high power for 5 minutes. Drain carrots, reserving liquid.

2. Combine liquid from carrots with lemon juice, 3/4 cup water, and raisins in a medium saucepan. Bring to a boil.

3. Stir in rice and lemon rind. Cover; remove from heat. Let stand 5 minutes. Stir in carrots.

Calories per serving: 148 Fat: 1 g. Sodium: 18 mg.
For exchange diets, count: 1 starch, 2 vegetable
Preparation time: 15 minutes

Menu *of the* Day

Turkey Breast on the Grill
Lemon Carrots with Rice
Pear Sauce
Gingersnap Cookie
Skim Milk

The Lord hath his way in the whirlwind and in the storm,
and the clouds are the dust of his feet.
–Nahum 1:3

September 29

Pepper Corn Barley

4 1-cup servings

1/2 cup reduced-fat Italian salad dressing	1 1/4 cups water
1 medium red pepper, chopped	1 tablespoon lime juice
1/2 cup chopped onion	1/8 teaspoon cumin
1 cup quick barley	1/4 teaspoon pepper
1 1/2 cups chicken broth	10-ounce package frozen whole kernel corn

1. In a large saucepan, heat Italian dressing. Add red pepper and onion, and cook over medium heat, stirring occasionally, for 5 minutes or until vegetables are tender.

2. Stir in barley and cook, stirring constantly, for 1 minute. Add broth, water, lime juice, cumin, and pepper. Cover and continue to simmer mixture for 20 minutes.

3. Add frozen corn and continue heating just until corn is tender.

Calories per serving: 176 Fat: 4 g. Sodium: 724 mg.
For exchange diets, count: 2 starch
Preparation time: 30 minutes

Menu of the Day

Broiled Pork Burger on a Bun
with your favorite Condiments
Pepper Corn Barley
Fresh Peach
Skim Milk

September 30

Fruited Barley

4 1-cup servings

1/2 cup quick barley
2 1/2 cups water
1/2 cup golden raisins
1/2 cup finely chopped prunes

1/2 cup finely chopped dried apricots
1 tablespoon brown sugar
1 tablespoon lemon juice

1. In a medium saucepan, combine barley and water. Bring mixture to a boil; cover and simmer for 20 minutes.

2. Add fruit and simmer for 5 more minutes.

3. Just before serving, add brown sugar and lemon juice.

Calories per serving: 170 Fat: 1 g. Sodium: 8 mg.
For exchange diets, count: 2 starch
Preparation time: 10 minutes Cooking time: 25 minutes

Menu *of the* Day

Round Steak in the Crockpot
with Reduced-Fat Cream of
Mushroom Soup
Fruited Barley
Fresh Broccoli with Reduced-
Calorie Cucumber Dressing
Frozen Vanilla Yogurt
with Raspberries on top
Decaf Coffee

*I would rather sit on a pumpkin and have it
all to myself than be crowded on a velvet cushion.*
—Henry David Thoreau

October 1

Kraut Casserole in the Crockpot
4 2-cup servings

4 strips bacon
1 cup chopped onion
32-ounce jar sauerkraut, drained and rinsed
1 cup peeled and chopped apples
1 large potato, peeled and shredded
1 cup no-added-salt chicken broth

1/4 cup brown sugar or equivalent in brown sugar substitute
1/4 teaspoon pepper
1/4 teaspoon thyme
1/2 cup dry vermouth or dry white wine
1/4 pound lean ham, cut into chunks (or may substitute leftover cooked pork)

1. Snip bacon into small pieces and place on a microwave broiling rack. Cover with a paper towel and cook on high power for 3 minutes. Drain bacon and place in Crockpot.

2. Add all remaining ingredients. Cook in Crockpot for minimum of 4 hours.

Optional microwave method: Microwave bacon as directed above; drain and place in a microwave-safe casserole dish. Add all remaining ingredients except ham. Cook uncovered on high power for 15 minutes. Add ham. Cook on 50 percent power for 3 minutes.

Calories per serving: 263 Fat: 6 g. Sodium: 920 mg.
(To reduce sodium, substitute cooked pork for ham and/or fresh cabbage for sauerkraut.)
For exchange diets, count: 1 starch, 1 lean meat, 1 fruit, 3 vegetable
Preparation time: 10 minutes Cooking time: Crockpot—4 hours Microwave—18 minutes

---

Menu *of the* Day

Kraut Casserole in the Crockpot
White Dinner Rolls
with Soft Margarine
Lime Sherbet
over Pineapple Tidbits
Skim Milk

Come, ye thankful people, come, / Raise the song of harvest home;
All is safely gathered in, / Ere the winter storms begin.
—"Come, Ye Thankful People, Come," Henry Alford

Discover the Mediterranean Diet

The rule of the Mediterranean Diet is to move vegetables and grains to the center of the plate. If you don't have time to change your routine diet, start by making it Mediterranean even once a month or once a week.

Here's how. Choose a variety of foods from Lists 1, 2, and 3 below. Add extra flavor with several items from List 4. For example, sauté minced garlic with black beans, artichokes, and rice. Sprinkle with Romano cheese before serving. What could be simpler?

List 1	*List 2*	*List 3*	*List 4*
Black-eyed peas	Artichokes	Barley	Feta cheese
Garbanzo beans	Broccoli	Buckwheat	Romano cheese
Kidney Beans	Carrots	Bulgur	Parmesan cheese
Lentils	Cauliflower	Cornmeal	Olive oil
Navy, pinto beans	Onions	Couscous	Black pepper
Soybeans/tofu	Peppers	Multigrain bread	Basil/Oregano
Split peas	Sweet potatoes	Pasta	Thyme/Rosemary
White beans	Tomatoes	Rice	Garlic

Menu *of the* Day

Sautéed Black Beans, Artichokes and Rice seasoned with Romano Cheese, Basil, and Garlic

Fresh Banana

Skim Milk

My grandmother had no use for whiners. Her constant theme was, "If you can't change it, change the way you think about it." —Maya Angelou

October 3

How to Stretch Before Exercise

Fall days are perfect for a walk in the leaves. Stretching regularly helps keep muscles and joints flexible, relieves stress, and reduces the risk of injury.

Stretch at least 5 to 10 minutes a day, especially after a brisk workout.

Don't stretch a cold muscle. Warm up first with a few minutes of moderate movement, preferably a slower, less vigorous version of your fitness activity.

Take your time. A stretch must generally be held for 20 to 30 seconds to be effective.

Don't bounce. A good stretch calls for a steady, controlled movement.

Do breathe during stretches, with slow, deep rhythmic breaths.

Don't overdo it. When you hold a stretch, you should feel some mild tension, never pain.

Menu of the Day

French Toast cooked in a no-stick skillet, topped with Nonfat Yogurt and All Fruit Jam
Reduced-Fat Cottage Cheese
Pineapple Orange Juice

Gathering a Harvest

And when ye reap the harvest of your land, thou shalt not wholly reap the corners of thy field, neither shalt thou gather the gleanings of the harvest. And thou shalt not glean thy vineyard, nor gather every grape of the vineyard; thou shalt leave them for the poor and stranger. —Leviticus 19:9-10

Hot Spiced Applesauce
4 servings

16-ounce jar sugar-free chunky applesauce   1/2 teaspoon cinnamon
1 teaspoon vanilla   1/4 teaspoon nutmeg

1. Combine ingredients in a microwave-safe bowl.

2. Cover and microwave on high power for 5 minutes. Spoon over ice milk.

Calories per serving: 60 Fat: 0 Sodium: 8 mg.
For exchange diets, count: 1 fruit
Preparation time: 10 minutes

Menu *of the* Day

Reduced-Fat Breaded
Fish Square on a Bun
Oven Baked French Fries
Mixed Vegetables
Hot Spiced Applesauce
over Vanilla Ice Milk
Skim Milk

The Lord bless thee, and keep thee:
the Lord make his face shine upon thee, and be gracious unto thee:
The Lord lift up his countenance upon thee, and give thee peace.
—Numbers 6:24-26

October 5

Is There a Sensible Alcohol Intake?

For a long time, Americans have considered alcohol an undesirable part of the diet due to negative social and medical impact associated with heavy alcohol consumption.

However, as a result of investigations of the "French Paradox" and other studies, alcohol has received a positive second look by nutritionists and consumers.

In women, wine consumption increases HDL cholesterol (the "good" kind). Beer and liquor consumption increases HDL cholesterol for both men and women. Compared with nondrinkers, drinking one can of beer, one glass of wine, or one shot of liquor increases HDL levels by 7 to 16 percent.

While alcohol may help protect against heart disease, alcohol abuse adversely affects physical, emotional, and mental health. Moderate alcohol consumption is strictly defined as 1 serving for women and 2 servings for men daily.

It's safe to conclude that more than 1 serving for women or 2 servings for men is beyond the currently defined healthy limit.

Menu *of the* Day

Steamed Quick Rice mixed with
Reduced-Fat Cream of Chicken
Soup, Chunky Chicken, Water
Chestnuts, and Green Peas
Hard Rolls
Sliced Cucumbers with
Reduced-Fat Italian Dressing
Sliced Pears
Skim Milk

While the earth remaineth, seedtime and harvest, and cold and heat, and summer and winter, and day and night shall not cease. —Genesis 8:22

Pan Roasted Chicken with Oranges

4 servings

4 skinless boneless chicken breasts
1 tablespoon olive oil
1 carrot, sliced into coins
1 white onion, sliced into thin wedges

1/2 cup dry white wine
1/2 cup no-added-salt chicken broth
1 teaspoon dried rosemary
11-ounce can mandarin oranges, drained

1. Preheat oven to 350°.

2. Place chicken breasts in a shallow baking pan.

3. Heat olive oil in a skillet and sauté carrots and onions for 2 minutes. Add all remaining ingredients and bring mixture to a boil. Cook for 3 minutes, then pour over chicken.

4. Bake uncovered for 40 minutes.

Calories per serving: 204 Fat: 6 g. Sodium: 75 mg.
For exchange diets, count: 3 lean meat, 1/2 fruit
Preparation time: 15 minutes Baking time: 40 minutes

Menu *of the* Day

Pan Roasted Chicken
with Oranges
Quick Rice
Steamed Broccoli
Red Grapes
Skim Milk

There is no season such delight can bring,
As summer, autumn, winter and the spring.
—Variety

October 7

How Adolescents Rate Satisfaction with Family Life

Family life research points out that adolescents who are more satisfied with their families engage in greater emotional disclosure with parents, are more compliant with parental expectations, and report greater quality of life.

Findings from a recent study point out the importance of looking beyond surface relationships. Family closeness, parental support, adaptability, and lack of punitiveness are more important predictors than is family structure.

Working with teenagers to build appropriate family rules and roles is vital. Studies underline the importance of guiding and disciplining teens without being punitive or coercive.

Inviting and involving teens in menu planning, grocery shopping, coupon clipping, recipe testing, food preparation, meal service, and cleanup provides a natural time to get close, promote emotional disclosure, and discuss family rules and roles.

Menu of the Day

Carryout Pizza
Chunky Raw Cauliflower
with Reduced-Fat Buttermilk
Ranch Dip
Fresh Strawberries
dipped in Vanilla Yogurt
Skim Milk

October 8

Coldly, sadly descends the autumn evening.
The field strewn with its dank yellow drifts of withered leaves,
and the elms, fade into dimness apace, silent; hardly a shout
from a few boys late their play! —Rugby Chapel

Salmon Salad for Company

4 ³/₄-cup servings

15-ounce can red salmon, drained and boned
2 tablespoons horseradish
1 teaspoon lemon juice

2/3 cup fat-free mayonnaise
1/2 teaspoon lemon pepper seasoning

Combine all ingredients and chill for 30 minutes. Serve with crackers or melba toast.

Calories per serving: 183 Fat: 6 g. Sodium: 1000 mg.
For exchange diets, count: 3 lean meat, 1/2 starch
Preparation time: 15 minutes Chilling time: 30 minutes

Menu *of the* Day

Salmon Salad for Company
Reduced-Fat Wheat Crackers
Fresh Apple Slices
Tomato Juice

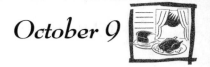
Celebrate Calcium!

The menu below supplies over 800 mg. of calcium. To help prevent osteoporosis, the National Osteoporosis Foundation offers these guidelines:

Eat a balanced, varied diet rich in calcium. Dairy foods contribute the bulk of dietary calcium, but other foods like salmon, tuna, sardines, broccoli, spinach, fortified orange juice, and cereal are supplementary sources.

Exercise regularly and participate in weight-bearing activities. Walking for 30 minutes three times a week is practical and beneficial.

Drink alcohol in moderation. For women, this means one beer, one glass of wine, or 2 ounces of spirits.

Be aware of your risk factors for osteoporosis:

    Age (post-menopausal women)

    Inactivity—Bone cells grow better with mechanical strain and stimulation

    Race—Caucasians and Asians are at greater risk.

    Small body frame and low body weight

    Diet chronically low in calcium

    Family history of osteoporosis

    Early menopause

    Anorexia nervosa

    Cigarette smoking

    Excessive alcohol intake

Menu *of the* Day

Tuna Salad Sandwich on
Wheat Bread with Fresh Spinach
Dill Pickle Garnish
Reduced-Fat Potato Chips
Leftover Fresh Fruits
with Vanilla Yogurt
Skim Milk

Have you called your momma today?
I sure wish I could call mine.
—Bear Bryant, spoken on a television commercial

Pepper Swiss Spread

8 ⅓-cup servings

12-ounce package reduced-fat Swiss cheese, shredded
2 large green peppers, chopped
1 teaspoon dry mustard

2/3 cup fat-free mayonnaise
1 teaspoon seasoned salt
6 dashes Tabasco sauce

Combine all ingredients and refrigerate for at least 6 hours. Taste improves with aging—24 hours is ideal. Use as a spread for crackers or on a rye bread sandwich.

Calories per serving: 154 Fat: 7 g. Sodium: 609 mg.
For exchange diets, count: 2 1/2 lean meat, 1 vegetable
Preparation time: 15 minutes Chilling time: 6 to 24 hours

Menu *of the* Day

Beef and Vegetable Soup
from a can
Pepper Swiss Spread
Rye Crackers
Dried Apricots
Skim Milk

The Good Lord can make you anything you want to be,
but you have to put everything in his hands.
—Mahalia Jackson, gospel singer

October 11

Sweet Skillet Carrots

4 servings

1 teaspoon margarine
1 tablespoon brown sugar
1 tablespoon grated orange rind

1/4 cup fresh squeezed orange juice
6 medium carrots, scrubbed and sliced into coins

Combine all ingredients in a large skillet. Cook uncovered over medium heat for 15 minutes or until liquid is evaporated and carrots are tender-crisp.

Calories per serving: 75 Fat: 1 g. Sodium: 50 mg.
For exchange diets, count: 1 starch
Preparation time: 5 minutes Cooking time: 15 minutes

Menu *of the* Day

Hamburger on a Bun
with Lettuce and Pickles
Sweet Skillet Carrots
Fresh Blueberries
Skim Milk

Minestrone
8 1½-cup servings

1 tablespoon vegetable oil
1 pound lean round steak, cut in 1/2-inch cubes
1 large onion, peeled and sliced
1/4 teaspoon minced garlic
4 cups no-added-salt beef broth
16-ounce can chunky tomatoes

1 teaspoon oregano
1/2 teaspoon thyme
1/2 teaspoon pepper
1/2 cup white rice
1/2 small head cabbage, shredded
Garnish: freshly grated Parmesan cheese

1. Heat oil in a large stockpot, and add cubes of round steak. Add onion and garlic. Cook until vegetables are tender.

2. Add all remaining ingredients. Cook for 30 minutes or until rice and cabbage are tender.

3. Ladle soup into bowls. Garnish with freshly grated Parmesan cheese if desired.

Calories per serving: 207 Fat: 6 g. Sodium: 775 mg.
   (To reduce sodium, use no-added-salt tomatoes.)
For exchange diets, count: 2 lean meat, 1 starch, 1 vegetable
Preparation time: 15 minutes Cooking time: 35 minutes

Menu *of the* Day

Minestrone
Toasted Onion Bagel sprinkled
with Parmesan Cheese
Italian Ice
Cranberry Juice

Cheddar 'n Onion Pie

8 slices

Non-stick cooking spray
4 medium size white or yellow onions, peeled and
   sliced very thin
9-inch deep-dish pie crust, unbaked
6 ounces reduced-fat cheddar cheese, shredded

3/4 cup liquid egg substitute or 3 eggs
2/3 cup evaporated skim milk
1/2 teaspoon salt
1/2 teaspoon white pepper
1 fresh tomato, peeled and cut into 6 slices

1. Preheat oven to 400°.

2. Sauté onions in a large skillet that has been sprayed generously with cooking spray.

3. Layer onions and cheese in the unbaked crust, ending with cheese.

4. Combine next four ingredients in a medium dish, beating lightly. Pour over cheese and onions.

5. Bake for 25 minutes. Place tomato slices on top, and bake for 5 more minutes.

Calories per 1-slice serving: 202 Fat: 10 g. Sodium: 601 mg.
For exchange diets, count: 1 starch, 1 1/2 lean meat, 1 fat
Preparation time: 20 minutes Baking time: 30 minutes

Menu of the Day

Cheddar 'n Onion Pie
Fresh Greens with
Reduced-Calorie Dressing
Baby Carrots
Grape Juice

October 14

Meditation to Read for a Prayer Group Just Getting Started

We will now get seated comfortably with our bodies relaxed and our minds stilled.

Where two or three are gathered together in my name, there am I in the midst of them. We become conscious of God's presence in our midst.

We give a few minutes' thought to who Jesus really is: God with us, Truth, Love, Forgiveness, Power, Release, Purpose.

As we become aware of God's presence, we ask for an outpouring of God's love and power upon every person in the group.

We ask that this group be united in fellowship and be made one in God's love by the Holy Spirit moving through each of us. We sit quietly in God's presence.

We read a selected Bible passage together.

Menu of the *Day*

Pizza:
Hot Roll Mix Crust, your favorite Sauce, Leftover Chunks of Vegetables, with Canadian Bacon and Part-Skim Mozzarella cheese

Salad Greens with
Reduced-Fat Dressing
Fresh Strawberries
Skim Milk

Day 2 of Saving Your Soul at Work: *Learn from whatever happens to you. When life throws us a situation that cannot be solved by what you know, seek and find the answer through Jesus.* —John Scherer from The Lutheran

October 15

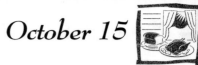

Meditation to Read for an Experienced Prayer Group

Prayer brings us into contact with God! What a glorious thought that I can come to him, talk with God, and experience his power. Why I have not given more time and thought to this adventure with you, I will never be able to explain.

O Christ, as you stand in our midst, your presence reminds me of the great amount of time that you gave to prayer when you were among us in the flesh. When I recall that you spent all night in prayer, that you prayed before every decision, that you showed constant dependence upon prayer—how ashamed I feel.

Your presence has been very real to me in times of distress, in the midst of tragedy, in times of helplessness. I long to know the way of prayer as a daily way of life. I wait here today for you to speak to me about this way of life for me.

As I sit in your presence a conviction is growing within me—prayer is the answer to my deepest need. From you comes a fullness for my emptiness; from you comes a calm and peace for my distressed mind; and from you comes a deep sense of life. Here is a real life adventure from this moment on.

In this awareness of your presence, the thrilling adventure of knowing you grips my mind. What is there to know about life with you? How can I relate this experience of you to daily problems? How glorious is the imagination of trying. It is good to know that others in this little group feel much the same as I do. Thank you for being in the midst of this group that is seeking to know the same spiritual reality that I am seeking.

We sit quietly listening to the still small voice of the spirit of God.

Menu *of the* Day

Roast Pork Loin with Beer
in the Crockpot
Boiled Potatoes
Steamed Carrots and Cabbage
Rye Bread
Vanilla Ice Milk
with Chopped Dates and
Warm Maple Syrup Topping
Skim Milk

October 16

Questions for a Prayer Group to Encourage Sharing

At what time in your life was God the most real?

Relate something of the reality of this personal experience.

What is the most vivid experience of prayer that you ever had?

What is the most pressing need in your life?

How can you truly know God so that His presence is real and meaningful in your total experience of life?

How can you effectively share with others what you have discovered about God?

Menu of the *Day*

Baked Mock Crab Tortilla: *Stuff a Flour Tortilla with Mock Crab and Chopped Green Chilies. Top with Reduced-Fat Cream of Mushroom Soup and Reduced-Fat Cheddar Cheese, then bake or microwave until bubbly*

Chopped Lettuce and Tomatoes

Fresh Pear

Skim Milk

Day 4 of Saving Your Soul at Work: *Have you ever heard anyone close to death say, "I wish I'd spent more time at the office"? Balance work with piano lessons, bird watching, hot tubbing, a good book, time alone, splitting wood, arranging flowers, or writing songs.* —John Scherer from The Lutheran

October 17

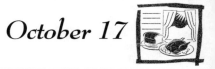

Mushroom Chicken

4 servings

4 boneless, skinless chicken breasts
1/2 teaspoon minced garlic
4 ounces mushrooms, sliced thin

4 green onions, diced
2 ounces reduced-fat mozzarella cheese, shredded

1. Preheat oven to 400°.

2. Arrange chicken breasts in a shallow baking dish. Rub minced garlic into the chicken.

3. Mix together mushrooms, onion, and shredded cheese, and sprinkle over the chicken. Bake for 25 minutes or until chicken is tender and juices run clear.

Calories per serving: 178 Fat: 4 g. Sodium: 235 mg.
For exchange diets, count: 3 lean meat, 1 vegetable
Preparation time: 10 minutes Baking time: 25 minutes

Menu *of the* Day

Mushroom Chicken
Brown Rice
Stewed Tomatoes
seasoned with Oregano
Sliced Kiwifruit
Skim Milk

Day 5 of Saving Your Soul at Work: *How much of your work is joy? How much of what you do from moment to moment is a beautiful manifestation of your spirit? Reconnect work and spirit by making each interaction an expression of who you are.* —John Scherer from The Lutheran

Sweet and Sour Green Bean Casserole

4 servings

4 slices bacon, diced and fried crisp
3 tablespoons vinegar
3 tablespoons sugar

1 green onion, diced
24-ounce can no-added-salt French-style green beans, drained

1. Preheat oven to 350°.

2. Combine crumbled bacon, vinegar, sugar, and onion in a skillet. Bring mixture to a boil and cook for 2 minutes.

3. Spoon drained green beans into a casserole dish. Pour bacon mixture over the beans, and stir to mix. Bake for 20 minutes.

Calories per serving: 73 Fat: 3 g. Sodium: 111 mg.
For exchange diets, count: 2 vegetable, 1/2 fat
Preparation time: 10 minutes Baking time: 20 minutes

Menu *of the* Day

Broiled Pork Chops
seasoned with Caraway Seed
Sweet and Sour
Green Bean Casserole
Rye Bread with Soft Margarine
Grapefruit Sections in Juice
Skim Milk

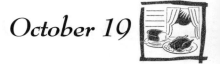
Reconnecting Work and Spirit

If you disagree with more than three of these statements, it may be time to reevaluate your work situation.

I can go to my boss with a real problem and expect to be heard.

I know how my work fits into the bigger picture at work.

My boss is committed to my personal and professional growth.

When I do excellent work, I am thanked for it.

I am excited about going to work almost every day.

Conflict at work is treated as a chance to learn.

At work, I am respected not only for what I do but for who I am.

Every day I see that my work is making a real difference in people's lives.

My work is close to what God would have me do.

Menu of the Day

Kidney Beans, Lean Browned
Hamburger, and Reduced-Fat
Cheddar Cheese mixed with Salsa,
stuffed in a Flour Tortilla

Sliced Green and Red Pepper
Strips on the side

Cantaloupe Wedges with
Raspberry Yogurt on top

Skim Milk

Go very lightly on the vices.
—Satchel Paige

Zesty Grits
8 ½-cup servings

3 cups no-added-salt chicken broth (or water)
3/4 cup quick grits
1/4 teaspoon celery salt
1/4 teaspoon onion salt
2 ounces reduced-fat cheddar cheese, grated

1 teaspoon Worcestershire sauce
1/2 teaspoon paprika
4 dashes Tabasco sauce
1/2 cup liquid egg substitute or 2 eggs
1 tablespoon grated Parmesan cheese

1. Bring broth or water to a boil. Add grits and cook for 3 minutes. Remove from heat.

2. Stir in all remaining ingredients and pour into a 2-quart microwave-safe casserole dish.

3. Microwave on high power for 10 minutes or until bubbly.

Calories per serving: 98 Fat: 2 g. Sodium: 343 mg.
For exchange diets, count: 1 starch
Preparation time: 10 minutes Microwave cooking time: 10 minutes

Menu *of the* Day

Grilled Chicken Breast
Zesty Grits
Fresh Green Pepper Rings
Pineapple Chunks in Juice
Vegetable Juice Cocktail

Creamy Baked Salmon

4 servings

15-ounce can red salmon, drained and flaked
1 large rib celery, cleaned and finely diced
1 green onion, diced

1/4 cup nonfat sour cream
1/2 teaspoon dry mustard
2 ounces shredded reduced-fat Swiss cheese,
   divided

1. Preheat oven to 350°.

2. Combine first 5 ingredients, and stir in half of the cheese.

3. Spoon into a shallow casserole dish. Sprinkle with remaining cheese. Bake for 20 minutes.

Calories per serving: 193 Fat: 6 g. Sodium: 736 mg.
For exchange diets, count: 3 lean meat, 1 vegetable
Preparation time: 10 minutes Baking time: 20 minutes

Menu *of the* Day

Creamy Baked Salmon
Butternut Squash with Dill Weed
Sliced Cucumbers with Oil
and Vinegar Dressing
Tropical Fruit Cocktail
Skim Milk

Shortcut Soup

Use one of these formulas to boost "staying" power of canned soup. If available, purchase reduced-sodium, reduced-fat soups to start with.

Chicken Noodle Soup + Canned Chicken + Stirfry Veggies

Beef Vegetable Soup + Leftover Roast Beef or Pork + Canned Tomatoes

Tomato Soup + Italian Veggies + Parmesan Cheese sprinkled on top

Cheese Soup + Salsa + Nonfat Sour Cream, served with Baked Tortilla Chips

Cream of Mushroom Soup + Diced Ham + Reduced-Fat Swiss Cheese

Cream of Chicken Soup + Canned Corn + Crumbled Bacon

Creamy Clam Chowder + Canned Clams + Canned Potato Slices

Cream of Potato Soup + Green Onions + Shredded Reduced-Fat Cheddar Cheese

---

Menu of the *Day*

Shortcut Soup
Bran Muffins from the deli
Green Grapes
Skim Milk

People see God every day;
they just don't always recognize Him.
—Pearl Bailey

October 23

Veggie Biscuit Ring

8 servings

2 tablespoons margarine, melted
1 very small zucchini, diced
2 green onions, diced
1 small green pepper, seeded and diced

Nonstick cooking spray
1/4 cup grated Parmesan cheese
12 refrigerated biscuits (2 cans), cut in half

1. Preheat oven to 350°.

2. Melt margarine in a skillet and sauté next three ingredients.

3. Spray a Bundt pan generously with cooking spray.

4. Place 1/3 of the biscuits in the bottom of the pan. Follow with layers of 1/3 of the vegetables and Parmesan cheese. Repeat layers with biscuits, vegetables, and cheese two more times.

5. Bake for 35 minutes. Turn out onto a large plate and serve warm.

Calories per serving: 104 Fat: 5 g. Sodium: 297 mg.
For exchange diets, count: 1 starch, 1/2 fat
Preparation time: 15 minutes Baking time: 35 minutes

Menu *of the* Day

Sirloin Steak on the Grill
Veggie Biscuit Ring
Baked Potato with Soft Margarine
Lemon Yogurt
over Fresh Nectarine
Skim Milk

Believe in life.
—W.E.B. Dubois, African-American scholar
and activist against colonialism

Midday Fuel Stop

By mid afternoon, do you feel tired, irritable, and stressed out?

Perhaps you should stop skipping or skimping on lunch.

The downward mental spiral is clear. Skimping on lunch means running on empty all afternoon. The low fuel supply masquerades as stress or fatigue. By dinner, starvation accelerates speed-eating past the true measure of fullness.

A little lunch could break the cycle, make the afternoon more productive, reduce stress, and improve dinnertime control. Evenings are the natural time for our stomachs and brains to rest.

Planning ahead for lunch is as easy as adding a few items to your shopping list and hauling them to the refrigerator at work. Start with three-packs of juice boxes, mozzarella cheese sticks, lean lunch meats, bagels, wheat crackers, whole fresh fruits, and boxes of raisins.

You'll save time and energy, and you'll actually feel better if you stop to refuel.

Menu *of the* Day

Chicken and Noodles
Cooked Wide Noodles, Chunks of
Chicken, Reduced-Fat Cream of
Chicken Soup, and Diced Pimiento

Bran Muffins
Celery Sticks
Orange Slices
Skim Milk

"Two Minutes to Grab Lunch" Ideas

Peanut butter on raisin bread, raw baby carrots, low-fat chocolate milk

Lean smoked turkey and pepper cheese on rye bread, tomato juice

Leftover pizza and fresh fruit

Cold chicken, dinner rolls, cherry tomatoes

Pita bread filled with leftover roast beef and horseradish, plums

Canned black bean soup, string cheese, baked tortilla chips

Granola bars, cottage cheese, pineapple

Leftover chili, tacos, or spaghetti, raw veggies and dip

Cold meatloaf sandwich, baked potato chips, apple

Frozen microwave dinner, fruit juice

Menu of the Day

Crockpot Chicken Breasts
in Marinara Sauce
Boiled Spaghetti
Green Salad with Reduced-Fat
Italian Dressing
Kiwifruit splashed with Lime Juice
Skim Milk

Hope is a gift we give ourselves,
and it remains when all else is gone.
—Naomi Judd

Vegetable Hash with Bacon
8 1-cup servings

2 tablespoons vegetable oil
6 red-skinned potatoes, washed, halved,
  and sliced very thin
8 ounces Canadian bacon, diced

1 green pepper, diced
1 yellow onion, diced
1 teaspoon salt
1/2 teaspoon fresh ground pepper

1. In a large skillet, heat oil over medium heat. Add sliced potatoes and cook for 15 to 18 minutes, covered.

2. Remove cover and add all remaining ingredients. Cover again and heat for 5 more minutes.

Calories per serving: 259 Fat: 6 g. Sodium: 717 mg.
   (To reduce sodium, substitute cooked diced pork for Canadian bacon.)
For exchange diets, count: 2 vegetable, 2 starch, 1 lean meat
Preparation time: 15 minutes Cooking time: 25 minutes

Menu *of the* Day

Vegetable Hash with Bacon
Breadsticks with Soft Margarine
Applesauce sprinkled with Sliced
Almonds and Raisins
Skim Milk

Sweet and Sour Red Cabbage
8 1-cup servings

1 medium red cabbage	2 tablespoons flour
1 small onion, sliced	1/2 cup water
2 tablespoons lemon juice	1/4 cup vinegar
4 slices bacon, diced	1/2 teaspoon salt
1/4 cup brown sugar	1/8 teaspoon black pepper

1. Remove outside leaves from the cabbage, and wash well.

2. Shred the cabbage, discarding tough center core.

3. In a casserole dish, combine shredded cabbage with sliced onion and lemon juice. Cover and microwave for 8 minutes.

4. Meanwhile, in a small skillet, fry diced bacon until crisp. Discard drippings. Remove bacon and allow to drain on a paper towel. In same skillet, combine brown sugar, flour, water, vinegar, salt, and pepper. Whisk mixture until smooth, then cook over medium heat until thick, about 5 minutes.

5. Pour sauce over cooked cabbage. Stir to mix. Stir in diced bacon.

6. Microwave for 3 more minutes on high power.

Calories per serving: 81 Fat: 1 g. Sodium: 16 mg.
For exchange diets, count: 1 starch
Preparation time: 25 minutes

Menu of the Day

Pork Roast in the Crockpot
Sweet and Sour Red Cabbage
Wheat Bread with Soft Margarine
Sliced Bananas and Apples
sprinkled with Lemon Juice
Skim Milk

---

*There is as much dignity in plowing a field
as in writing a poem. —Booker T. Washington*

Preparing for Halloween

Gaelic custom called for an autumn festival on the last day of October to mark the beginning of winter. Giant bonfires became symbolic to honor the sun god and to frighten away evil spirits.

The custom of jack-o-lanterns began in the early United States after a plentiful fall harvest of pumpkins. Taffy pulls, corn-popping parties, and hayrides became part of the celebration.

Consider these inexpensive ways to encourage fall fellowship.

Invite friends and family to an old-fashioned scavenger hunt: Assign teams to go around the neighborhood looking for common items—an acorn, a feather, a thimble, a mini-pumpkin, an ear of Indian corn, etc.

Start early in the month and let the kids design their own simple costume to make. Instead of buying masks, let the kids paint their faces with face crayons.

"Hide and Seek" is a tradition but can be scary on a dark night. Provide flashlights for party participants.

Give healthy treats. Chocolate candy bars are expensive and full of saturated fat. Consider giving your trick-or-treaters a choice of small boxes or packets of nuts, raisins, or dried fruit; single-serve cartons of 100% fruit juice; sticks of sugarless gum; single-serve boxes of dry cereal; packaged fruit rolls; single-serve packets of microwave popcorn; or commercially baked and wrapped muffins.

Menu *of the* Day

Broiled Pork Burger on a Bun
with Alfalfa Sprouts for Crunch
Butternut Squash
Fresh Pear
Skim Milk

God does not ask your ability or inability.
He asks only your availability.
—Mary Kay Ash

Pumpkin Poppy Seed Cake
16 slices

1 package 94% fat-free yellow cake mix
1 1/4 cups solid pack pumpkin
2/3 cup orange juice
3 eggs or 3/4 cup liquid egg substitute

2 tablespoons poppy seeds
2 tablespoons finely grated orange rind
Non-stick cooking spray

1. Preheat oven to 350°.

2. Combine cake mix, pumpkin, orange juice, and eggs in a large mixing bowl. Beat at low speed for 30 seconds. Beat at medium speed for 3 more minutes. Fold in poppy seeds and orange rind.

3. Pour into a Bundt pan that has been sprayed with cooking spray. Bake for 35 minutes.

4. Cool for 10 minutes, then invert onto a wire rack to cool completely, at least 30 minutes. Serve with orange or lemon sherbet.

Calories per 1-slice serving: 153 Fat: 3 g. Sodium: 245 mg.
For exchange diets, count: 2 starch
Preparation time: 15 minutes Baking time: 35 minutes Cooling time: 40 minutes

---

Menu *of the* Day

Baked Potato with Toppings:
Reduced-Fat Ham and Cheese,
Chopped Onions, Dill Weed

Raw Broccoli Dippers with
Reduced-Fat Salad Dressing Dip
Pumpkin Poppy Seed Cake
Skim Milk

When we do the best we can,
we never know what miracles may result.
—Helen Keller

Halloween Salad

4 ³⁄₄-cup servings

2 cups shredded carrots
1 small can mandarin oranges, drained
1/4 cup raisins
1 cup nonfat plain yogurt
2 tablespoons light mayonnaise

1 tablespoon lemon juice
2 tablespoons brown sugar or substitute
1 teaspoon cinnamon
2 tablespoons chopped walnuts

1. Combine carrots, oranges, and raisins in salad bowl.

2. In small mixing bowl, combine all remaining ingredients except walnuts for dressing. Stir to mix, then pour dressing over carrots. Sprinkle walnuts on top before serving.

Calories per serving: 112 Fat: 4 g. Sodium: 53 mg.
For exchange diets, count: 1 starch, 1 fat
Preparation time: 15 minutes

Menu *of the* Day

Broiled Turkey Breast
basted with Teriyaki Sauce
Quick Rice mixed with
Steamed Stirfry Vegetables
Halloween Salad
Skim Milk

Pumpkin Soup
4 1½-cup servings

This recipe is one of the author's favorites.
It freezes well in individual containers for a lingering taste of autumn.

1 tablespoon margarine
1 cup chopped onion
1/2 cup sliced celery
1/4 teaspoon garlic powder
3 cups no-added-salt chicken broth

1/4 teaspoon salt
1/2 teaspoon white pepper
16-ounce can solid pack pumpkin
1 cup evaporated skim milk
2 scallions, finely chopped

1. In 2-quart saucepan, melt margarine. Add onion, celery, and garlic powder, cooking until vegetables are soft. Add broth, salt, and pepper, and simmer for 15 minutes.

2. Stir in pumpkin and evaporated skim milk. Cook for 5 minutes over medium heat.

3. Pour into a blender container and blend on low speed about 30 seconds or until creamy. Ladle into soup bowls. Top with chopped scallions, and serve.

Calories per serving: 120 Fat: 1 g. Sodium: 215 mg.
For exchange diets, count: 1 starch, 2 vegetable
Preparation time: 30 minutes

Menu *of the* Day

Pumpkin Soup
Broiled Hamburger on a Bun
with Lettuce and Pickles
Fun Size Candy Bar
Skim Milk

Thankful Celebration

**In every thing give thanks:
for this is the will of God in Christ Jesus.
—I Thessalonians 5:18**

The excitement and beauty of the harvest are nearly over and we wake up to the grayness of November. So what if this month is recognized for having the fewest sunny days? We have full and thankful hearts and we are preparing for the holidays.

Your kitchen will be made glad with the smell of chili and the steam from soups and chowder. You can begin freezing treats for gifts and guests (like Chex Mix and fruitcake).

Your mind races to the picture of Thanksgiving dinner... roasting and carving the turkey, whipping up the meanest sweet potatoes, and spoiling your diners with cran-raspberry sauce and marble cheesecake.

You control Christmas craziness better than ever before. You learn about the legend of the Christmas tree and mistletoe, you turn out the perfect prime rib. You reflect on the meaning of Christmas giving and define it with your own values and budget (instead of the department store flyer) in mind.

You reread the Christmas story. You marvel at Mary. She was so young and such a wonder.

And the moment will come at the end of this two month celebration when you reflect on the meaning of *Daily Bread*. It was a gift you gave yourself when you bought this book.

Give thanks with me for this daily feeding of food and spirit, faith and comfort, love and beauty, utility and laughter. It was sent from above.

*I will give thanks for the sheer wonder of life, dipped day upon day
from eternal springs, and held to the thirsting lips of all creatures.
—Lilly Gracia Christensen, Lutheran Woman Today
Used with permission.*

November 1

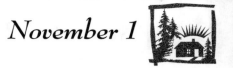

Fruit, Nuts, and Rice
4 ¾-cup servings

2 cups no-added-salt chicken broth
2/3 cup wild rice
Non-stick cooking spray
2 green onions, chopped fine

1 rib celery, chopped fine
2 tablespoons chopped parsley
2 tablespoons chopped walnuts
1/4 cup dried cranberries or raisins

1. Bring broth to a boil. Add rice and reduce heat to simmer for 20 minutes.

2. Meanwhile, spray a skillet with cooking spray. Add onions, celery, and parsley. Sauté over medium heat for 5 minutes, then add to rice.

3. Simmer rice and vegetables another 20 minutes. Mix in nuts and dried cranberries during last 10 minutes of cooking.

Calories per serving: 168 Fat: 2 g. Sodium: 21 mg.
For exchange diets, count: 2 starch
Preparation time: 10 minutes Cooking time: 40 minutes

Menu of the Day

Grilled Ham Steak
with Pineapple Ring Garnish
Fruit, Nuts, and Rice
Wheat Rolls and Soft Margarine
Skim Milk

Thankful Celebration

November 2

I will give thanks for the beauty of God's wide world, the fragrance of rain and the lilt of wind, the marvel of clouds and mountains and seas.
Lilly Gracia Christensen, Lutheran Woman Today
Used with permission.

Winter Workouts

Staying fit during the winter isn't impossible, even in the northland.

Try it on ice—Ice skating is a great cardiovascular workout for the whole family.

Inhale/exhale—A brisk refreshing walk in the winter can be exhilarating. Enjoy beautiful scenery of the winter wonderland.

Whistle while you work—Winter chores, like shoveling, scraping car windows, and decorating the house with lights can be good for your arms and waist. Do these chores with vigor!

Re-energize your home life—Take advantage of being indoors by organizing the basement or attic or deep cleaning those bedroom closets.

Be a kid again—Sledding is one of the most popular pastimes during the winter. Not only do you work your legs, buttocks, and arms each time you climb the steep hill, you speed your heart on the way down. If you're afraid of the wild ride, just walk down the hill and offer to bring the sled up for the kids.

Keep it up—Keep healthy snacks handy to maintain energy levels as you play. Staying warm in cold temperatures requires extra calories and fluids.

Menu *of the* Day

Chunky Chicken with
Green Chilies, Green Onion,
and Reduced-Fat Cream of
Mushroom Soup baked in a Flour
Tortilla topped with Part-Skim
Monterey Jack Cheese
Cherry Tomatoes
Fresh Grapes
Skim Milk

I will give thanks for the simple grace of laughter, silver-clear above sounds of strife. —Lilly Gracia Christensen, Lutheran Woman Today *Used with permission.*

November 3

Cherry Angel Refrigerated Dessert

12 servings

1 prepared angel food cake
3-ounce package instant lemon pudding mix
1 1/2 cups skim milk

1 cup nonfat sour cream
21-ounce can reduced-sugar cherry pie filling

1. Tear the angel food cake into bite-size pieces. Place pieces in a 13- by 9-inch pan.

2. In a mixing bowl, combine the pudding mix, milk, and sour cream. Beat on medium speed until thick, about 2 minutes. Spread over the cake.

3. Spoon pie filling on top, and chill for at least 1 hour. This dessert keeps for 24 hours.

Calories per serving: 157 Fat: 0 Sodium: 367 mg.
For exchange diets, count: 2 starch
Preparation time: 15 minutes Chilling time: 1 hour

Menu of the Day

Tuna Salad on a bed of Lettuce
Buttermilk Biscuits from a tube
Red Onion and Cucumber Slices
with Reduced-Fat Italian Dressing
Cherry Angel Refrigerated Dessert
Hot Tea

Thankful Celebration

I will give thanks for the challenge of new beginnings, of goals attained and vistas opening, of failures forgiven and hope new-sprung.
—Lilly Gracia Christensen, Lutheran Woman Today
Used with permission.

Apple Rum Cheesecake
Serves 16

Crust:
1 1/2 cups crushed graham crackers
1 tablespoon sugar
3 tablespoons reduced-fat margarine, melted

Cheesecake:
8-ounce package nonfat cream cheese, softened
1/2 cup sugar
2 eggs or 1/2 cup liquid egg substitute
1 teaspoon vanilla

Topping:
4 large Macintosh apples, washed, peeled, and sliced thin
1/3 cup sugar
1 teaspoon cinnamon
2 tablespoons chopped pecans
1/3 cup apple jelly
2 teaspoons rum extract

1. Preheat oven to 350°.

2. Combine cracker crumbs, sugar, and melted margarine. Press into the bottom of a 9-inch springform pan and bake for 10 minutes.

3. In a medium mixing bowl, combine softened cream cheese and sugar until well blended. Add the eggs and vanilla and pour over baked crust.

4. Combine sugar and cinnamon. Toss apples with sugar-cinnamon mixture. Spoon over cream cheese. Sprinkle with chopped nuts. Bake for 1 hour and 10 minutes.

5. Remove from oven. Combine apple jelly and rum extract in a 1-cup glass measure; microwave for 45 seconds to melt. Spoon over cheesecake. Refrigerate this dessert for at least 1 hour or until serving time. Loosen cake from rim of pan and remove carefully.

Calories per serving: 180 Fat: 7 g. Sodium: 158 mg.
For exchange diets, count: 1 starch, 1 fruit, 1 fat
Preparation time: 20 minutes Baking time: 1 hour, 20 minutes
Chilling time: 1 hour

Menu *of the* Day

Broiled Pork Chops
Butternut Squash
seasoned with Allspice
Celery Sticks
Apple Rum Cheesecake
Skim Milk

I will give thanks for the unspeakable privilege of working with God,
bearing together a fragment of the world's dread burden of sin
—Lilly Gracia Christensen, Lutheran Woman Today
Used with permission.

November 5

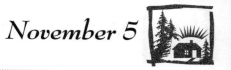

Hamburger and Potato Soup
8 2-cup servings

1 pound lean ground beef	4 cups no-added-salt beef broth
4 large potatoes, peeled and cubed	1 teaspoon celery salt
1 small onion, chopped	1 teaspoon black pepper
24 ounces no-added-salt tomato sauce	1 teaspoon Tabasco sauce

1. Brown the ground beef in a stockpot. Drain well. Return meat to the pot and add all remaining ingredients.

2. Bring mixture to a boil, reduce heat, and simmer for 30 minutes.

Calories per serving: 252 Fat: 7 g. Sodium: 309 mg.
For exchange diets, count: 2 lean meat, 1 starch, 2 vegetable
Preparation time: 20 minutes Cooking time: 30 minutes

Menu of the Day

Hamburger and Potato Soup
Soda Crackers
Green Grapes
Skim Milk

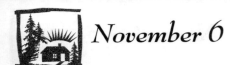

I will give thanks for the high vision of earth's great souls, whom neither sword nor fire nor want nor hate could swerve from running the race, nor from straining toward the beckoning goal. —Lilly Gracia Christensen, Lutheran Woman Today. *Used with permission.*

Party Popcorn
4 2-cup servings

8 cups popped popcorn
1 tablespoon dill weed
2 teaspoons finely grated lemon rind

1/4 teaspoon garlic powder
1/2 teaspoon pepper
2 tablespoons margarine, melted

1. Place popped corn in a 3-quart baking pan.

2. Mix seasonings with melted margarine. Pour over popped corn and stir.

3. Bake at 200° for 1 hour, stirring every 15 minutes. Cool to room temperature and transfer to an airtight container. To use after several days, simply rewarm in the oven at 200° for 10 minutes.

Calories per 2-cup serving: 96 Fat: 6 g. Sodium: 66 mg.
For exchange diets, count: 1/2 starch, 1 fat
Preparation time: 15 minutes Baking time: 1 hour

Menu of the *Day*

Snack Supper
Party Popcorn
Mini Frozen
Canadian Bacon Pizzas
Fresh Vegetable Dippers
with Reduced-Fat Dip
Pineapple Juice

I will give thanks for the sacredness of human suffering, for the ministry of sorrow and pain, leading up close to the heart of God, slipping our hands like children's into the almighty palm. —Lilly Gracia Christensen, Lutheran Woman Today. *Used with permission.*

November 7

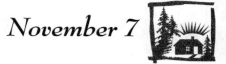

Is There "Heart" in Your Christmas Shopping?

Are you having trouble deciding what to get for whom?

Sometimes it is hard to stay sensitive to what Christmas is really about in the midst of the season's near-frantic activity. When you plan for Christmas this year, search your heart first and remember:

God so loved the world, that he gave his only begotten Son, that whosoever believes in him should not perish, but have everlasting life.

Unto you is born this day...a Savior, who is Christ the Lord.

God was in Christ reconciling the world to himself.

We have seen and do testify that the Father sent the Son to be the Savior of the world.

Christmas can be beautiful. God's love for us in Jesus Christ makes it possible for us to love God and one another.

Put your favorite ministry of Christ at the top of your Christmas list this year. Missions overseas and at home tell the story of Jesus and his love.

And if just one person hears and believes, the angels in heaven will rejoice.

Menu of the Day

Broiled Hamburger with Sautéed Mushrooms on a Wheat Bun
Steamed Broccoli with Margarine
Fresh Orange
Skim Milk

Thankful Celebration

I will give thanks for the reality of love rooted in God flowing in perfect freedom, blasting barriers and welding humanity into the kinship of spirit.
—Lilly Gracia Christensen, Lutheran Woman Today
Used with permission.

Crockpot Cranberry Pork Roast

8 3-ounce servings

1 1/2 pound boneless pork loin
8-ounce can jellied cranberry sauce
1/4 cup orange juice

1/2 teaspoon dry mustard
1/8 teaspoon cloves

1. Place pork loin in the Crockpot.

2. In a small bowl, mash cranberry sauce smooth. Fold in orange juice, dry mustard, and cloves. Pour over roast. Cook on low heat for 6 hours.

Calories per serving: 195 Fat: 4 g. Sodium: 69 mg.
For exchange diets, count: 4 very lean meat, 1 fruit
Preparation time: 10 minutes Cooking time: 6 hours

Menu of the Day

Crockpot Cranberry Pork Roast
Boiled Potatoes
Steamed Carrots with Dill Weed
Chilled Tropical Fruit Cocktail
Skim Milk

I will give thanks for the undimmed power of the cross, planted deep in the heart of the universe, eternal embodiment and revelation of the divine love.
—Lilly Gracia Christensen, Lutheran Woman Today
Used with permission.

November 9

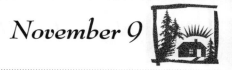

Chunky Lemon Fruit Salad
4 1-cup servings

1 apple
1 pear
1 banana

1 kiwifruit
2 tablespoons frozen lemonade concentrate
(not diluted)

1. Cut fruits into bite-sized chunks; place chunks in a salad bowl.

2. Spoon lemonade concentrate over the fruits. Mix gently, then cover and refrigerate until serving time. This salad lasts 24 hours.

Calories per serving: 86 Fat: 0 Sodium: 2 mg.
For exchange diets, count: 1 1/2 fruit
Preparation time: 10 minutes

Menu of the Day

Baked Cod or Halibut
with Basil and No-Added-Salt
Chunky Tomatoes
Quick Rice sprinkled
with Parmesan Cheese
Chunky Lemon Fruit Salad
Skim Milk

Thankful Celebration

November 10

I will give thanks for the changelessness of God from day to day and from age to age. —Lilly Gracia Christensen. Lutheran Woman Today Used with permission.

Vegetable Chowder with Bacon

4 1½-cup servings

6 slices bacon
1 small can no-added-salt chicken broth
2 cups finely chopped potatoes
1 cup shredded carrots

1/2 cup chopped onion
1/2 teaspoon curry powder
1/8 teaspoon pepper
12-ounce can evaporated skim milk

1. Broil bacon until crisp, then crumble into pieces.

2. Meanwhile, in 3-quart kettle, combine broth and vegetables. Steam vegetables until tender. Stir in curry, pepper, bacon, and evaporated skim milk. Heat through, about 10 minutes over medium heat. Do not boil!

Calories per serving: 243 Fat: 5 g. Sodium: 304 mg.
For exchange diets, count: 1 vegetable, 2 starch, 1 fat
Preparation time: 25 minutes

Menu *of the* Day

Vegetable Chowder with Bacon
Hard Rolls with Soft Margarine
Pineapple Rings
with Lemon Yogurt on top
Skim Milk

I will give thanks for the gifts of a grateful heart, sharing in the building of a timeless temple, a temple not made with hands—a temple of praise which God eternally inhabits. —Lilly Gracia Christensen, Lutheran Woman Today. Used with permission.

November 11

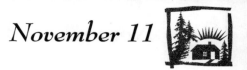

Oat Bran Banana Bread
24 ½-slice servings

3/4 cup water
1/2 cup mashed banana
1 egg
1/2 cup oat bran
2 3/4 cups bread flour

3 tablespoons sugar
1 1/2 teaspoons salt
1 1/2 tablespoons nonfat dry milk
1 1/2 teaspoons dry yeast

1. Recipe is meant for large (3 cups flour) loaf.

2. Add ingredients to bread machine pan in order listed (recipe was tested with a Hitachi Automatic Home Bakery). If your machine calls for dry ingredients first, then invert the order of ingredients.

3. Program for "Bread" or regular setting. Push "Start" and remove bread from machine approximately 4 hours later.

Calories per serving: 124 Fat: 1 g. Sodium: 67 mg.
For exchange diets, count: 1/2 starch
Preparation time: 10 minutes Baking time: 4 hours

Menu *of the* Day

Your favorite Meatloaf
Mashed Potatoes
Chilled Sweet and Sour Bean
Salad from the deli or can
Oat Bran Banana Bread
Skim Milk

Thankful Celebration

I will give thanks for the terrible patience of God, loving to the uttermost pouring out the most precious of oblations on the cold, unresponsive altar of the unrepentant heart. —Lilly Gracia Christensen, Lutheran Woman Today. Used with permission.

Survive the Holidays Without Weight Gain

Nobody said, "Ready, get set, gorge!" So getting through November and December without that bloated feeling is entirely up to you. Here are some secrets:

Out-Smart the Buffet Line

Plan ahead. Never go to a party on an empty stomach. Have an apple, some skim milk, or a few crackers before you go.

Quench your thirst first. When you arrive at a party, make the water or diet soda station your first stop. Once your thirst is handled, you can decide what sounds best to eat.

Bring a fresh fruit or vegetable platter to any gathering and watch it disappear. You can ensure your own success and share it with others.

Watch the dabs and licks. A little dab of real mayo or a lick of fudge adds up.

Decide on a favorite "splurge" item before you go. Help yourself to a small portion, then sit down and enjoy every bite.

Menu of the Day

Grilled Canadian Bacon,
Tomato, and Lettuce Sandwiches
on Wheat Toast
Whole Kernel Corn seasoned with
Dried Onion and flakes of Thyme
Ice Milk with Dried Pineapple
or Dates on top
Skim Milk

God is a generous giver, wanting us to have every good thing.
...He offers happiness. Take it. He offers peace. Take it.
He offers renewal of body, mind, and spirit.
—Norman Vincent Peale

November 13

Survive the Holidays Without Weight Gain

Be a Hostess Without the "Mostest"

You can clobber holiday cheer with any announcement that the menu is "low fat" or "low calorie." Don't say a word about your low-fat dip or fat-free dessert and just wait for the compliments to roll in.

If you're cutting portions of a baked dessert or molded salad, go small!

Use a small spoon in the pasta or potato salad to encourage reasonable servings.

Allow guests to serve themselves and don't feel obliged to pile your guests' plates as if the meal is their last.

You don't need 10 foods on the menu for the food service to be praised. Showcasing one or two pretty and delicious items will be a lasting remembrance for your family and friends.

Go ahead and send all the leftovers home with the guests. You won't be throwing them out a week later and the guests will have an edible present the next day.

Menu of the Day

Broiled Salmon Steaks
with Fresh Lemon Wedges
Baked Potato
Steamed Carrots
Fresh Blueberries
Skim Milk

Thankful Celebration

We shall come one day to a heaven where we shall gratefully know that God's great refusals were sometimes the true answers to our truest prayer. –P.T. Forsyth

Survive the Holidays Without Weight Gain

One Day at a Time

The busier we get at holiday time, the easier it is to forget good food choices. If you really want to see January in the same size, today's the day to get out the food diary. Recording your food intake (even on a running tablet in your mind) will help curb mindless munching.

Skipping meals is a classic mistake. Take time for three planned food encounters. It's OK to push breakfast back to 10 a.m. if you're meeting a friend at the mall. You can grab a bagel and an orange juice there and call it breakfast. But think ahead.

Fit exercise into your holiday plans. Take a brisk walk or pop in a half hour exercise video before the big office party. Exercise burns calories and also reduces stress and out-of-control eating.

Know your demons. For me, it's fudge, cookie baking, real candy cane ice cream, and 4-year-aged cheddar cheese. You might have to lock up and hide your sins, so you can enjoy a bite here and there and make the treat last the season.

Menu *of the* Day

Beef Cubes in the Crockpot with
chunks of Potato, Onion, Carrot,
and Celery in No-Added-Salt
Tomato Soup
Whole Grain Bread
from the bakery
Red Grapes
Skim Milk

*Like my father quoted from his simple catechism,
"Trust your future to the things you love."*
–Diane Sawyer

November 15

It's Your Turn to Roast the Turkey
Tips on turning out a perfect bird:

Purchase: Allow 3/4 to 1 pound of turkey per person to be served.

Preparation for roasting: Thaw a frozen turkey breast side up. Estimate at least one day of thawing for every 6 pounds of turkey. Do not thaw at room temperature. Remove neck and giblets from thawed body cavity. Rinse the turkey inside and out with cool water, and pat dry with paper towels. Stuff turkey lightly if desired. Return legs to tuck position, if untucked. Insert a meat thermometer into the deepest part of the thigh. Place turkey, breast up, on a flat rack in a shallow pan. Brush skin with vegetable oil. Place in preheated 325° oven. When skin is golden brown, shield the breast loosely with a tent of foil to prevent overbrowning. Roast to an internal temperature of 180° in the thigh, 170° in the breast, and 160° in the stuffing. Begin checking for doneness 30 minutes before anticipated end of cooking.

General guideline to estimate cooking time:

Weight of Turkey	Cooking Time in Hours	
	stuffed	unstuffed
10-18 pound	4-4½	3-3½
18-22 pound	4½-5	3½-4
22-24 pound	5-5½	4-4½
24-29 pound	5½-6½	4½-5

When appropriate temperature has been attained, remove turkey from the oven, cover, and allow to rest at room temperature 20 to 30 minutes before carving.

Menu of the Day
Diced Chicken stir-fried with Garlic, Thinly-Sliced Broccoli and Water Chestnuts, seasoned with Teriyaki Sauce
Quick Rice
Green Grapes
Skim Milk

*A baby is God's opinion
that the world should go on.
–Carl Sandburg*

How to Carve the Turkey

Thanksgiving is almost here. A well-made sharp carving knife and two-pronged kitchen fork will steady the bird and allow you to carve easily and safely.

Remove the leg and wing: Arrange the turkey breast side up on a large cutting board. Cut through the skin between the wing and breast. Press the wing outward to locate the joint, then slice down through the joint. Remove the thigh in the same fashion.

Carve the drumstick and thigh: Cut the leg joint to separate the drumstick and thigh. Slice the drumstick meat lengthwise along the bone; turn leg and slice again. Repeat twice more. Place the thigh flat side down and slice meat parallel to the bone.

Carve the breast: Hold the carving fork along the breast bone. Carve parallel to the breast bone, slicing diagonally through the meat.

Menu of the Day

Grilled Reduced-Fat Swiss
Cheese and Ham Sandwiches
Steamed Asparagus
with Lemon Juice
Chilled Fruit Cocktail
with Piña Colada Yogurt on top
Herb Tea

The only limit to our realization of tomorrow will be our doubts of today. Let us move forward with strong and active faith.
–Franklin Delano Roosevelt

November 17

Pineapple Cranberry Upside Down Cake
24 servings

1/4 cup soft margarine
1/2 cup packed brown sugar
1 cup fresh cranberries

15-ounce can chunk pineapple in juice, drained
and juice reserved
18-ounce package reduced-fat yellow cake mix

1. Preheat oven to 350°.

2. Measure margarine into a 13- by 9-inch baking pan and place in the warming oven.

3. Sprinkle sugar, cranberries, and pineapple over the melted margarine.

4. Prepare cake mix according to package directions and spread over the fruit. Bake for 40 minutes. Cool for 5 minutes, then invert onto a large serving plate.

Calories per serving: 133 Fat: 3 g. Sodium: 174 mg.
For exchange diets, count: 1 starch, 1 fruit
Preparation time: 15 minutes Baking time: 40 minutes Cooling time: 5 minutes

---

Menu of the Day

Reduced-Fat Breaded
Fish Square on a Bun
Steamed Sugar Snap Peas
Pineapple Cranberry
Upside Down Cake
Skim Milk

Thankful Celebration

There is a land of the living and a land of the dead,
and the bridge is love. —Thornton Wilder

Lemony Sweet Potatoes
4 ¾-cup servings

24-ounce can sweet potatoes
1 1/2 teaspoons finely grated lemon rind

1/4 teaspoon ground red pepper
1 green onion, diced

1. Preheat oven to 400° (if using a conventional oven).

2. Pour sweet potatoes into a microwave-safe baking dish. Use a hand masher to mash potatoes to desired smoothness. Fold in lemon rind, pepper, and onion.

3. Cover and microwave on 70 percent power for 15 minutes, or bake for 30 minutes.

Calories per serving: 161 Fat: 0 Sodium: 119 mg.
For exchange diets, count: 2 starch
Preparation time: 10 minutes Microwave cooking time: 15 minutes
  Conventional oven cooking time: 30 minutes

Menu *of the* Day

Grilled Turkey Breast
seasoned with Paprika
Lemony Sweet Potatoes
Green Salad
with Reduced-Fat Dressing
Apricot Sauce
Skim Milk

Cherish all your happy moments:
they make a fine cushion for old age.
—Booth Tarkington

November 19

Chocolate Marble Cheesecake
12 slices

6-ounce prepared chocolate crumb crust
8-ounce package light (50% reduced-fat) cream
  cheese
14-ounce can fat-free sweetened condensed milk

1 egg or 1/4 cup liquid egg substitute
1/2 teaspoon vanilla
1/4 cup semisweet chocolate chips, melted

1. Preheat oven to 350°.

2. In a small mixing bowl, beat cream cheese until fluffy. Gradually add sweetened condensed milk until smooth. Add egg and vanilla. Mix well.

3. Reserve 1/4 cup of batter. Add melted chocolate chips to this batter. (To melt chocolate chips, microwave in glass measuring cup at 70 percent power for 1 minute.)

4. Pour vanilla batter into prepared crust. Spoon chocolate batter over the vanilla batter.

5. Use a knife or spatula to gently swirl through the batters to marble. Bake for 35 to 40 minutes or until the center of the pie is set.

6. Cool, then chill at least 1 hour in the refrigerator. Refrigerate leftovers.

Calories per 1-slice serving: 194 Fat: 8 g. Sodium: 234 mg.
For exchange diets, count: 1 starch, 1 fruit, 1 fat
Preparation time: 15 minutes Baking time: 35 minutes
    Chilling time: 1 hour

Menu of the Day

Crockpot Roasted Chicken
with Dried Apricots and Celery
Quick Rice with Margarine
Steamed Japanese Vegetables
Chocolate Marble Cheesecake
Decaf Coffee

Thankful Celebration

Walt Whitman said: "I find letters from heaven dropped
in the street and every one is signed by God's name.
Thanksgiving is one of those signed letters.
Anyone can open it and see what it says." —Garrison Keillor

Baby Carrots in Red Wine Vinegar

8 ¾-cup servings

1 pound baby carrots, each cut into 4 strips
  lengthwise
1 red pepper, diced
1 green pepper, diced

4 green onions, diced
1/3 cup reduced-fat red wine vinegar salad dressing
  (such as Seven Seas)

Combine all ingredients in a salad bowl. Cover and refrigerate at least 30 minutes or until serving time. This salad lasts one week.

Calories per serving: 78 Fat: 2 g. Sodium: 118 mg.
For exchange diets, count: 1 starch
Preparation time: 15 minutes Chilling time: 30 minutes

Menu *of the* Day

Broiled Hamburger on a Kaiser
Roll with Lettuce and Pickles
Baby Carrots in Red Wine Vinegar
Crushed Pineapple and Raisins
with Nonfat Vanilla Yogurt
Sugar-Free Lemonade

Viva November Chili
8 1½-cup servings

1/2 pound lean ground beef
1 small white onion, chopped fine
2 ribs celery, diced
1 teaspoon garlic
1 teaspoon oregano
1 teaspoon basil

3 14-ounce cans no-added-salt chopped tomatoes
16-ounce can chili-style beans
16-ounce can kidney beans
1/2 cup water
2 tablespoons chili powder
1/2 teaspoon ground thyme

1. Brown ground beef with onion and celery in a stockpot over medium heat for 5 minutes. Drain meat and vegetables in a colander for 5 minutes.

2. Return meat and vegetables to the stockpot and add all remaining ingredients. Simmer for at least 30 minutes or up to 90 minutes.

Calories per serving: 161 Fat: 5 g. Sodium: 189 mg.
For exchange diets, count: 1 lean meat, 1 starch, 1 vegetable
Preparation time: 10 minutes Cooking time: 30 minutes

Menu of the *Day*

Viva November Chili
Corn Bread Muffins from a mix
Sliced Kiwifruit
Skim Milk

Deep in their roots all flowers keep the light.
—Theodore Roethke

Cranberry-Stuffed Baked Apples
4 servings

4 cooking apples, such as Granny Smith, Pippin,
  or Macintosh
1/2 cup dried cranberries
2 tablespoons chopped walnuts

1/4 cup brown sugar
1 teaspoon cinnamon
1 tablespoon soft margarine

1. Preheat oven to 375°.

2. Wash and core apples, then remove one-half inch from the bottom of each so they sit flat in a baking dish.

3. Combine all remaining ingredients in a small mixing bowl.

4. Stuff the apples with filling, generously mounding on top.

5. Bake for 25 minutes. Serve warm.

Calories per serving: 166 Fat: 4 g. Sodium: 23 mg.
For exchange diets, count: 2 fruit, 1 fat
Preparation time: 15 minutes Baking time: 25 minutes

Menu *of the* Day

Cold Roast Beef from the deli
on an Onion Roll
Whole Kernel Corn
with Rosemary
Cranberry-Stuffed Baked Apples
Skim Milk

Managing Gas and Bloating

Whether we happen to overeat at the holiday party or talk with our mouth full, everyone suffers from gas and bloating now and then.

The most common causes of excessive gas are:

> Swallowing excess air while eating or drinking

> Foods moving through the intestinal tract too rapidly to allow for reabsorption of gas

> Eating foods that are gas-producing

If you suffer from gas:

> Try to eat slowly. Chew with your mouth closed and avoid gulping food. Try putting your fork down often during the meal.

> Stop chewing gum, or if you do, keep your mouth closed.

> If you have added new high-fiber foods to your diet (cranberries, sweet potatoes, pumpkin, fresh apples, raisins, and nuts are examples), expect to experience temporary symptoms of gas. It generally takes a month to 6 weeks for your intestinal tract to adjust to added fiber.

> Watch out for carbonated drinks. They promote bloating and belching.

> Try eating yogurt with live bacteria cultures. The bacteria decrease gas production in the lower intestine.

> And remember the most effective remedy, exercise your gas pain away.

Menu *of the* Day

Tuna Salad and shredded Pepper
Jack Cheese on an Onion Bagel
Reduced-Fat Potato Chips
Steamed Green Beans
seasoned with Dill Weed
Peach Slices
Skim Milk

Thankful Celebration

November 24

Pass on This Holiday Message of Hope and Love
for the Grieving Hearts You Know and Love

Is there—anywhere—a remedy for grief? Our misery, like our joy in other days, is shared by those who love us best. Even the very wise, the very great are bewildered in the face of grief. The great poet Dante said it well: "There is no greater sorrow than to recall in misery the time when we were happy." Reality is real. Denying the dark never forced a dawning day. Running from sorrow never shortened the road to recovery by a single footstep.

Your present sorrow—which is truly yours and valuable to you as your past gladness—is a certain sign of your life's good fortune.

Does this seem incredible, unfeeling to be reminded of your good fortune? Think then of the truly unfortunate. These are the people who will never know your suffering—because they have never known your happiness. These are the people who have not ever really loved, not ever really been loved in return.

For tears are the end companion of laughter. Only those who have loved greatly will grieve greatly. And the love that has brought them to grief is the love that will bring them consolation. Let us meet a dark hour as we met the bright ones—filled with hope and empty of fear. The measure of our love is the measure of our lives. The weight of grief is in proportion to our love, and love is greater than grief. A remedy then—even for this? Yes. In your own heart, in your own spirit, the comfort you seek awaits discovery. Look for it. Claim it. It's yours.

Reverend Peter Pintus,
Reprinted by John Karras, *Des Moines Register* columnist

Menu of the **Day**

Chicken and Vegetable Soup from
a can with Extra Canned Chicken
and Stirfry Vegetables tossed in
Broiled French Bread
Pineapple Chunks
and Sliced Bananas
Skim Milk

What feeling is so nice as a child's hand in yours?
So small, so soft and warm, like a kitten huddling
in the shelter of your clasp. —Marjorie Holmes

November 25

Cran Raspberry Sauce
8 ⅓-cup servings

Even the kids will like this sauce.

1 pound fresh cranberries
1 1/2 cups water

3/4 cup sugar
16-ounce package frozen raspberries

1. In a 2-quart saucepan, combine cranberries and water and bring to a boil. Boil for 5 minutes. Add sugar and raspberries and boil for another 5 minutes.

2. Pour into a heat-proof serving bowl and chill at least 30 minutes. This sauce will be chunky. If you prefer a smooth sauce, run the mixture through a food processor and process to desired texture before chilling. Serve with poultry.

Calories per serving: 156 Fat: 0 Sodium: 1 mg.
For exchange diets, count. 2 1/2 fruit
Preparation time: 15 minutes Chilling time: 30 minutes

Menu *of the* Day

Roast Chicken
Baked Potatoes
Cran Raspberry Sauce
Steamed Asparagus
Sherbet
Skim Milk

*The heart leans on its silence, / And God, with a gentle nod
Writes with the chalk of winter / On the blackboard of the land.
—Alma Robison Higbee*

Not Your Grandma's Fruitcake
36 1-slice servings

This is described by originator Nancy Hill, RD, as the
ultimate holiday fruitcake for people who don't like candied fruit.

1 1/2 cups flour
1 cup sugar
1/2 teaspoon salt
1 1/2 teaspoons baking powder
3 cups pitted whole dates
1/3 cup large pecan halves

1 cup whole Brazil nutmeats
8-ounce jar whole maraschino cherries, drained
4 large bananas
4 eggs or 1 cup liquid egg substitute
Non-stick cooking spray

1. Preheat oven to 300°.

2. Sift flour with sugar, salt, and baking powder into a large bowl. Add dates, nuts, and maraschino cherries, and stir to coat all of the nuts and fruits with the flour mixture.

3. In another bowl, beat bananas until mashed. Add eggs and continue beating until well blended and mixture is fluffy. Fold in flour mixture.

4. Pour into a large loaf pan that has been sprayed with cooking spray. Pan will be very full. Bake for 1 3/4 to 2 hours or until cake springs back when center is touched.

5. Cool in the pan on a rack for 15 minutes. Remove cake from pan. Cool completely, then wrap with foil and store in a cool place. Allow cake to stand overnight before slicing.

Calories per serving: 183 Fat: 6 g. Sodium: 36 mg.
For exchange diets, count: 1 fruit, 1 fat, 1 starch
Preparation time: 15 minutes Baking time: 2 hours
Standing time: overnight

Menu *of the* Day

Veggie and Ham Omelet
Not Your Grandma's Fruitcake
Chilled Grapefruit
and Mandarin Orange Slices
Skim Milk

Nature cannot be surprised in undress.
Beauty breaks in everywhere.
–Ralph Waldo Emerson

November 27

Almond Bark Pretzel Treats
24 servings, 4 pretzels each

12-ounce bag Christmas tree shaped pretzels   6 ounces almond bark (may also use brick chocolate)

1. Melt almond bark in a deep saucepan on the stovetop or in a deep mixing bowl in the microwave oven per package directions.

2. Use a long thin knife or chopstick to dip pretzels in melted almond bark, covering both sides. Allow pretzels to dry on wax paper. Store in a covered plastic container.

Calories per serving: 102 Fat: 3 g. Sodium: 112 mg.
For exchange diets, count: 1 starch, 1/2 fat
Preparation time: 30 minutes

Menu of the Day
....
Reduced-Fat Spicy Pork
Sausage Link on a Bun
Kraut and Mustard Toppings
Baked Potato Chips
Chilled Tropical Fruit Cocktail
Almond Bark Pretzel Treats
Skim Milk

Thankful Celebration

November 28

Every man shall give as he is able, according to the blessing of the Lord thy God which He hath given thee. —Deuteronomy 16:17

Tutti Fruity Bars
12 servings

Non-stick cooking spray
1/4 cup margarine
8 ounces marshmallows
1/2 teaspoon vanilla

1/4 cup chopped candied red cherries
1/4 cup chopped candied green cherries
5 cups crisped rice cereal

1. Spray an 11- by 7-inch baking dish with cooking spray.

2. Microwave margarine and marshmallows in a large glass bowl on high power for 4 minutes, stopping to stir twice. Stir in vanilla and cherries briskly. Gently fold in crisped rice cereal.

3. Press into prepared pan, and cut into 12 bars. Cover tightly.

Calories per serving: 141 Fat: 3 g. Sodium: 181 mg.
For exchange diets, count: 1 starch, 1 fruit
Preparation time: 15 minutes

Menu *of the* Day

Salmon, Cucumber, and Tomato
Slices on a bed of Lettuce with
Reduced-Fat Ranch Dressing
Wheat Crackers
Peaches in Juice
Tutti Fruity Bars
Skim Milk

Ask for These Titles when Buying Christmas Music

Gospel Tunes

"Christmas With the Boys Choir of Harlem"

Cyrus Chestnut, "Blessed Quietness"

John P. Kee and the New Life Community Choir, "A Special Christmas Gift"

"An Angel Tree Christmas," produced by Barny Robertson

Classic Gifts of Song

Roberto Alagna, "Our Christmas Songs for You"

Kathleen Battle and Christopher Parkening, "Angel's Glory"

"Ensemble Organum," by the Anonymous 4

Ethan James, "The Ancient Music of Christmas"

"In the Spirit," by Jessye Norman

"Bach's Christmas Oratorio" by Tom Koopman

Menu of the Day

Your favorite Meatballs,
broiled and drained
Steamed Cabbage and Carrots
seasoned with Dill Seed
Wheat Rolls with Soft Margarine
Crushed Pineapple and Pear Slices
Skim Milk

Freely ye have received, freely give.
—Matthew 10:8

Hot Turkey Salad

8 ¾-cup servings

4 cups cubed cooked turkey
2 cups diced celery
1/4 cup slivered almonds
1/2 teaspoon salt
1/2 teaspoon dried thyme

1/2 teaspoon pepper
1 cup nonfat mayonnaise
2 ounces reduced-fat cheddar cheese
1/2 cup finely crushed baked potato chips

1. Preheat oven to 425°.

2. Combine first eight ingredients in a 2-quart casserole dish.

3. Sprinkle crushed potato chips on top. Bake, uncovered for 15 minutes or until heated through.

Calories per serving: 149 Fat: 3 g. Sodium: 693 mg.
For exchange diets, count: 2 lean meat, 1/2 starch
Preparation time: 15 minutes Baking time: 15 minutes

Menu *of the* Day

Hot Turkey Salad
Rye Bread
Coleslaw from the deli
Applesauce
Skim Milk

*Dear God, Did you think that Christmas would turn out
like this when you started it? Love, Wendy (age 7)
–from* Dear God, Children's Letters to God, *by David Heller*

December 1

Quick Cocktail Sauce
1/2 cup or 4 2-tablespoon servings

1/3 cup catsup

2 tablespoons prepared horseradish

1 tablespoon chunky salsa

1. Mix all ingredients together in a small bowl. Cover and refrigerate until use.

2. Serve with cold crab, shrimp, or salmon. This keeps for 2 weeks.

Calories per serving: 25 Fat: 0 Sodium: 240 mg.
For exchange diets, count: 1 vegetable
Preparation time: 5 minutes

Menu of the Day

Boiled Shrimp
with Quick Cocktail Sauce

Crunchy Breadsticks with
Reduced-Fat Soft Cheese as a dip

Fresh Vegetable Relishes
with Reduced-Fat Dip

Reduced-Fat Chocolate Chip
Mint Ice Cream

Decaf Coffee

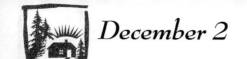

December 2

What Shall You Give This Christmas?
The gift of acceptance
The gift of seeing the best in people
—Dan Sugarman

Legend of the Holiday Plants

The Christmas Tree

Probably the most popular holiday tradition is the Christmas tree. According to legend, Martin Luther was inspired by the beauty of evergreens one Christmas Eve. He cut down a tree, brought it home, and decorated it with candles to imitate the starry skies of Bethlehem. By the early 1900s, the Christmas tree had spread to nearly every household in the United States.

Keep a live tree green by cutting off 1 to 2 inches of trunk and immersing it in a bucket of water overnight before placing it in the stand. Never allow the water to dry out from the stand.

The Poinsettia

The poinsettia is another long-standing holiday tradition. The plant is native to Mexico, where the Aztec Indians used the colorful branches to make a reddish purple dye. Following the Spanish conquest and the introduction of Christianity, poinsettias were used in Christian celebrations and nativity processions. In 1825, poinsettias were introduced to the United States.

Menu *of the* Day

**Stop at the taco stand
to carry home dinner**
Soft and Hard
Chicken or Beef Tacos
Refried Beans
Loads of Lettuce,
Tomatoes, and Salsa
Orange Juice

Give me good digestion, Lord, and also something to digest;
but where and how that something comes I leave to Thee, who knoweth best.
—Sir Henry Webb of Cardiff

December 3

Legend of the Holiday Plants

The Mistletoe

A holiday plant with a gay tradition is mistletoe. Mistletoe is a semi-parasitic plant with leathery leaves and small white berries. Mistletoe plants make their own food, but must obtain water and minerals from a host plant. Ancient traditions state that mistletoe could bestow health and good luck. It was associated with fertility by Welsh farmers. The most popular tradition involving mistletoe concerns marriage. It was believed that kissing under the mistletoe increased the possibility of marriage in the upcoming year.

The Yule Log

The Vikings began the solstice festival called Yuletide. It signified banishment of the year's evil and rekindling of the hearthfire, a symbol of home. It was a time to forget malice, forgive freely, and clear up all misunderstandings. The Yule log was freshly cut in the forest, decorated, and brought into the house on Christmas Eve. Part of the log was saved to start the next year's fire.

Menu of the Day

Broiled Pork Chops
dotted with Teriyaki Sauce
Steamed Yams
with Allspice and Raisins
Green Beans with Parsley
Orange Sherbet
Skim Milk

Eat thy bread with joy,
and drink thy wine with a merry heart.
–Ecclesiastes 9:7

Eggnog Pudding
4 servings

2 cups skim milk
1 package sugar-free vanilla pudding and pie filling

1/2 teaspoon rum extract
1/4 teaspoon ground nutmeg

1. Pour milk into a medium saucepan. Add pudding mix. Cook over medium heat according to package directions until thick. Stir in rum and nutmeg.

2. Pour into individual pudding dishes. Cover, and refrigerate for at least an hour.

Calories per serving: 69 Fat: 0 Sodium: 66 mg.
For exchange diets, count: 1 starch
Preparation time: 10 minutes Chilling time: 1 hour

Menu of the Day

Carryout Chili
from the supermarket
Broiled Onion Bagels
with Soft Margarine
Radishes and Celery Sticks
Eggnog Pudding
Cranapple Juice

*Every man should eat and drink
and enjoy the good of all his labor,
it is the gift of God. —Ecclesiastes 3:13*

December 5

Low-Fat Chex Mix
8 ½-cup servings

2 cups Rice Chex cereal
2 cups Corn Chex cereal
2 cups Wheat Chex cereal
2 cups mini-knot pretzels
3 tablespoons reduced-fat margarine, melted

1/4 teaspoon garlic powder
1/4 teaspoon seasoned salt
2 teaspoons lemon juice
4 teaspoons Worcestershire sauce

1. Preheat oven to 325°.

2. Combine cereals with pretzels in a 13- by 9-inch metal pan.

3. Combine remaining ingredients in a small bowl and pour over the cereal mixture. Stir gently until well coated.

4. Bake for 45 minutes, stirring every 15 minutes.

5. Spread on paper towels to cool. Store in a covered plastic container.

Calories per serving: 147 Fat: 4 g. Sodium: 530 mg.
For exchange diets, count: 2 starch
Preparation time: 10 minutes Baking time: 45 minutes

Menu *of the* Day

Holiday Snack Buffet
Reduced-Fat Summer Sausage
Mozzarella Cheese Sticks
Low-Fat Chex Mix
Fresh Apple Slices
with Reduced-Fat Caramel Dip
Apple Cider

It is a wicked world in which the power of any individual to cause suffering is so great and power to do good is so slight; but here we are in the time of our beloved national feasting and signs of loving Providence are everywhere.
—Garrison Keillor

Giving Gifts from St. Nick on Dec. 6

St. Nicholas was a priest who lived in Asia Minor during the fourth century A.D. According to legend, he furnished dowries for three poor girls whose father couldn't afford to pay them. He did this at night by throwing sacks of coins into the girl's rooms. This is how the custom of nighttime visits from St. Nick originated. St. Nick's Day is celebrated on Dec. 6 with simple gifts such as Christmas stamps, Christmas music tapes, books about Christmas, personalized ornaments, Christmas socks, or napkins or paper plates.

How to Welcome Children

Thoughts on being a gracious hostess to young visitors this holiday season:

Ages 0-2: Have on hand a few rattles or stimulating toys, which go a long way toward distracting a fussy baby. Let the visiting mom know she can use your refrigerator and microwave for preparing food and formula. Offer breast-feeding moms a private, quiet room and comfortable chair.

Ages 2-5: Preschoolers need physical exercise. If the weather is nice, try to visit a park once a day. In prolonged bad weather, look for an indoor swimming pool or indoor playground. Blocks and puzzles are big hits with toddlers. So are coloring and finger painting. Preschoolers probably will prefer sleeping in the same room as their parents. Provide a couch, daybed, or rented cot.

Ages 6-10: School-age children enjoy books, videos, trips to the movie theater, bowling, skating, and playgrounds. Ask parents what their children are interested in. If you own a computer, check out some game software from the library.

Menu of the *Day*

Broiled Chicken Breast
dotted with Soy Sauce and Ginger
Steamed Vegetable Pasta
Sugar Snap Peas
Frozen Banana
Skim Milk

---

*Memory triggered by smell is a powerful thing, bigger than life
—perhaps better than life. For holiday smells are, more often than not,
pleasant ghosts of lives shared. —Kurt Ullrich*

December 7

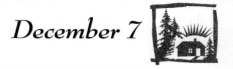

Add Fun, Subtract Expense to Holiday Traditions

Consider paper chains, bread dough ornaments, cookies, popcorn strings, starched bows, decorated pine cones, or pretty Christmas cards to hang on your tree.

If you love to bake cookies, but shouldn't eat them, fasten cut out sugar cookies to a plain green wreath. All you need is some ribbon or fish line. Poke a tiny hole in the top of each cookie with a toothpick before you bake it. Decorate with colored sugar, then bake and cool.

Prepare a video or audiotaped greeting for special family members you won't see at Christmas. It will likely mean more than an expensive gift.

Display Christmas books on open shelves. Open the Bible to Luke 2:1-20 and place a pretty bookmark at the place of the Christmas story.

Spend some time at the dinner table or before bed reading the Christmas cards together.

Menu of the Day

Get Ready for Christmas!
Wrap Presents, Decorate,
or Write Cards
Enjoy Chinese or Italian Takeout
*Almost all Chinese entrées are low
in fat except for breaded and fried
meats and vegetables. With Italian
dishes, choose the meatless or lean
beef fillings instead of sausage.*

Let us always give thanks / For the food we eat,
For family who loves us / And friends that we meet.
—Joan Marie Arbogast

Turkey Roasted on the Gas Grill
12 4-ounce servings

Ask dad to put on his coat and cook the bird!

12-14 pound turkey, thawed if frozen
Non-stick cooking spray

Dried seasonings of choice (suggest pepper, marjoram, thyme, rosemary, poultry seasoning, garlic, onion powder, oregano, or basil)
1 cup no-added-salt chicken broth

1. Place a medium-size disposable foil roasting pan on the cold grill to check if the grill lid will close. If necessary, fold in the sides of the pan.

2. Light one side of the gas grill. Heat on high for 5 minutes, then reduce heat to medium.

3. Remove giblets, neck, and fat from the turkey and discard. Rinse the turkey, and fold skin flap under back. Spray with cooking spray and rub in desired seasonings.

4. Place turkey, breast side up, in the foil pan. Insert a meat thermometer in the center of the thigh next to the body, not touching the bone. Place pan on unheated side of the grill. Add chicken broth and close lid.

5. Grill for 1 1/4 hours. Rotate the pan half a turn and grill for 1 to 1 1/2 hours longer, until a meat thermometer registers 180°. Remove turkey to a serving platter or carving board. Let rest for 30 minutes for juicier meat and easy carving.

Menu *of the* Day

Turkey Roasted on the Gas Grill
Stuffing from a mix
Steamed Green Beans
Pineapple Chunks
Skim Milk

Calories per serving: 191 Fat: 5 g. Sodium: 84 mg.
For exchange diets, count: 5 very lean meat
Preparation time: 10 minutes Roasting time: 2 1/2 hours

Prayer for Peace at Christmas:
Fountain of patience and compassion, open our hearts to listen well.
Word of life, open our hearts to proclaim true peace.
—Women of the ELCA Third Triennial Convention Closing Litany, 1996

December 9

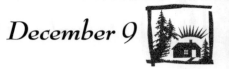

Dried Fruit Gift Pack

32 1-ounce servings

Fix this pretty gift for someone who can do without cookies and candy.

Empty 3-pound coffee can with a lid
1 yard pretty holiday fabric
1/2 pound dried apricots

1/2 pound dried pears
1/2 pound dried apples
1/2 pound dried pineapple

1. Clean coffee can well.

2. Lay the fabric out on a table, printed side down, and place the can in the center.

3. Wrap the fabric up around the can and press the edges down into the middle.

4. Place a clear plastic bag in the can, on top of the fabric. Layer bits of dried fruit into the bag, packing it tightly so the fabric stays weighted down. Close the bag with a twist tie. Place cover on the can.

Calories per serving: 83 Fat: 0 Sodium: 3 mg.
For exchange diets, count: 1 1/2 fruit
Preparation time: 20 minutes

Menu *of the* Day

Sloppy Joes on a Bun using
Lean Ground Pork and a
Favorite Bottled Barbecue Sauce
Mixed Vegetables
Sliced Strawberries and Bananas
Skim Milk

Thankful Celebration

Prayer for Peace at Christmas:
Creator of humankind, let our voices shatter walls of hatred.
—Women of the ELCA Third Triennial Convention Closing Litany, 1996

Chocolate Challa
24 slices

1 package dry yeast
1/4 cup lukewarm water
1 cup boiling water
1 tablespoon vegetable oil
1 1/2 teaspoons salt
1 1/2 teaspoons sugar
1 egg, well beaten, or 1/4 cup liquid egg substitute

2/3 cup cocoa
3 1/3 cups flour
Flour to coat work surface
Non-stick cooking spray
1 egg
1 teaspoon cold water

1. Soften yeast in lukewarm water in a glass measuring cup.

2. In a large mixing bowl, combine boiling water, oil, salt, and sugar. Stir until sugar is dissolved. When mixture has cooled to lukewarm, add softened yeast. Add beaten eggs. Stir in cocoa and 1 1/2 cups of flour, beating until smooth.

3. Allow dough to rest for 10 minutes. Add remaining flour and turn dough out onto a floured board, kneading until smooth and elastic. Allow dough to rise until double in bulk.

4. Knead again until dough is fine grained.

5. Cut the dough into 3 parts. Roll each part into thin long strips. Braid three strips together, starting from the center. Place braided dough on a baking sheet that has been sprayed with cooking spray. Allow dough to rise 1 hour.

6. Preheat oven to 350°. Beat 1 egg with 1 teaspoon cold water. Brush surface of dough with egg and water mixture and bake for 25 minutes or until golden brown.

Calories per 1-slice serving: 144 Fat: 1 g. Sodium: 102 mg.
For exchange diets, count: 2 starch
Preparation time: 45 minutes First rising time: 2 hours
    Second rising time: 1 hour Baking time: 25 minutes

Menu *of the* Day

Fresh Veggie and
Lean Ham Omelet
Chocolate Challa
Leftover Fresh Fruits
marinated in Cranberry Juice
Skim Milk

Prayer for Peace at Christmas:
Friend of the poor, move us to question unshared wealth.
—Women of the ELCA Third Triennial Convention Closing Litany, 1996

December 11

Mulled Wine
8 4-ounce servings

1 1/2 cups water
1/2 cup sugar
2 oranges, sliced into wagon wheels and
    then quartered

2 4-inch cinnamon sticks
10 whole cloves
750 ml bottle dry red wine
1/4 cup brandy

1. In a large saucepan, combine water, sugar, and half of oranges. Bring mixture to a boil, then add cinnamon sticks and cloves. Simmer uncovered for 10 minutes. Remove oranges and spices with a slotted spoon and discard.

2. Add wine and brandy to the pan and keep warm over medium-low heat. Serve in heat-proof mugs and garnish with remaining orange slices.

Calories per serving: 148 Fat: 0 Sodium: 62 mg.
For exchange diets, count: 1 fruit
Preparation time: 15 minutes

Menu *of the* Day

Round Steak and Beer in the
Crockpot with chunks of Potato,
Carrot, Celery, and Onion
Shredded Cabbage
with Reduced-Fat Dressing
White Roll with Soft Margarine
Applesauce
Mulled Wine

December 12

Controlling Christmas Craziness

Don't go crazy this holiday. Relax and enjoy these gift tips.

1. Start early. The right gift takes thinking time, not shopping time. Use key words to describe your giftees; once you have an idea, get it on a list.

2. Break the shopping down into small, "doable" loads. Work from your list, stopping to pick things up when it is most convenient.

3. Buy it when you see it. When the perfect thing hits you, go ahead and grab it.

4. You can choose to do all of your shopping without leaving the house. Order on-line or from mail order catalogs. Your local stores may deliver, and regional stores will ship.

5. Locate a gift-wrapping service provided by local charity fund-raisers.

6. Team up with a friend and wrap gifts together.

7. Use gift bags.

8. Assume advertised specials will be sold out.

9. Step out of tradition and ask that your friends make a donation to your church or a charity instead of buying you a gift.

Menu *of the* Day

Browned Ground Turkey and
Chunky Marinara Sauce over
Spaghetti Noodles
Sliced Cucumbers, Onions,
and Red Pepper with
Reduced-Fat Italian Dressing
Broiled French Bread
Frozen Blueberries
with Vanilla Yogurt on top
Skim Milk

Day 2 of Controlling Christmas Craziness

Cards and Cookies...

1. Look at Christmas cards as a time saver. You can complete a half dozen cards in the time it takes to catch up with one person on the phone. It probably costs less too.

2. Do five or six cards a day. The whole list probably cannot be wiped out on a Saturday morning.

3. Use a short note to bring the person up to date on major happenings. The recipient will be pleased no matter how much you say.

4. In a real pinch? Send a sincere e-mail message.

5. Stage a cookie exchange with four friends, even during lunch break at the office. Everyone makes a batch, brings plastic bags, and shares the joy.

6. When the cookie cutter becomes tiresome, roll and cut plain, tinted cookie dough into 3-inch circles; sprinkle with colored sugar. Add a hole at the top if you want to make ornaments, then bake. Or cut the circles into pie wedges. Add a piece of dough at the bottom for a tree trunk. When baked they look like Christmas trees.

7. Buy plain sugar cookies from the bakery or deli and decorate them yourself. Melt chocolate chips in a plastic sandwich bag in the microwave. Snip a corner out of the bag and drizzle chocolate designs on the cookies.

Menu of the Day

Tuna Melts:
Waterpacked Tuna on an English Muffin broiled with Reduced-Fat Colby Cheese on top

Steamed Carrots seasoned
with Dried Rosemary

Reduced-Fat Lemon
Sandwich Cookies

Skim Milk

Where do I start to tell about the God I know?
Do I start with the sky so dark at night you cannot see it but only see
through it, pale blue at dawn, brilliantly bright at mid-day, dusty orange
as the sun sinks? —Kristine Franke Hill, Lutheran Woman Today

Day 3 of Controlling Christmas Craziness

Projects and Parties...

1. Forget staying up late to handcraft a load of gifts. If you didn't start your craft projects in November, it's probably too late.

2. When you take your turn at hosting holiday gatherings, delegate specific menu items that will come together to form the perfect menu.

3. Get out of your apron altogether. Buy carryout frozen dishes, throw the wrappers in the trash, and arrange the food on your best holiday dishes.

4. Instant centerpieces: cranberries in a footed glass bowl or fresh fruit with sprigs of holly on a silver tray.

5. Buy extra-long cinnamon sticks, and tie them in bundles of two or three with plaid ribbon. Arrange them on dining or coffee tables.

6. No time or too cold for outdoor Christmas lights? Put your Christmas tree in front of a picture window and call it a light show.

7. Still some dust on the woodwork? Dim the lights, burn plenty of candles, turn up the Christmas tunes, and enjoy!

Menu *of the* Day

Apple Juice and Pork Chops
in the skillet
Braise with Sliced Cabbage,
Onions, Apples, and Caraway Seed

Rye Bread from the deli
Peach and Pear Slices
Skim Milk

Where do I start to tell about God?
Should I start with the people, all the people without whom I would have wasted away to nothing, died a thousand deaths—physically, spiritually, emotionally—long ago. —Kristine Franke Hill, Lutheran Woman Today

Fruit and Cheese Tostada
4 tostada

1 medium Granny Smith apple, diced
1/4 cup diced dates or golden raisins
1 tablespoon fresh lemon juice
1 tablespoon dried parsley

1 teaspoon dried rosemary
1 tablespoon honey
4 ounces feta cheese, crumbled
4 large flour tortillas

1. Preheat broiler to low.

2. Mix first seven ingredients together in a mixing bowl.

3. Arrange flour tortillas on a baking sheet. Divide cheese and fruit mixture among the tortillas.

4. Broil under low heat for 5 minutes. Serve warm and eat with a fork.

Calories per tostada: 290 Fat: 10 g. Sodium: 567 mg.
For exchange diets, count: 1 lean meat, 1 fat, 1 1/2 starch, 1 fruit
Preparation time: 10 minutes Broiling time: 5 minutes

Menu *of the* Day

Tomato Juice
Fruit and Cheese Tostadas
Fresh Spinach
with Reduced-Fat Dressing
Hot Chocolate
with a Candy Cane to stir

Thankful Celebration

Where should I begin to tell about God?
Let me begin at the center where everything comes together,
at Bethlehem where a child was born and laid in a manger.
—*Kristine Franke Hill*, Lutheran Woman Today

Holiday Seafood Marinade
4 4-ounce servings

Marinade:
2/3 cup fresh lemon juice
1 cup chopped fresh tomato or canned chunky
tomatoes, drained well
2 green onions, chopped fine
1 seeded jalapeño pepper, chopped fine

2 tablespoons chopped fresh cilantro
2 tablespoons ketchup
4 drops hot pepper sauce
Seafood:
2 cups cooked shrimp
1 cup cooked scallops or mock crab

1. Mix ingredients for marinade in a glass bowl. Stir in seafood.

2. Refrigerate at least 4 hours or overnight. This keeps for 3 days.

Calories per serving: 212 Fat: 4 g. Sodium: 428 mg.
For exchange diets, count: 5 very lean meat, 2 vegetable
Preparation time: 10 minutes Marinating time: 4 hours

Menu *of the* Day

Holiday Seafood Marinade
Assorted Reduced-Fat
Cheese and Crackers
Sliced Apples and Grapes
Sparkling Grape Juice

Where do I start to tell God who I am?
Do I start with words that profess my trust in God:
I believe in God the Father Almighty.
–Kristine Franke Hill, Lutheran Woman Today

December 17
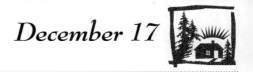

Make Holiday House Cleaning Efficient!

1. Use an extension cord when vacuuming so you don't have to keep looking for outlets.

2. When cleaning things on a shelf, move items to one side, clean the surface, then put them back. You waste energy by moving everything from a shelf to another place while you clean.

3. To easily remove scum from soap dishes, let them sit in a sink full of hot water, or if they cannot be removed from the wall, put a hot wet sponge on them to soften the soap scum.

4. If you're going to be baking something that spatters, line your oven bottom with tin foil, then throw it away.

5. If you don't have time to wash the bed sheets, you can freshen them up by turning them over and putting the top of the sheet at the bottom of the bed. The undersides of the sheets will feel clean.

Menu *of the* Day

Carryout Chicken from the deli
Don't eat the skin!

Carryout Vegetable Pasta Salad
with Clear Dressing

Carryout Baked Beans

Skim Milk

Where do I start to tell God who I am?
Do I begin by making myself useful? Giving of myself
to others in imitation of how God has given for me?
–Kristine Franke Hill, Lutheran Woman Today

Day 2 of Holiday Housekeeping Tips

1. Schedule your work. Many projects do not need to be done every week, such as cleaning the refrigerator or chandeliers or wiping up fingerprints on woodwork. Fit projects in when they are most convenient.

2. Sweep floors, rather than washing them, every other time you clean.

3. When wet mopping a floor, use a towel or an old T-shirt to get the corners.

4. To clean a microwave oven easily, let a cup of water boil in it for a few minutes. That will steam off much of the grime.

5. If your tablecloth has a few minor spills after a holiday meal, consider using a sponge with a towel underneath to spot clean.

Menu of the *Day*

Carryout Veggie Pizza
Green Salad with Reduced-Fat
Italian Dressing
Raspberry Sherbet
with Diced Kiwifruit on top
Skim Milk

Where do I start to tell God who I am?
I start with all these—just a start—and I ask God to move me beyond
this meager beginning to a whole life of giving, thanking, and serving.
—Kristine Franke Hill, Lutheran Woman Today

December 19
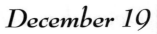

Crab Cakes
4 2-cake servings

Non-stick cooking spray
1/2 cup fat-free mayonnaise
1 large egg
1 teaspoon Old Bay seasoning
1 teaspoon pepper

1 teaspoon lemon juice
1 teaspoon Worcestershire sauce
1 teaspoon garlic powder
1 pound crabmeat
1/4 cup bread or cracker crumbs

1. Spray skillet or griddle with cooking spray. Preheat over medium heat.

2. Combine all remaining ingredients in a mixing bowl.

3. Form 8 small patties from the crab mixture and cook over medium heat until golden brown, about 7 minutes on each side. Serve with red seafood sauce or reduced-fat tartar sauce.

Calories per serving: 178 Fat: 3 g. Sodium: 1323 mg.
For exchange diets, count: 2 lean meat, 1 starch
Preparation time: 20 minutes

Menu of the *Day*

Crab Cakes
Steamed Red Potatoes
with Dill Weed
Raw Broccoli Chunks with
Reduced-Fat Ranch Dressing Dip
Skim Milk

Thankful Celebration

An angel can be that voice inside you, the voice of goodness,
telling you the right thing to do.
—Roma Downey, angel actress on CBS's Touched by an Angel

Sweet and Sour Broiled Ribs
8 3-ounce servings

6 pounds pork spareribs, cut into 8 portions
Water
1/2 cup light molasses

2 tablespoons balsamic vinegar
2 tablespoons prepared mustard
1 tablespoon hot pepper sauce

1. In a large saucepan over high heat, heat ribs and enough water to cover to boiling. Reduce heat to low; cover and simmer for 45 minutes or until ribs are tender. Drain.

2. Meanwhile, in a medium bowl, combine molasses, vinegar, mustard, and sauce.

3. Preheat boiler. Place ribs on broiling rack and brush with sauce.

4. Broil ribs for 15 minutes about 8 inches from broiler element. Brush at least 3 times with sauce.

Calories per serving: 242 Fat: 11 g. Sodium: 105 mg.
For exchange diets, count: 3 lean meat, 1 fruit, 1/2 fat
Preparation time: 10 minutes Boiling time: 45 minutes Broiling time: 15 minutes

Menu of the *Day*

Sweet and Sour Broiled Ribs
Whole Kernel Corn
garnished with Pimiento
Cabbage Salad from the deli
Fresh Tangelo
Skim Milk

I pray this Christmas, Lord, for light / To see beyond the gloom of night,
For grace to grow and understand, / The warmth to lend a helpful hand,
A surer faith, a greener thumb / The humblest heart in Christendom.
—Corinna Marsh

December 21
First Day of Winter

Quick Mexican Chicken
4 4-ounce servings

4 4-ounce skinless, boneless chicken breasts, thawed

1 cup chunky no-added-salt salsa

2 ounces shredded part-skim Monterey Jack cheese

1. Preheat oven to 400°.

2. Place chicken breasts in a non-stick baking dish. Pour salsa on top. Cover and bake for 20 to 25 minutes.

3. Remove cover and sprinkle with cheese. Return to the oven uncovered for 5 minutes. Serve over rice.

Calories per serving: 207 Fat: 6 g. Sodium: 190 mg.
For exchange diets, count: 5 very lean meat, 1 vegetable
Preparation time: 10 minutes Baking time: 25 minutes

Menu *of the* Day

Quick Mexican Chicken
White Rice with Green Chiles
mixed in
Fresh Apple and Orange Slices
Skim Milk

Thankful Celebration

In those days a decree went out from Emperor Augustus that all the world should be registered. —Luke 2:1

Ham and Cheese Biscuits
12 biscuits

2 cups bread flour
1 teaspoon baking powder
1/2 teaspoon salt
1/2 teaspoon baking soda

1 cup skim milk
1/2 cup nonfat mayonnaise
2 ounces lean ham, chopped fine
2 ounces reduced-fat cheddar cheese, shredded

1. Preheat oven to 425°. Line 12 muffin cups with papers.

2. In a large bowl, combine bread flour, baking powder, salt, and baking soda.

3. Combine remaining ingredients in another bowl; stir liquid mixture into dry ingredients just until moist.

4. Fill muffin cups and bake for 16 minutes or until golden brown.

Calories per serving: 107 Fat: 1 g. Sodium: 531 mg.
For exchange diets, count: 1 lean meat, 1 starch
Preparation time: 15 minutes Baking time: 16 minutes

Menu *of the* Day

Clam Chowder from a can
Ham and Cheese Biscuits
Granny Smith Apple Slices
Leftover Christmas Candy
Herb Tea

Joseph also went from the town of Nazareth in Galilee to Judea, to the city of David called Bethlehem, because he was descended from the house and family of David. —Luke 2:4

December 23

Parmesan Canes
6 canes

11-ounce can refrigerated soft breadsticks

1/2 cup grated Parmesan cheese

2 tablespoons soft margarine, melted

1. Preheat oven to 350°.

2. Remove breadsticks from the tube, and cut in half making 2 shorter sticks. Dip one side of breadsticks in melted margarine and then in grated cheese.

3. Twist and shape into candy canes on an ungreased baking sheet, cheese side up.

4. Bake for 16 minutes or until golden brown.

Calories per 1-cane serving: 105 Fat: 5 g. Sodium: 307 mg.
For exchange diets, count: 1 starch, 1/2 fat
Preparation time: 10 minutes Baking time: 16 minutes

Menu *of the* Day

Sirloin and Vegetable Kabobs
seasoned with Barbecue Sauce

Parmesan Canes

Green Salad
with Reduced-Fat Dressing

Raspberry Sherbet

Decaf Coffee

December 24

And she gave birth to her firstborn son and wrapped him in bands of cloth and laid him in a manger, because there was no place for them in the inn.
–Luke 2:5-7

Six Steps to a Perfect Prime Rib

A rib roast is one of the most tender cuts available and is easy to prepare. It may be cooked to any doneness, but for optimum flavor and tenderness, cook beef rib roasts rare to medium. Beef rib roasts will yield about three 3-ounce cooked, trimmed servings per pound. Bone-in rib roasts yield about two 3-ounce, cooked trimmed servings per pound.

1. Place roast, fat side up, on rack in open roasting pan. If using a bone-in rib roast, the ribs form the rack that keeps the meat above the drippings.

2. Season either before or after cooking.

3. Insert meat thermometer into the thickest part of the roast, not touching bone or fat.

4. Do not add water. Do not cover.

5. Roast at 300° to 325° until the meat thermometer registers 5° to 10° below the desired doneness. During the standing time, roast will continue to rise 5° to 10° and reach the final meat thermometer reading. (Oven does not have to be preheated.)

	Minutes per pound	Internal Temp
Rare	17–19	135–140
Medium-Rare	20–22	145–150
Medium	23–25	155–160
Well Done	27–30	165–170

6. Allow roast to stand tented with foil 15 to 20 minutes before serving. Temperature will rise, and roast will be easier to carve.

Menu *of the* Day

Prime Rib of Beef
Steamed Rice
with Stirfry Vegetables
French Bread
Green Salad
with Reduced-Fat Dressing
Low-Fat Cherry Nut Ice Milk
Decaf Coffee

In that region there were shepherds living in the fields, keeping watch over their flock by night. And the angel of the Lord stood before them, and the glory of the Lord shone around them, and they were terrified.
—Luke 2:8-11

December 25

Keep a Christmas Journal

Several years ago, I found something called *The Family Christmas Album* on an after-Christmas sale table. I picked it up as a present to myself and have enjoyed it more every year. The journal is one that anyone could easily copy using a pretty holiday bound notebook. It has blank pages titled for:

The Place	Christmas Day
The Family	Boxing Day
Children	The Aftermath
The Friends	Funny Incidents
The Preparations	Particular Successes
Special Outings	Improvements for Next Year
Christmas Eve	Notes

I also keep two copies of our family Christmas card in the journal (one for each of my children to claim one day).

I usually write in the journal between Christmas and the New Year. I always ask the kids for their input on the various pages. My enjoyment of the season has deepened by reflecting back on the special joys and predictable disasters that each year brings.

Menu *of the* Day

Baked Ham drizzled with Maple Syrup and Orange Marmalade
Mashed Potatoes
Green Beans baked with Reduced-Fat Mushroom Soup
Brown-and-Serve Wheat Rolls
Cranberry Salad from the deli
Pumpkin Ice Cream
Sparkling Red Wine

Thankful Celebration

December 26

Go now with God, choose not to go alone.
Go in the faith that there is no wilderness so vast
that God is not already there to show you the way.
—Lutheran Woman Today

Returning to Normal

Immense amounts of hubbub and excitement combine to produce the magical countdown to Christmas, but now it is time to get back to normal.

What to do with leftovers?

Remove leftovers to shallow containers or dishes.

Cover food tightly with plastic wrap or foil.

Place leftovers in the coldest part of the refrigerator, usually near an interior shelf where cold air enters.

How long will it keep in the refrigerator?

Turkey lasts two days.

Ham lasts five days.

Mashed potatoes last two days.

Stuffing lasts two days.

Eggnog lasts five days after the "sell" date.

Menu *of the* Day

Beef and Vegetable Soup from a
can with Mixed Veggies tossed in
Wheat Crackers
Low-Fat Cottage Cheese
and Peach Slices
Leftover Christmas Cookies
Skim Milk

For I was hungry and ye gave me meat: I was thirsty, and ye gave me drink: I was a stranger, and ye took me in: Naked, and ye clothed me: I was sick, and ye visited me: I was in prison, and ye came unto me.
—Matthew 25:35-36

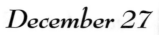 December 27

Returning to Normal

Cleaning out the fridge and freezing leftovers

Make sure your freezer registers 0 degrees or lower.

Wrap leftovers as tightly as possible.

Do not refreeze food that has been frozen and thawed.

Freezer Life

Turkey and other poultry—six months

Beef roast—six months

Pork roast—three months

Cured ham—one month

Meat and poultry casseroles, including stuffing—three months

Bread, cake, and cookies—three months

Soft cheese—three months

Hard cheese—eight weeks

Menu of the Day

Cold Sliced Leftover Turkey
or Ham on Toast with
Light Mayonnaise
Steamed Cauliflower with
Reduced-Fat Cheese
sprinkled on top
Fresh Apple Slices
and Vanilla Yogurt
Skim Milk

---

*Whatsoever good thing any man doeth,
the same shall he receive of the Lord.*
–Ephesians 6:8

Returning to Normal

Storing Decorations

Use specially made plastic panels to wrap light cords, tucking each up against the last to avoid crossovers. Tape the end in place or tuck it under the adjacent cord. Panels, sold at hardware and home stores, are generally less than two dollars each. Or make your own from stiff cardboard.

Try storing your lights in a 5-gallon bucket, circling the light cords in the bucket and separating strands with a circle of cardboard cut to fit.

Check light cords for cuts and bare spots that could start a fire.

Recycle your tree. Check with your local environmental service office or waste hauler. If curbside pickup is available, a special yard waste sticker may be required.

Reflect on the reason for the season. Think back to a sentimental card or loving interaction with a family member or friend. Take time to write thank-you notes.

Menu *of the* Day

Macaroni and Cheese from a box
Steamed California Blend Veggies
Leftover Bread or Fruitcake
Fresh Orange
Skim Milk

Since I was 24 there never was any vagueness in
my plans or ideas as to what God's work was for me.
—Florence Nightingale

Quick Italian Chicken
4 4-ounce servings

4 4-ounce skinless, boneless chicken breasts,
thawed

1 cup chunky no-added-salt marinara sauce
1/2 cup shredded Parmesan cheese

1. Preheat oven to 400°.

2. Place chicken breasts in a non-stick baking dish. Pour sauce on top.

3. Cover and bake for 25 minutes. Remove cover and sprinkle with cheese. Return
chicken to the oven uncovered for 5 minutes. Serve over pasta.

Calories per serving: 232 Fat: 8 g. Sodium: 190 mg.
For exchange diets, count: 5 very lean meat, 1/2 fat, 1 vegetable
Preparation time: 10 minutes Baking time: 30 minutes

Menu *of the* Day

Quick Italian Chicken
Tender Cooked Pasta
sprinkled with Oregano
Broiled French Bread
Sliced Kiwifruit
with Pineapple Tidbits
Skim Milk

Thankful Celebration

Have courage for the great sorrows of life, and patience for the small ones. And when you have accomplished your daily tasks, go to sleep in peace. God is awake. —Victor Hugo

Microwave Caramel Corn

10 2-cup servings

Non-stick cooking spray
20 cups popped popcorn
1 cup packed brown sugar
1/4 cup light corn syrup

1/2 teaspoon salt
1/2 cup reduced-fat margarine
1 teaspoon vanilla
1/2 teaspoon baking soda

1. Spray the inside of a large brown paper bag with cooking spray. Add popped popcorn.

2. Combine sugar, syrup, salt, and margarine in a quart-size glass measuring cup. Microwave on high for 2 minutes. Stir and microwave again for 3 more minutes. Add vanilla and baking soda. Stir well.

3. Pour sugar mixture over the popcorn, and stir with a long-handled wooden spoon. Fold the top of the sack. Place in microwave oven and microwave on high power for 1 minute. Shake and cook again for 1 minute. Shake, and cook for 30 seconds, then shake again and cook for 30 more seconds.

4. Pour onto aluminum foil and let cool.

Calories per serving: 204 Fat: 5 g. Sodium: 263 mg.
For exchange diets, count: 2 starch, 1 fat
Preparation time: 20 minutes

Menu *of the* Day

Broiled Halibut Steaks
marinated in Pineapple Juice
and Teriyaki Sauce
Baked Potato with Nonfat
Sour Cream and Dill Weed
Steamed Sugar Snap Peas
with Water Chestnuts
Frozen Strawberry Yogurt
Herb Tea
For an Afternoon or Evening Treat:
Microwave Caramel Corn

Lord, you have consecrated unto us / This fresh new year, to do with as we will,
A calendar unturned, a blessed / First page for us to fill
—Helen Harrington

December 31

Sweet and Sour Cocktail Meatballs
24 2-meatball servings

1 1/2 pounds lean ground beef
8-ounce can water chestnuts, drained and chopped
1 egg, beaten, or 1/4 cup liquid egg substitute
1/3 cup dry bread crumbs
1 tablespoon Worcestershire sauce

1 cup beer
1/2 cup brown sugar
1/4 cup vinegar
1/4 cup catsup
2 tablespoons cornstarch

1. In a large bowl, combine ground beef, water chestnuts, egg, bread crumbs, and Worcestershire sauce.

2. Shape into 48 meatballs. Place on a broiling rack and broil for 6 minutes or until done.

3. In a skillet, combine all remaining ingredients. Use a wire whisk to stir over medium heat, uncovered, until mixture thickens.

4. Transfer sauce to a Crockpot or chafing dish. Transfer broiled meatballs into the sauce, and keep warm. Serve with toothpicks.

Calories per serving: 101 Fat: 4 g. Sodium: 92 mg.
For exchange diets, count: 1 lean meat, 1 fruit
Preparation time: 20 minutes Broiling time: 6 minutes

Menu *of the* Day

New Year's Eve Buffet
Sweet and Sour Cocktail Meatballs
Assorted Reduced-Fat Cheese
Sesame Seed Melba Crackers
Splurge on
Fresh Vegetable Dippers:
Brocciflower Tops, Red Pepper
Rings, Sugar Snap Peas,
Asparagus, Yellow Squash Rings

Reduced-Fat Dip from
the produce section
Fresh Pineapple Wedges
on a skewer
Hot Cocoa with a splash of
Peppermint Schnapps or
Peppermint Extract

SOUL GOALS TO SAVOR FOR THE NEW YEAR

I want to delight God.

I want to "practice heaven" by enjoying God now.

I want to have a part in advancing God's kingdom.

I want to remain open to the unexpected plans God may have for my life.

I want to grow in love and graciousness in my relationships.

I want to laugh more.

I want to think less like a victim and more like a survivor.

I want to excel in prayer.

from *She Can Laugh at the Days to Come* by Valerie Bell.
Copyright 1996 by Valerie Bell. Used by permission of Zondervan Publishing House

REFERENCES

Abbinante, Julie. *Cooking with Angels*. Minneapolis: Chronimed Publishing, 1995.

Anderson, John Louis. *Scandinavian Humor*. Minneapolis: Nordbook, 1986.

Angelou, Maya. *Phenomenal Woman*. New York: Random House, 1994.

Bell, Janet. *Famous Black Quotations*. New York: Warner Books, 1995.

Baird, Pat. *Be Good to Your Gut*. Cambridge, Massachusetts: Blackwell Science, 1996.

Bartlett, John. *Familiar Quotations*. Boston: Little, Brown and Company, 1980.

Barwick, Dee Danner. *A Treasury of Days*. Norwalk, Connecticut: C. R. Gibson, 1983.

Barwick, Dee Danner. *Great Words of Our Time*. Kansas City: Hallmark Editions, 1970.

Beilenson, Esther. *Thinking of You*. White Plains, New York: Peter Pauper Press, Inc., 1993.

Birnes, Nancy. *Cheaper and Better*. New York: Shadow Lawn Press, 1987.

Christing, Adam. *Comedy Comes Clean*. New York: Crown Trade Paperbacks, 1996.

Clairmont, Patsy. *365 Ways God Uses Cracked Pots*. Wheaton, Illinois: Tyndale House Publications, Inc., 1996.

Davidoff, Henry. *The Pocket Book of Quotations*. New York: Pocket Books, 1952.

Dixon, Monica. *Love the Body You Were Born With*. New York: Perigee Books, 1996.

Dunham, Maxie. *Living Prayer*. Nashville: Upper Room Books, 1994.

"Five ways to put your imagination to work." *Des Moines Register,* February 4, 1996, page 1E.

Family Christmas Album. London: Alan Hutchinson Publishing, Inc., 1993.

Foster, Richard J. *Coming Home*. San Francisco: HarperCollins, 1994.

Franklin, Linda. *Our Old Fashioned Country Diary*. South Salen, New York: Michel Publishing, Ltd., 1992.

Fraser, Laura. "Annals of dieting." *Vogue*. May 1996, page 210.

Freeman, M. *The Book of Southern Wisdom*. Nashville: Walnut Grove Press, 1994.

Fulghum, Robert. *All I Really Needed to Know I Learned in Kindergarten*. New York: Ballantine Books, 1986.

Garnett, Emmeline. *Seasons*. New York: Bell Books, 1966.

Goudge, Elizabeth. *A Book of Comfort*. New York: Coward-McCann, Inc., 1964.

Harvey, Gail. *Poems of Nature*. New York: Gramercy Books, 1989.

"Health and spirituality." *Mayo Clinic Health Letter.* November 1996, page 4.

Heller, David. *Dear God*. New York: Perigee Books, 1987.

Hutchinson, Woods. *A Handbook of Health*. Cambridge: The Riverside Press, 1922.

Johnson, Pearl Patterson. *Who Tells the Crocuses It's Spring?* Philadephia: Countryside Press, 1971.

Kano, Susan. *Making Peace with Food*. New York: Harper and Row, 1989.

Kelleher, Susan. "Make a change for the better." *Des Moines Register,* January 5, 1997, page 5E.

Knuckles, Barbara. "The lies of spirituality." *Today's Christian Woman,* November 1996, page 52.

Levine, Mark. *Complete Book of Bible Quotations from the New Testament.* New York: Pocket Books, 1986.

Levine, Mark. *Complete Book of Bible Quotations from the Old Testament.* New York: Pocket Books, 1986.

Lichtman, Susan. "Do the next right thing." *Lutheran Woman Today.* November 1996, page 12.

Life Application Bible. Iowa Falls, Iowa: World Bible Publishers, Inc., 1989.

Longacre, Doris. *More with Less Cookbook.* Scottdale, Pennsylvania: Herald Press, 1976.

Lutheran Book of Worship. Minneapolis: Augsburg Publishing House, 1978.

Moyers, Bill. "The resurgence of faith." *USA Weekend,* October 11, 1996.

McWilliams, John-Roger and Peter McWilliams. *Do It.* Los Angeles: Prelude Press, 1991.

Min, Linda. "Alcohol consumption and increased HDL levels." *Nutrition Close-Up.* 13:4, 1996, page 3.

Montapert, Alfred. *Words of Wisdom to Live By.* Los Angeles: Books of Value, 1986.

Petty, Jo. *Apples of Gold.* Norwalk, Connecticut: The C. R. Gibson Company, 1962.

Ruehlmann, Virginia. *Blossoms of Friendship.* Tarrytown, New York: Fleming H. Revell Company, 1984.

Quotabale Quotes. Montreal: The Reader's Digest Association, Inc., 1997.

Ruehlmann, Virginia. *From the Heart.* Grand Rapids: Fleming H. Revell, 1992.

Ruehlmann, Virginia. *When I Must Leave You.* Old Tappan, New Jersey: Fleming H. Revell Company, 1972.

Schafter, Renate. "One woman's story." *Today's Christian Woman,* May 1996, page 30.

Schwartz, Michael. "The new biology of body weight regulation." *Journal of The American Dietetic Association,* 1997. 97:54-60.

Spurlock, Ellen. "Holiday plants." *Market Basket,* December 1, 1996, page 118.

The Quotable Woman. Philadelphia: Running Press, 1991.

Trygstad, Susan and Jay. "A prayer sampler." *Lutheran Woman Today.* May 1996, page 2.

Tudor, Tasha. *All for Love.* New York: Philomel Books, 1984.

Wagner, Guy. *Acorns of Wit and Wisdom.* Cedar Falls: J.S. Latta, 1989.

Williamson, Marianne. *A Return to Love.* New York: HarperCollins, 1993.

Wilson, Neil. *The Handbook of Bible Application.* Wheaton, Illinois: Tyndale House Publishers, Inc., 1992.

Yates, Susan. "Whatever happened to family meals?" *Today's Christian Woman.* November 1996, page 33.

INDEX OF RECIPES

Index